Guide to the
LEED® Green Associate™
V4 Exam

GUIDE
TO THE
LEED®
GREEN
Associate™ V4 Exam

Michelle Cottrell, LEED AP BD+C

WILEY

Cover design: Wiley

This book is printed on acid-free paper. ∞

Copyright © 2014 by John Wiley & Sons, Inc. All rights reserved.

Published by John Wiley & Sons, Inc., Hoboken, New Jersey.
Published simultaneously in Canada.

For general information about our other products and services, please contact our Customer Care
Department within the United States at (800) 762-2974, outside the United States at (317) 572-3993 or
fax (317) 572-4002.

Wiley publishes in a variety of print and electronic formats and by print-on-demand. Some material
included with standard print versions of this book may not be included in e-books or in print-on-
demand. If this book refers to media such as a CD or DVD that is not included in the version you
purchased, you may download this material at http://booksupport.wiley.com. For more information
about Wiley products, visit www.wiley.com.

Library of Congress Cataloging-in-Publication Data:
Cottrell, Michelle.
  [Guide to the LEED Green Associate Exam]
  Guide to the LEED Green Associate V4 Exam / Michelle Cottrell.—Second edition.
    pages cm—(Wiley series in sustainable design)
  Revised edition of: Guide to the LEED Green Associate Exam.
  Includes index.
    ISBN 978-1-118-87031-0 (paperback), ISBN 978-1-118-87024-2 (ebk),
ISBN 978-1-118-87027-3 (ebk)
  1. Leadership in Energy and Environmental Design Green Building Rating System—
Examinations—Study guides.   2. Sustainable construction—Examinations—Study guides.
  3. Sustainable buildings—Design and construction.   I. Title.
  TH880.C68 2014
  720'.47076—dc23
                                                                        2014025603

Printed in the United States of America

10 9 8 7 6 5 4 3 2 1

Contents

Acknowledgments

To all my students and readers, thank you so much for all the feedback, suggestions, and insight for the second edition of this study guide. Your questions and eagerness to learn continues to inspire me.

I would like to thank each of the image contributors, as the exam prep series would not be the same without your added visual integrity. Each of you helped to maintain my excitement about the book, as the readers will appreciate as well. Preparing for the exam with the added help of your images will greatly help them to remember the strategies of the rating system.

Melissa Mayer, Editorial Assistant, at John Wiley & Sons—I enjoyed the opportunity to work with you and look forward to continuing my writing efforts with Wiley. You were incredibly supportive and motivating—for that I cannot thank you enough. Amanda, Kerstin, Amy, and Nancy—your support during production has always made the process streamlined and enjoyable. Thank you, Lisa Ryan at Stellar Searches, for helping me with yet another index!

A tremendous thank you to my family and friends for all of your support, motivation, interest, and patience. I really cannot thank you all enough!

Mom, thank you for taking care of Izzy while I was on the road, for always sending me home with your delicious meals, and for all the surprises after I finished each chapter.

This past year has been incredibly enlightening, as I am always on a quest to better myself and grow. I have been fortunate enough to reconnect with a very special person from my past who has not only been extremely supportive and motivating, but makes me strive even harder to meet my goals, both personally and professionally. Juan, this is just the beginning of our next chapter together. . . .

Introduction

Guide to the LEED®Green Associate V4 Exam is the resource to prepare for the Leadership in Energy and Environmental Design (LEED®) Green Associate exam. This exam prep guide provides a road map to studying for the LEED Green Associate exam as administered by Green Building Certification Institute (GBCI™). *Guide to the LEED Green Associate V4 Exam* is aimed at those professionals seeking knowledge about the basic knowledge and understanding that is required in order to pass the exam and earn the LEED Green Associate accreditation.

As a means to introduce myself, I am a LEED consultant and an education provider, focused on sustainable design and building operation concepts. I have traveled the country helping many students to prepare for the LEED Green Associate and LEED Accredited Professional (AP) exams. The LEED Green Associate class typically is a one-day seminar and reviews all of the information as presented in this book. During this class, I share my LEED project experiences and study tips in order to help make sense of this challenging information and present it in a logical format to help streamline the studying efforts for my students. This book breaks down the difficult information to be retained into a coherent and straightforward approach, as compared to simply repeating what would be found in the study reference material outlined by GBCI.

EXAM PREP GUIDE STRUCTURE

Guide to the LEED Green Associate V4 Exam is organized into three parts as a method to break down the information to comprehend. First, an introduction is needed to review the concepts and processes, in order to then understand the next part, the technologies and strategies to implement. Finally, the appendices include charts and diagrams summarizing the critical information, as well as other resources to narrow down the amount of information to be studied as preparation to sit for the LEED Green Associate exam. The composition of the book is as follows:

Part I: Ramping Up is composed of the following information:

- Chapter 1: Understanding the Credentialing Process
- Chapter 2: Introduction to the Concepts of Sustainable Design
- Chapter 3: Integrative Process
- Chapter 4: Third-Party Verification
- Chapter 5: The LEED Green Building Certification Program
- Chapter 6: Essential LEED Concepts

Part II: Diving In: The Strategies and Technologies of LEED details the categories that are included in the rating systems, as well as the strategies to achieve each basic concept contained within. Part II details the critical information to be retained for the exam.

In this part of the book, the following LEED categories are reviewed:

- Chapter 7: Location and Transportation
- Chapter 8: Sustainable Sites
- Chapter 9: Water Efficiency
- Chapter 10: Energy and Atmosphere
- Chapter 11: Materials and Resources
- Chapter 12: Indoor Environmental Quality
- Chapter 13: Innovation and Regional Priority

Part III: Study Tips and Appendices is dedicated to summarizing the critical information, details, and concepts to retain, as well as providing an overview of the testing center environment. The appendices include additional resources to help after Part I and Part II of this book have been completed.

STUDY TIPS! are located throughout the book as tools to help stay focused on the pertinent information. They will include things to remember and point out side note–type information. Sample exam questions (in terms of format and content) are also found in the book, as well as more basic quiz questions placed sporadically throughout.

While reading though this book, be sure to also keep an eye out for FLASH-CARD TIPS!, as they will help to depict the important aspects for the exam and act as an indicator to create critical flashcards. All of the FLASHCARD TIPS! referenced throughout the book are collected at the end, following the index, although it is suggested that you make your own to enhance your studying. It is recommended to purchase plain white cards, as well as the color-coded flashcards (i.e., pink, yellow, blue, green, and purple). Use the white ones for the information to be covered in Part I and the color-coded cards for Part II of this exam prep book. The FLASHCARD TIPS! suggest a starting point for flashcard creation, but feel free to make more as needed. If you decide to make your own with the help of the FLASHCARD TIPS!, be sure to refer to the flashcards at the end of the book for some additional suggestions. If you decide to use the flashcards from the end of the book, you can always use markers or highlighters to color-code them if you wish.

One of the main concepts of sustainable design is the integrative fashion in which green buildings are designed and constructed. It is critical to understand how strategies and technologies have synergies and trade-offs. For example, green roofs can have an impact on a construction budget but can help save on operational energy costs, which may present a breakeven or surplus. Green roofs also have synergistic qualities, as they can help reduce the heat burden on a building, as well as help to manage rainwater (Figure I.1). These types of concepts will be discussed in greater detail in Part II of this exam prep guide, but for now be sure to look for these BAIT TIPS! throughout Part II to help bring the concepts together.

After the first edition of this book, I received feedback from some of the readers eager for more information than you are required to know for the exam. I learned that most of the individuals preparing for the Green Associate exam are

TIP **Study:** Keep an eye out for these STUDY TIPS!, as they will point out the intricacies and nuances to remember.

 Be sure to spot these FLASHCARD TIPS! to create flashcards along the way. Use the white cards for Part I and the color-coded ones for Part II.

 Be sure to look out for these Bring-All-of-It-Together Tips, which are referred to as BAIT TIPS! These tips will reinforce the important concepts and bring all of it together as synergies and trade-offs are pointed out for green building strategies and technologies.

Figure I.1 The CCI Center in Pittsburgh earned its gold certification under the LEED for Existing Buildings: Operations & Maintenance rating system by reducing the amount of rainwater runoff from the site, increasing the amount of open space, promoting biodiversity, reducing cooling loads, and reducing the impacts of the urban heat-island effect by implementing a vegetated roof. *Photo courtesy of Conservation Consultants, Inc.*

looking to enter into green building but are not quite sure what part they wish play. If you are one of these individuals, be sure to look out for CAREER TIPS! throughout Part II. These tips will depict which team member typically contributes to implementing different green building strategies and the type of education they typically have.

Did you unsuccessfully attempt to pass the previous version of the LEED Green Associate Exam? If you started studying but were unable to sit for the previous version of the exam, look for V3V4! tips for insight on the changes from LEED 2009.

Another new addition to this edition of *Guide to the LEED Green Associate V4 Exam* is the Online Resources section. With the new version of the LEED Rating Systems, U.S. Green Building Council (USGBC®) has posted numerous videos and articles to help educate the industry about the benefits of green building strategies and how to implement them into different project types. Visit these links to access these incredible resources.

Career: Interested in a career in sustainability? Look out for these CAREER TIPS! for more information on which professional typically is responsible for the different strategies and concepts identified in Part II.

V3V4: Need clarification on the changes from LEED 2009? Look for these V3V4! tips for more information.

STUDY SCHEDULE

Week	Chapters	Pages
1	Part I: Ramping Up (Chapters 1–3)	1–30
2	Part I: Ramping Up (Chapters 4–6)	31–64
3	Part II: Location and Transportation and Sustainable Sites (Chapters 7 and 8)	65–96
4	Part II: Water Efficiency and Energy & Atmosphere (Chapters 9 and 10)	97–130
5	Part II: Materials & Resources (Chapter 11)	131–150
6	Part II: Indoor Environmental Quality, Innovation and Regional Priority (Chapters 12 and 13)	151–174
7	Part III: Study Tips (Chapter 14), Study Flashcards, rewrite your Cheat Sheet a few times, and take online Practice Exams	175–182
8	Register and Take LEED Green Associate Exam!!	

As the preceding table shows, it is recommended that you read through Parts I and II of this exam prep book within six weeks. Introductory terminology from Part I should be absorbed to get on the right path to understand the more critical exam-oriented information presented in Part II. The goal is to create a complete set of flashcards during the first six weeks while reading through the material, thus allowing the following week (seventh week of studying) to focus on memorizing and studying the flashcards, followed by taking a few online practice exams which are available at www.wiley.com/go/leedgreenassociate.

Although the exam format and structure will be reviewed in Part III of this book, there is one component that should be revealed up front. When at the testing center and about to take the exam, there will be an opportunity to make a "cheat sheet" of sorts. Although you will not be allowed to bring any paper, books, or pencils into the exam area, you will be supplied with blank paper and a pencil (or a dry-erase board and a marker). So now that you know this opportunity is there, let's take advantage of it! Therefore, as a concept, strategy, referenced standard, or requirement is presented in this exam prep guide, make note of it on one single sheet of paper. At the end of Part II, this "cheat sheet" should be reviewed and then rewritten with the critical information you determine that you might forget during the exam. You are the only one who knows your weaknesses in terms of the information you need to learn—I can only make recommendations and suggestions. During Week Seven, you should rewrite your cheat sheet two to three more times. The more you write and rewrite your cheat sheet, the better chance you will have for actually retaining the information. It is also advised that you monitor the time it takes to generate your cheat sheet, as time will be limited on exam day.

If you maintain the recommended study schedule, six weeks from now a set of flashcards will be created and your cheat sheet started. Then you will have one week of straight studying time focused on the material in your flashcards. After studying your flashcards, it is recommended that you take a few online practice exams to test your knowledge. The approach to these sample exams is described in Part III, Chapter 14, of this book, including the next steps for the cheat sheet. After a few practice exams, an assessment of your preparation should be completed to determine if you are ready for the exam. Your exam date should be scheduled at that time.

Before focusing on the exam material, be sure to read through Chapter 1 to understand the exam registration and application process of the LEED Green Associate exam.

TIP **Study:** After taking a few practice exams, you may want to add to your cheat sheet and/or your flashcards.

TIP **Study:** Eager for even more information? Check out the Online Resources section at the end of each chapter for links to videos and websites with more information.

PART I

RAMPING UP

CHAPTER 1

UNDERSTANDING THE CREDENTIALING PROCESS

BEFORE DIVING INTO THE EFFORT OF STUDYING and preparing for the LEED® Green Associate™ exam, there are quite a few things to review. Whenever I teach an exam prep course, this topic is not typically addressed until the end of the class, as it is easier to digest at that point; but it is important to present this information here in the first chapter, to make sure the test is applicable and appropriate for you. This chapter will provide the important concepts of the tiered credentialing system to ensure that the components and the exam registration process are understood.

This initial information begins with the credentialing system for LEED accreditation, as it involves three tiers:

1. LEED Green Associate

2. LEED Accredited Professional (AP) with Specialty

3. LEED Fellow

THE TIERS OF THE CREDENTIALING PROCESS

The first step of comprehending the credentialing process begins with a brief understanding of the basics of LEED. LEED is the acronym for Leadership in Energy and Environmental Design, signifying a green building rating system designed to evaluate projects and award them certification based on their performance. The U.S. Green Building Council's (USGBC®) website indicates that LEED is a "nationally accepted benchmark for the design, construction, and operation of high performance green buildings."[1] USGBC created the LEED Green Building Rating System™ back in the 1990s as a tool for the public and private commercial real estate markets to help evaluate the performance of the built environment. It now has become "the most widely recognized and widely used green building program across the globe."[2]

 TIP **Study:** Notice the LEED acronym does **not** contain an "S" at the end. Therefore, please note this first lesson: when referring to LEED, please do not say "LEEDS," as it is quite important to refer to the acronym correctly.

 Use white index cards to create flashcards to remember the acronyms for USGBC and LEED.

LEED Green Associate

The **LEED Green Associate** tier is applicable for individuals with a basic understanding of green building systems and technologies. These individuals have been tested on the key components of the different LEED green building rating systems and the certification process. This level of credentialing is the first step to becoming a LEED Accredited Professional.

The LEED Green Associate exam is geared toward all persons involved in the world of sustainable design, construction, and operations, beyond just the typical architecture and engineering design students and professionals. Therefore, the exam is available for lawyers, accountants, contractors, owners, and developers as well. Any person interested in the field of sustainable design and green building is eligible to sit for the exam, especially those with LEED project experience. For those who wish to sit without LEED project experience or are not employed in the field, it is recommended to attend an educational course focused in sustainable design.

LEED Accredited Professional with Specialty

The second tier, **LEED AP™ with Specialty**, is divided into five types (of specialties):

1. *LEED AP Building Design + Construction* (BD+C). This exam includes concepts related to new construction and major renovations in the commercial, residential, educational, and healthcare sectors. The project types include new construction, core and shell, schools, retail, hospitality, data centers, warehouses and distribution centers, healthcare, homes, and midrise multifamily residential structures.

2. *LEED AP Interior Design + Construction* (ID+C). This exam contains questions related to tenant improvement and fit-out project knowledge for commercial interior, retail, and hospitality professionals.

3. *LEED AP Operations + Maintenance* (O+M). This exam covers existing building project knowledge specific to operations and maintenance issues of commercial facilities, schools, retail facilities, hospitality facilities, data centers, and warehouses and distribution centers.

4. *LEED AP Homes.* This exam applies to professionals practicing in the residential market.

5. *LEED AP Neighborhood Development* (ND). This exam tests whole or partial neighborhood development project knowledge.

 TIP While there is an additional application fee to separate the LEED AP exam into two different test dates, it is highly recommended to take the LEED Green Associate exam one day and take the AP specialty exam on another.

Because the LEED Green Associate credentialing tier is the first step to obtaining LEED AP status, the LEED AP exams are thought of in a two-part exam process beginning with the LEED Green Associate exam. You have the option to decide whether you wish to take both exams in one day or break the exam into two different testing appointments. The exams are quite challenging and mind intensive, and can be exhausting, so bear this in mind when deciding on which option to pursue.

LEED project experience is no longer required in order to be able to sit for any of the LEED AP specialty exams. These exams cover more in-depth knowledge of each of the prerequisites and credits of the LEED Rating Systems, the requirements to comply including documentation and calculations, and the technologies involved with the corresponding rating system. These exams are therefore applicable for those professionals working on LEED registered projects or those who worked on projects that have earned certification.

LEED Fellow

Finally, the third tier of the credentialing system, **LEED Fellow**, is the highest level of credentialing. It is meant to signify a demonstration of accomplishments, experience, and proficiency within the sustainable design and construction community. These individuals are considered to be "the most exceptional professionals in the green building industry" because they have made a significant contribution to green building and sustainability at a regional, national or global level."[3] These professionals have established extraordinary achievement in the following:

- Technical knowledge and skill.
- A history of exemplary leadership in green building significant contributions in teaching, mentoring, or research with proven outcomes.
- A history of highly impactful commitment, service, and advocacy for green building and sustainability.[4]

LEED Professional Certificates™

LEED Professional Certificates are available to individuals interested in the residential market and are seeking the LEED for Homes Green Rater credential. The Green Classroom Professional certificate is available to individuals eager to create green schools in which to work and teach.

THE EXAM REGISTRATION PROCESS

Now that there is an understanding about the three tiers of the credentialing system and whom each tier is geared for, it is time to review the process for registering for the exam. The first step involves visiting the USGBC website at www. usgbc.org and downloading the *LEED Green Associate Candidate Handbook* found in the LEED Credentials section of the website.

 Study: USGBC updates the candidate handbooks for each of the exam types at the beginning of each month, so make sure to have the most current version.

Each of the candidate handbooks details the following information:

- Study materials—including exam format, timing, references, and sample questions.
- How to register for the exam—including the registration period, eligibility requirements, and exam fees.
- How to schedule your exam—including confirmation, canceling, and rescheduling your test date.
- A pre-exam checklist.
- What to expect on the day of your exam—including name requirements, scoring, and testing center regulations.
- What to do after your exam—including the Credentialing Maintenance Program (i.e., continuing education requirements) and certificates.

Although the intention of this exam prep book is to consolidate all of the information needed to prepare for the LEED Green Associate exam, some of the references are updated from time to time. Therefore, this book contains similar information as found in the handbooks to add efficiency, but it is best advised to reference the latest version of the handbook appropriate to the LEED Green Associate credentialing tier for the most recent exam information.

 The exam is offered in English but translation is available to non-native English speakers. Refer to the *LEED Green Associate Candidate Handbook* for more information.

Once the handbook is downloaded and reviewed, the next step includes establishing an account with the USGBC website if you have not already done so. To set up a new account, go to www.usgbc.org/registration/create-user. It

TIP **Study:** It is not only important to refer to LEED correctly, but also to the projects and professionals involved. Remember buildings are **certified** and people are **accredited**. People will never be able to become LEED certified professionals—remember, there are LEED APs and not LEED CPs.

Additionally, LEED **certification** is meant for projects and buildings, not products. Not only will a LEED certified professional not be found, but also neither will a LEED certified chair, air-conditioning unit, appliance, paint, or glue.

TIP If you work for a member organization of USGBC, be sure to connect your USGBC account in order to take advantage of the member discount available for the exam fee.

TIP Remember, employees of USGBC member companies and full-time students can take advantage of reduced exam fees.

TIP To reschedule or cancel an exam date, please consult the *LEED Green Associate Candidate Handbook* for explicit instructions. They are quite meticulous about the procedure, so it is advised to be aware of the details to avoid risking a loss in fees paid.

is critical to sign up and create the account with USGBC consistent with the account holder's name as it appears on the identification to be used to check in at the testing center. If they do not match on the day of the exam, exam fees may be lost, and the opportunity to take the exam may be forfeited. If your existing account with USGBC is not consistent with your identification, refer to the LEED Green Associate Handbook for instructions.

REGISTER!

Once an account is established with USGBC, the next step is to register for the exam. It is advised not to register for the exam any longer than one month prior to your desired exam date. To register for the exam, visit www.usgbc.org/leed/credentials, click on "Register for the Exam," input the required information, and pay the exam fee. An approved registration is valid for up to one year, once the exam fees are paid. After the fee has been paid, you will be redirected to Prometric to schedule your exam.

SCHEDULE!

The next step is scheduling an appointment to take the exam at a Prometric testing center. As stated previously, it is advised to hold off from selecting an exam date until further along in the preparation for the exam. In the introduction of this exam prep book, a study and reading schedule is suggested. It is best recommended to start studying and determine the level of knowledge of the test content before scheduling an exam date.

When ready to schedule an exam date, please visit www.prometric.com/gbci or, if signed into your account at the USGBC website, follow the links to the Prometric website to schedule a day to take the exam, from the "Credentials" section. After an exam date is scheduled, a confirmation code is displayed on the screen. Keep this code! This code will be needed should the selected exam date need to be canceled, confirmed, or rescheduled with Prometric. A confirmation email will be sent from Prometric shortly after scheduling.

In addition, it is important to remember that candidates will have three allowed testing attempts per one-year registration period. In the event that a retake is necessary (even though this is not the plan!), test-takers will need to pay an additional fee for the exam. Refer to the *Green Associate Candidate Handbook* for more information on this rule.

WHY EARN LEED CREDENTIALS?

Just like green buildings are evaluated based on triple bottom criteria (social, economic, and environmental), deciding whether to earn LEED credentials can be approached in the same fashion, as there are individual, employer, and industry benefits to examine. From an individualistic standpoint, earning the LEED Green Associate credential will grant a professional with a differentiator to market to a potential employer or client, provide them with exposure on the USGBC website database of LEED professionals, and earn them a certificate to display and recognition as a professional on the LEED certification process. An employer would also benefit by earning the eligibility to participate on LEED projects, as more projects are requiring LEED credentials for team members; building the firm's credentials when responding to requests for proposals (RFPs) and requests for qualifications (RFQs); and having the opportunity to encourage other staff members to aim for the same credential to help the firm to evolve. Finally, the market would also benefit as more professionals earn the LEED Green Associate credential by helping the built environment to become more sustainable and the market to evolve, transform, and grow.

QUIZ TIME!

*These questions are formatted just as they would be on the exam. Notice the question indicates how many answers to select. The proper number of correct answers is required on the exam, as partial credit is **not** awarded.*

In an effort to present information to you in multiple ways and help you learn, you may find questions asking about information that is new to you, that you did not read about throughout the book.

Q1.1   How many types of credentials for LEED AP with Specialty are available? (Choose one)

   A. 5

   B. 6

   C. 3

   D. 4

   E. 2

Q1.2   Is it possible to sit for the LEED Green Associate exam and the LEED AP ID+C exam in one day?

   A. Yes

   B. No

Q1.3   Is LEED project experience needed in order to sit for the LEED AP O+M exam?

   A. Yes

   B. No

Q1.4   How long is the exam registration period valid? (Choose one)

   A. One week

   B. One month

   C. 3 months

   D. One year

   E. It never expires

Q1.5   What does LEED stand for? (Choose one)

   A. Leadership in Energy Efficient Design

   B. Leadership in Efficient and Effective Design

    C. Leadership in Energy and Environmental Design

    D. Leadership in Environmental and Energy Design

ONLINE RESOURCES

Access information about the available credentials and certificates at www.usgbc.org/leed/credentials#certificates.

    Create a USGBC account at www.usgbc.org/registration/create-user.

    Register for the LEED Green Associate exam at www.usgbc.org/exam-registration/exam?exam=2773636.

    Schedule your exam at www.prometric.com/gbci.

NOTES

1. USGBC website, www.usgbc.org/Docs/Archive/General/Docs3330.pdf.

2. USGBC website, www.usgbc.org/about.

3. USGBC website, www.usgbc.org/articles/learn-how-become-leed-fellow.

4. Ibid.

CHAPTER 2

INTRODUCTION TO THE CONCEPTS OF SUSTAINABLE DESIGN

AS MENTIONED EARLIER, IT IS CRITICAL TO be on the right path of understanding the basic concepts before jumping into the details of Leadership in Energy and Environmental Design (LEED®) strategies and technologies. Therefore, sustainability and green building are described and detailed as a starting point. What is *sustainability*? The U.S. Environmental Protection Agency's (EPA) website indicates that "sustainability creates and maintains the conditions under which humans and nature can exist in productive harmony, that permit fulfilling the social, economic, and other requirements of present and future generations."[1] For the purposes of LEED, it is important to take a step further beyond sustainability and think of sustainable design and green building concepts. Within the design industry, sustainable design and sustainable building concepts are interchangeable with the term *green building*, "a process that applies to buildings, their sites, their interiors, their operations, and the communities in which they are situated."[2] Green building strategies encompasses more than reduced environmental impact but can improve the conditions for the planet and interior environments for building occupants. It's a holistic approach to finding responsible solutions within the build environment.

When referring to green buildings, it is understood that the buildings are sensitive to the environment, but one might wonder how exactly? Green buildings are more efficient and use resources wisely, as they take energy, water, and materials into account (Figure 2.1). But "how do they use resources more efficiently?" one might ask. To answer this question, it is important to think of the different aspects of a building, for instance:

- *Site selection.* Is the project a redevelopment in an urban area or does it support urban sprawl? How close is the project to public transportation to reduce the amount of cars coming and going? How will the building need to be situated in order to take advantage of the natural breezes for ventilation and daylight to reduce the need for artificial lighting within the building?

- *Design of the building systems, such as mechanical equipment, building envelope, and lighting systems.* How do they work together? Were they designed independently of each other? Is the heat emitted from the lighting

 Set aside white index cards to create flashcards to remember the concepts of sustainable design throughout this chapter.

Figure 2.1 The BASF North American Headquarters project in Florham Park, New Jersey, incorporates multiple green building strategies within the base building and the tenant space, helping the project to earn platinum certification under both the LEED for Core & Shell™ and LEED for Commercial Interiors™ rating systems. *Photo courtesy of BASF Corporation*

> **TIP**
>
> **Study:** When thinking of green buildings, it is important to think of not only how the building is designed to function and how it is constructed, but also the environmental impacts from operations and maintenance.

fixtures accounted for? Are there gaps in the envelope that allow conditioned air to escape?

- *Construction processes.* Think about the people on site during construction—are they being exposed to harmful fumes and gases? Are precautions being taken to reduce the chances for mold growth or other contaminants?

- *Operations of the building.* What kind of items are purchased to support business? What about cleaning procedures?

- *Maintenance.* When was the last time equipment was tested to ensure it is performing appropriately? Are there procedures in place to monitor for leaks?

- *Waste management.* How is construction waste addressed? What about the garbage generated during operations? Is it going to the landfill? Who knows where those containers are going?!

THE BENEFITS OF GREEN BUILDINGS

Hopefully, the previous questions started to generate some thoughts of what is involved with green buildings. If not, maybe evaluating the benefits of green buildings might help, beginning with a review of the traditional buildings statistics and how they impact our planet. The U.S. Green Building Council (USGBC®) has compiled information from the Energy Information Administration and the U.S. Geological Survey on the impacts of buildings on our natural resources in the United States. According to the *Green Building and LEED Core Concepts Guide,* buildings account for:

24 to 50 percent of energy use

72 percent of electricity consumption

38 percent of carbon dioxide (CO_2) emissions

14 percent of potable water consumption

30 percent of waste output

40 percent of raw materials use[3]

It is important to digest the 38 percent CO_2 emissions statistic, as this percentage puts buildings at the top of the list, followed by transportation and industry. Buildings have a bigger impact on greenhouse gas emissions—the biggest actually! "Greenhouse gas emissions come from many components of the built environment, including building systems and energy use, transportation, water use and treatment, land-cover change, materials and construction."[4] At 38 percent, there is a push for the market to find better ways to design, construct, and operate buildings. Numerous state and local governments have become aware of this need to raise the preceding minimal building code requirements to help reduce the emissions from buildings and facilities and improve public health, safety, and environmental quality. As a result, the International Green Construction Code (IGCC) has been developed to work in tandem with traditional building codes and give the industry a basis of smart public policy.

When looking at the statistics for green buildings, including LEED-certified buildings, the General Services Administration (GSA) indicates that these projects have been able to achieve the following:

26 percent energy use reduction

33 percent lower CO_2 emissions

13 percent reduction in maintenance costs[5]

These percentages reflect the benefits in the economic bottom line, but these green buildings have also reduced their impact on the environment, as well as demonstrated an improved indoor environment (in terms of air quality) and contribution to the community. Indoor air quality is extremely important when analyzing the benefits of green buildings, as the Environmental Protection Agency (EPA) reports Americans "spend, on average, 90 percent or more of their time indoors."[6] Green buildings have resulted in 27 percent higher levels of satisfaction[7] and allowed students the opportunity to perform better.[8] So as you can see, green building is more than strategies to reduce greenhouse gas emissions.

The Triple Bottom Line

The values of green buildings are summarized in three components: environmental, economic, and health and community. In the green building industry, these three concepts are defined as the *triple bottom line* (Figure 2.2). A conventional project usually assesses only the singular component of the economic prosperity for the project. However, when determining the goals for a project seeking LEED certification, the process typically begins with assessing the goals in comparison to the *triple* bottom line values. For example, should a client wish to install a green roof on their building, the team would assess the financial implications as compared to the environmental impacts versus the community

Study: Write it, read it, say it, and hear it as many times as possible. The more senses you involve in your studying efforts, the more information you will be able to retain.

Study: The IGCC includes ASHRAE 189.1 as an alternative compliance path.

Make a flashcard to remember the percentages of savings of green buildings.

Study: The term *triple bottom line* was first used in a book by John Elkington, *Cannibals with Forks: The Triple Bottom Line of 21st Century Business.*

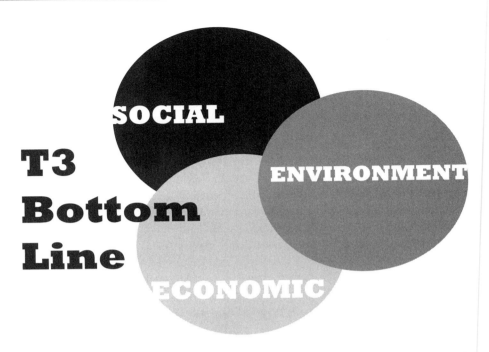

Figure 2.2 The triple bottom line.

benefits. These types of details will be discussed later, but understanding the three types of benefits is important at this time.

SYSTEMS THINKING

Systems thinking is an important concept as related to sustainable design, as the built environment is composed of a series of interrelated systems that form a whole and therefore not only impact each other but many other components as well. "Systems include materials, resources, energy, people, and information, as well as the complex interactions and flows between these elements across space and through time."[9]

The idea behind this concept is to remind us that all the different components within the built environment do not work in isolation. There are small systems and large systems; in either case, they are infinite in the sense that they do not end. For example, granite brought into a building from the outside is used as a countertop for years and then disposed of. This is an example of an open system, when materials are released in some form of sewage, solid waste, or pollution. A more sustainable solution is to mimic nature and slow the passing of materials and resources through the system by designing closed systems. The challenge is to remember how the systems are related to one another, as one decision can have a ripple effect. Understanding the trade-offs and synergies of green building strategies will be discussed in Part II of this book and are summarized in Appendix E. For now, it is important to understand the process of systems thinking.

Feedback Loops

Feedback loops help to describe how the concept of systems thinking works. There are two types of feedback loops: negative and positive. The *Green Building and LEED Core Concepts Guide* uses a thermostat as an example of a **negative feedback loop**, since the mechanical system is enabled to self-correct and, in turn, stabilize itself.[10]

Positive feedback loops are perpetual and ongoing. Population growth, urban sprawl, and climate change are all examples of positive feedback loops, as every stage stimulates the next. Let's use Ashburn, Virginia, a town 30 miles west of Washington, D.C., as a prime example of urban sprawl. With building height restrictions in Washington, D.C., development has pushed out from the urban core demanding more and more infrastructure. Not only have utilities been expanded west, but the Washington Metro is following suit with a planned expansion of the Silver line to Dulles Airport and beyond. These types of expansion only encourage and support more growth.

What can we learn from the two types of feedback loops? Think about older buildings without the technology currently available, including sensors and controls. How do they account for fluctuations throughout the day or different seasons? The same holds true for newer buildings with sensors in need of repair or that are blocked. Basically, it comes down to information. Without information, the systems cannot respond. How can we change the mind-set of staff members who do not shut off their computers at night if we do not have the data to convince them to use energy more efficiently? The key is to make the information not only available but also convenient. This is known as the **Prius effect**. If users are given real-time information, they tend to react and respond to the feedback loop.

 Make two flashcards to remember positive and negative feedback loops.

 Make another flashcard to remember the Prius effect.

Leverage Points

"To influence the behavior of a system, it is important to find the **leverage points**—places where a small intervention can yield large changes. Providing building occupants with real-time energy information is an example of using a leverage point to alter behavior."[11] It is obviously a lot more cost effective and sustainable to alter the behavior of use, as compared to modifying the entire mechanical system.

As part of systems thinking, it is important to understand the different scales at which leverage points can be utilized. As previously mentioned, changing from an open system to a closed system is more sustainable. This concept can apply on a project-by-project basis or on a larger scale. The *Green Building and LEED Core Concepts Guide* provides an example of Interface Flooring, a carpet manufacturer, and how they shifted from just manufacturing and selling carpet to servicing the carpet. This expansion of service transitioned the company to a more sustainable model, reducing waste and improving performance.

LIFE-CYCLE APPROACH

Green building projects are encouraged to question all phases of a project, a material or product, and service. These types of questions include: Where did it come from? What happens to them after they are no longer useful? What impacts do they have along the way? When thinking about these types of aspects, project teams are taking a life-cycle approach to decision making (Figure 2.3).

Figure 2.3 The ebony oak wood for the reception desk and other areas at One Haworth Center in Holland, Michigan, was recovered from the Great Lakes and other waterways to avoid depleting old-growth forests. *Photo courtesy of Haworth Inc.*

TIP **Study:** Chapter 11 discusses the environmental components of LCAs of building materials and products.

The life-cycle approach for a building starts before a site has been selected, and continues through design, construction, operations, refurbishment, and renovation. Ideally, a building's life cycle avoids demolition and the building is adapted and reused. Think back to the concept of systems thinking and closing the system.

Project teams are encouraged to apply life-cycle thinking when evaluating environmental impacts related to a building, not just products and materials. To do this, they can choose between two methodologies: life-cycle assessment (LCA) and **life-cycle cost** (LCC). LCA is discussed in more detail in Chapter 11. LCC includes the purchase price, fuel, installation, operation, maintenance, disposal, finance charges, and replacement costs for each technology and strategy proposed to determine the appropriateness of the solution specific to the project, from an environmental and economic perspective.

DO GREEN BUILDINGS COST MORE?

When assessing the cost of any type of project, it is important to understand the different types of costs involved. Traditionally, only two types of costs are detailed in a project's pro forma: hard costs and soft costs. Hard costs are defined as while soft costs are related to the fees for professional services including legal and design. Soft costs also include pre- and postconstruction-related expenses, such as insurance.

USGBC has promoted many studies, including one from Davis Langdon, indicating that green building does not have to cost more. "There are expensive green buildings, and there are expensive conventional buildings. Certification as a green building was not a significant indicator of construction cost."[12] This is especially true if the project starts the process early in the design phases. In the next chapter, you will learn about the integrative process and the need for an iterative approach to discover alternative technologies, systems, and materials. Before working on a green building project, one might misconceive these concepts and processes to be a burdensome cost added on to a project's budget. This kind of mind-set is lacking the long-term view of operational savings of high-performance equipment and systems. Therefore, it is important to bridge the gap between capital and operating budgets to understand the value of green building technologies and strategies. For example, the first or up-front cost of installing photovoltaic panels, high-efficiency mechanical systems, or an indoor water wall to improve indoor air quality may not fit in a typical budget, but if the utility cost savings were considered and evaluated, either one might make more sense. Another case in point, first costs may also be higher in a traditionally designed project because of the lack of integration. For example, a mechanical engineer may specify a larger mechanical system than what is actually needed because they may not realize that high-performance windows were specified by the architect, along with building insulation with a higher R-value. Remember, the economic bottom line is important, but a green building also evaluates the environmental and social impacts and benefits.

QUIZ TIME!

These questions are formatted just as they would be on the exam. Notice the question indicates how many answers to select. The proper number of correct answers is required on the exam, as partial credit is not awarded.

In an effort to present information to you in multiple ways and help you learn, you may find questions asking about information that is new to you, that you did not read about throughout the book.

Q2.1   Which of the following is an environmental benefit of green building? (Choose one)

    A. Conserve natural resources

    B. Reduce solid waste

    C. Improve air and water quality

    D. Enhance and protect ecosystems and biodiversity

    E. All of the above

Q2.2 How much time, on average, do Americans spend indoors? (Choose one)

A. 10 percent

B. 90 percent

C. 65 percent

D. 35 percent

Q2.3 According to the Department of Energy's website, space heating is the largest energy use in the United States, followed by lighting. True or false?

A. True

B. False

Q2.4 Which of the following describes a high-performance green building? (Choose one)

A. Conserves water and energy

B. Uses spaces, materials, and resources efficiently

C. Minimizes construction waste

D. Creates a healthy indoor environment

E. All of the above

Q2.5 Which of the following statements are true? (Choose two)

A. The built environment refers to any man-made environment.

B. The built environment refers to any element in nature.

C. The built environment provides structure for human activity.

D. The built environment refers to animal-made shelters.

E. The built environment includes individual buildings and not neighborhoods.

Q2.6 When working on a green building project, when is the best time to incorporate an integrative design approach? (Choose one)

A. Schematic design

B. Construction documents

C. Design development

D. Beginning of construction

E. Substantial completion

Q2.7 Life-cycle assessments (LCAs) are a beneficial tool to determine which of the following? (Choose one)

A. Environmental benefits and potential impacts of a material, product, or technology

B. Economics of building systems during the life of the building

C. Environmental impacts of materials during construction

D. Social impacts of policies during a fiscal year

E. Maintenance implications, including cost, during the life of the building

Q2.8 The project team is looking to conduct a life-cycle cost analysis as a method of evaluating alternative flooring products. Which of the following should they take into consideration as inputs to that analysis? (Choose two)

A. First costs, excluding the cost of installation

B. First costs, including the cost of installation

C. Maintenance, life expectancy, and replacement cost

D. Maintenance and replacement cost, but not life expectancy

NOTES

1. EPA website, www.epa.gov/sustainability/basicinfo.htm.

2. USGBC, *Green Building and LEED Core Concepts Guide,* 3rd ed. (2014), 5.

3. Ibid., p. 3.

4. Ibid., p. 8.

5. GSA Public Buildings Service, "Assessing Green Building Performance: A Post Occupancy Evaluation of 12 GSA Buildings" (2008).

6. Environmental Protection Agency. "The Inside Story: A Guide to Indoor Air Quality." U.S. EPA/Office of Air and Radiation. Office of Radiation and Indoor Air (6609J) Cosponsored with the Consumer Product Safety Commission, EPA 402-K-93-007, www.epa.gov/iaq/pubs/insidestory.html.

7. See note 5.

8. USGBC, *Green Building and LEED Core Concepts Guide,* p. 6.

9. Ibid., p. 19.

10. Ibid., p. 21.

11. Ibid., p. 24.

12. L. F. Matthiessen and P. Morris, "Cost of Green Revisited: Reexamining the Feasibility and Cost Impact of Sustainable Design in the Light of Increased Market Adoption" (http://sustainability.ucr.edu/docs/leed-cost-of-green.pdf, Davis Langdon, 2007), www.davislangdon.com.

CHAPTER **3**

INTEGRATIVE
PROCESS

CHAPTER 2 PREPARED YOU WITH THE CONCEPTS and benefits of sustainable design, but you might be thinking, "This sounds great, but how does a project team coordinate the triple bottom line concepts successfully?" The answer is simple: the integrative process.

Before diving into an explanation of the integrative process, perhaps it would be helpful to identify the different project team members and then review the conventional process of designing and constructing a project to truly understand the importance and key aspects of the integrative process.

Set aside white index cards to create flashcards to remember the concepts of integrative design throughout this chapter.

THE PROJECT TEAM MEMBERS

Understanding the processes of design and construction, from a traditional or conventional standpoint versus that of sustainable projects, begins with an understanding of the players involved in the process:

Architect. Responsible for the design of green building strategies, including overall site planning and interior spaces.

MEP engineer. Responsible for the design of the energy and water systems of a building, more specifically, the mechanical, electrical, and plumbing components, including thermal impacts.

Landscape architect. Responsible for the selection of trees and plants, the impacts of shading, and water efficiency for irrigation; also responsible for vegetated roof design.

Civil engineer. Responsible for site design, including rainwater management, open space requirements, and site protection.

Contractor. Typically referred to as the GC, short for general contractor. Responsible for the demolition (if required) and construction of a facility, including site work.

Facility manager. Also referred to as a building engineer. Responsible for maintaining a building and its site during operations.

Commissioning authority (CxA). Responsible for the commissioning process, including drawing review during design and equipment installation and performance review during construction.

Owner. Defines the triple bottom line goals and selects the team members for a project. Can be a developer and does not have to be the end user.

End users/occupants. The inhabitants of a building and therefore should be the main priority when designing for comfort and productivity.

For those not familiar with the professionals involved, create flashcards for each to remember their roles and importance.

19

THE TRADITIONAL APPROACH

With a traditionally designed project, an owner may hire a civil engineer or environmental team once they select a piece of property. Once the environmental reports are completed and they have an idea of how their building can fit on the site, the site plan is handed off to an architect. The architect then works with the owner to detail the program requirements (known as the programming phase) and then begins to design the building (known as the schematic design phase). The architect then works with an engineering team (typically composed of mechanical, electrical, and plumbing engineers and a structural engineer, if needed, depending on the project type). These professionals typically work independently of each other to complete their tasks (known as the design development phase). Remember with a traditionally designed project, the architect has already designed the building and is now handing off the plans to the engineers to fit the building systems into the building that was designed without their input. Once the basic design elements are established, each professional works to complete a set of construction documents (CDs). Notice that the responsibilities are segmented just as the communication is fragmented.

What happens next with the CDs varies with different project types. Typically, these documents are first issued for permit review by the local municipality. It is quite common for most conventional project types to send the CDs out for bid to a number of contractors about the same time as the drawings are issued for permit review (known as a design-bid-build project type).

At this point in a design-bid-build project type, the contractor is given a short period of time in which to evaluate the drawings and provide the owner with a fee to provide demolition services (if required) and to construct the building, including site development work. They are given an opportunity in which they can submit questions (known as requests for information, or RFIs) about the requirements or design elements during this bidding process, but then they are held to the quote they provide. Remember, the contractor was not engaged during the previous design phases, so they are not familiar with the project and have to dive in quickly, sometimes making assumptions about the construction requirements. Most of the time, projects are awarded based on the lowest bid, but think about the implications of doing so. If the lowest bidder wins the job, where are they cutting corners? Is quality being compromised? Was a critical element omitted? No one likes to lose money, as that is just bad business, but is this really the best way to select a contractor?

Once the permit is received, the contractor is selected, and the construction cost is agreed upon, the phases of the design process are over and the construction process begins. Just as the design process has four phases, the construction process does as well. Construction commences the process, traditionally with little involvement from the design team. The next phase, substantial completion, includes the final inspection process and when the owner issues a "punch list." The owner compiles a punch list while walking the space with the contractor and notes any problems requiring the contractor's attention. Final completion is next, followed by the certification of occupancy. Once the certificate of occupancy is received, the building is then permitted to be occupied.

TIP | **Study:** Notice when all the players were introduced to the project and how they all worked in a linear and independent fashion for the traditional approach.

THE INTEGRATIVE APPROACH TO DESIGN AND CONSTRUCTION

Project teams working on sustainable projects are encouraged to balance the triple bottom line concepts, as mentioned in Chapter 2. The integrative process helps project teams to find the synergies between the various components of a building and the property in which it resides. When compared to the traditional project delivery method, the integrative process for sustainable design projects requires a different approach, a different mind-set, perhaps requiring new skills for critical thinking, teamwork, and communication to "enhance the efficiency and effectiveness of every system."[1] As you will find, the process is more than a checklist or using building information modeling (BIM). The integrative process requires input and participation from every project team member, especially in the early stages, to understand the building systems interrelationships and discover opportunities for increased performance, efficiencies, and environmental benefits.

This chapter will explain the collaborative process and the tasks to be completed during the three stages of the integrative process:

 Create a flashcard to remember the three stages of the integrative process.

- Discovery

- Design and construction

- Occupancy, operations, and performance feedback

Discovery

The first phase of the integrative process is considered to be the most important, as the discovery phase expands the concepts of the conventional design phase of predesign, to ensure that a project's environmental goals are established early and cost effectively. If you remember, the tasks within the predesign phase typically occur prior to site selection or immediately afterward. Traditionally, the owner would engage one or two consultants, where the integrative process encourages participation and input from the entire team to ensure proper site selection and analysis. The discovery phase also encourages goal-setting exercises from the triple bottom line perspective.

During this phase, project teams are encouraged to implement the following five foundation principles for successful practice[2]:

- *Process matters.* With the right process, successful outcomes are inevitable.

- *Get in early.* The earlier the better to ensure the least expensive approach. For master planning projects, project teams should start the integrative process at the early stages of land-use planning; preferably, new construction projects should start prior to purchasing the land, and existing building projects should start before making any changes to policies, renovations, or other operational function.

- *Follow through.* Commitment to green building practices should be made as early as possible and kept throughout the life of the project. Continued commitment is the only way to ensure that the strategies implemented remain effective. Ongoing training should be included in the commitment, as it "ensures knowledgeable operation and maintenance of these strategies and technologies, as well as an opportunity to provide feedback on the challenges faced and lessons learned."[3]

■ *Look beyond first costs to long-term savings.* One of the hardest aspects of the integrative process for project teams to digest is cost. As mentioned in the previous chapter, implementing green building strategies and concepts does not have to cost more. The key is to understand that there is a shift to up-front investments in high-performance systems to increase efficiency to witness savings during operations.

■ *Include and collaborate.* Bring a multidisciplinary team of professionals together with the community to look at the project from a holistic manner in a collaborative setting.

An Iterative Process

When approaching a green building project, teams must move away from a linear approach, as it can lead to inefficient solutions. The traditional process of handing off work to the next person after a task is completed is replaced with collaborations of small groups working as a whole, "to develop the project design and plan collaboratively. Ideas are continually being developed by the entire team, researched and refined by smaller groups, and then brought back to the team to consider critical next steps and make final decisions."[4]

The cyclical nature of the iterative process allows for numerous feedback loops to allow for establishing goals and assessing design, construction, and operational strategies against those goals:[5]

■ Establish clear goals and overarching commitments.

■ Brainstorm and develop creative solutions.

■ Research and refine ideas.

■ Explore synergies between specific strategies.

■ Establish metrics for measuring success.

■ Set new goals based on the work that has been done.

For a project seeking Leadership in Energy and Environmental Design (LEED®) certification, the owner is encouraged engage a number of consultants during the discovery phase to assist in selecting the property or tenant space. They may retain an architect to evaluate the site for building orientation options to capitalize on natural ventilation or daylighting opportunities. They may hire a civil engineer to research the rainwater codes and to determine access to public transportation. A consultant may be engaged to assist with evaluating the triple bottom line goals. Think about the benefits of bringing the landscape architect and the civil engineer on board simultaneously so they could work together to reveal the opportunities to use rainwater collection for irrigation needs.

The iterative process allows for feedback loop opportunities to discuss these types of synergies. These feedback opportunities can range from small task groups to team meetings, stakeholder meetings, and goal setting meetings. These goal-setting meetings, or *charrettes,* are a key component of the iterative process, as they bring together stakeholders and professionals from different disciplines and experiences to brainstorm and collaborate to produce specific deliverables (Figure 3.1).

 TIP   **Study:** Charrettes are named after the carts that carried French architecture students' models to their final review (often as the students frantically completed their work en route with the help of friends).[6]

TIP   **Study:** The term *stakeholder* encompasses more than just decision makers and includes those who must live with the decisions and those who must carry them out.[7]

Figure 3.1 Conducting charrettes helps to facilitate critical thinking and collaborations between disciplines to find synergies between a building and its site. *Photo courtesy of Moshier Studio*

Team Selection

Successful projects are tied to a common understanding of goals, intentions, and commitment of the entire project team. Contracts that address these parameters ensure an identification of roles and responsibilities, and therefore eliminate confusion for the duration of the project, although sometimes it is difficult for the team to achieve this level of understanding before the goals of the project are defined.

After the charrette, the owner can distribute a request for qualifications (RFQ) based on the requirements of the project to find the best-suited consultants, depending on the project type. This can include the roles of the attendees of the charrette, or it can be used to find the missing disciplines required, such as a lighting designer or landscape architect. It might include past experience with green building or LEED-certified projects and/or LEED-credentialed professionals, whether Green Associates™ or LEED Accredited Professionals.

Remember, in the traditional approach, the owner engages different team members in a linear fashion, missing the opportunity to take advantage of the

Create a flashcard to remember what an IPD is.

different expertise and input of the professionals involved. Design-build and **integrative project delivery** (IPD) contract projects reap the collaborative benefits by bringing the project team together during the integrative process, as opposed to the tradition design-bid-build approach. Where design-bid-build projects seek the *lowest* bid, risking quality, design-build and IPD projects suggest that bids should be selected based on the *best low* bid. When design-build contracts are not possible, the owner should include qualification prerequisites in the request for proposal (RFP) in order to ensure an experienced team will be engaged.

Design and Construction

You will find Chapter 6 will describe the LEED Work Plan, a series of steps of the LEED certification process. As part of this work plan, you will find the discovery aspect of the integrative process is repetitive and ongoing through most of the design phases. As the project moves forward, the following tasks are addressed during the integrative process of design and construction:

- Goal setting
- Observation of the site
- Exploration and selection of technologies and strategies
- Implementation

Goal Setting

TIP **Study:** Project goals and their associated metrics and targets can be both quantitative and qualitative.[9]

The process of establishing the triple bottom line goals to ensure success has been emphasized and encouraged since Chapter 2. It is critical for a project teams to set clear and defined goals accompanied by "**metrics,** things that can be measured, and **targets,** levels of achievement that should be reached."[8] For example, an owner might establish water efficiency as a goal using the metric of the amount of potable water needed for irrigation. The target could stipulate a 50 percent reduction. As with most building systems in a facility, there are many aspects to water efficiency, and so a team would also need to develop metrics and targets for rainwater and vegetation, as they can impact the water efficiency goal of the project. Integrative project teams wishing to pursue LEED certification for their project scan refer to one of the LEED reference guides to help get an idea about different metrics and targets of the environmental goals.

Observation of the Site

TIP **Study:** GIS can also provide indicators of how a site is likely to evolve over time, such as growth project displays and targeted development areas.

Once the goals are defined, project teams are encouraged to study perspective sites or tenant spaces, to ensure the established goals can be met prior to selection. Project teams with a thorough understanding of the characteristics and attributes of the site (or an existing facility) are able to transition goals into action. Site assessment could include "observing the place, people, wildlife, plants, and weather," or engaging consultants, such as ecologists, hydrologists, and anthropologists, to collect systematic data.[10] Geographical information systems (GIS) aid assessment efforts with layered map data showing "soils, infrastructure, shade, wind patterns, species distribution, land uses, demographics, roads and transit routes, traffic patterns, walkways and barriers, material flows, and solid waste pathways."[11] GIS technology allows project teams to look at the site within itself, as well as the regional scale.

Understanding the existing infrastructure, roads, sidewalks, utility supply can help identify key cost components as well as how the project will be integrated into a community. Identifying the plants and wildlife will help with preservation, irrigation, and open space goals. What is the condition of the soil? How about the existing perviousness of the site? What about the microclimates? Understanding how the sun impacts the site is also an important factor relative to achieving project goals. There may be adjacent buildings hindering views or daylighting opportunities. What is the purpose of the buildings? Do they complement the project? In keeping consistent with the iterative process, before moving to the next step of integrative process, it is important to refer back to the project goals to identify synergies with the site findings.

Exploration and Selection of Technologies and Strategies

As you see, the concept of the integrative process is to spend more time up front during discovery to identify synergies, to ultimately "save time and money in both the short and the long term while optimizing resources."[12] The collaborative discovery sessions identified the cumulative understandings of system interactions to be integrated during this next phase. During this phase, strategies and technologies are explored, evaluated, and selected using systems thinking, a concept introduced in the previous chapter. When evaluating options, project teams are encouraged to refer back to the triple bottom line concepts to account for economic factors, such as cost; environmental impacts, such as carbon emissions; and social impacts, such as community involvement. "Sustainable design means finding not only the measures that perform best in a model but also the solutions that will perform best over the life of the project."[13]

During the design phase, project teams use tools, such as energy modeling and BIM, to find efficiencies and conflicts with their design intentions. They can model the proposed building systems to evaluate and predict the performance of the components specific to the elements and the project's location and site. These technologies allow the design team to specify systems and equipment sized appropriately for the specific building. Because the tools allow for the project to be evaluated from a three-dimensional perspective, design teams will also have the opportunity to find conflicts with building components and systems. The design teams can even use these tools to determine the estimated energy and water savings as compared to implementing traditional building systems and technologies. These tools are used throughout the design phase in an iterative fashion to bring more information, and ultimately efficiency, to the project.

Results of an energy model or review comments from the commissioning agent can unfortunately bring economic constraints to the table. When this occurs, project teams must avoid reverting back to the traditional method of value engineering (VE). When project teams need to reduce costs they traditionally look to up-front, first costs, forgetting about the long-term savings. With a conventional project, VE would typically take place when the bidding contractors respond with a construction cost much higher than anticipated by the owner and design professionals (since it is the first time these team members are involved in a project). In response to this high price, the design team begins to remove design elements from the original scope of work to try to get the construction cost better aligned with the project budget. However, with an integrative project

VE exercises are encouraged to "keep the big picture in mind and include all the stakeholders so that the decisions support the project goals."[14]

Existing buildings are encouraged to take the following seven steps when evaluation strategies to implement[15]:

- Set goals.
- Benchmark performance.
- Identify improvement opportunities.
- Prioritize and align improvement opportunities with the project goals.
- Implement the program.
- Measure performance and undergo third-party verification.
- Set revised or new goals.

Implementation

The implementation phase of the integrative process occurs during construction. During this phase, it is important to remember to avoid environmental damage caused by construction activities, compromising the project's commitment to sustainability by implementing the management plans consistent with the project goals. For a design-build project this might include a construction activity pollution prevention plan (discussed in Chapter 8), a waste management plan (discussed in Chapter 11), or an indoor environmental quality management plan (discussed in Chapter 12). For operations and maintenance projects, it is a bit trickier and might need to be approached as an ongoing process. Continual tweaking and training sessions will optimize operation and maintenance programs. In either case, all implementation changes should be well documented not only to track performance but for third-party verification as well.

Occupancy, Operations, and Performance Feedback

In this last phase of the integrative process, performance is measured and verified and feedback structures are setup to identify opportunities for improvement. "Feedback is critical to determining success in achieving performance targets, informing building operations, and taking corrective action when targets are missed."[16]

Ongoing Performance

A truly sustainable project is never truly complete just because the construction crew has left and the space is occupied, or when a capital improvement project is finished. Optimizing performance is extremely important and therefore proper data collection is necessary to discover inefficiencies. Facility teams must be trained to how to perform inspections, be familiar with the systems to collect the relative data, how to interpret the data, and be able to identify inconsistencies or unusual values to locate areas needing attentions or repair. Facility teams are not the only important participants of occupancy but the occupants themselves are, too. "Orientation and training of the occupants and personnel must be repeated as new tenants move in, staff is hired, and lessons are learned. Education of building occupants encourages their full participation in sustainability opportunities."[17]

QUIZ TIME!

These questions are formatted just as they would be on the exam. Notice the question indicates how many answers to select. The proper number of correct answers is required on the exam, as partial credit is not awarded.

In an effort to present information to you in multiple ways and help you learn, you may find questions asking about information that is new to you, that you did not read about throughout the book.

Q3.1 Which of the following are true statements concerning charrettes? (Choose two)

    A. An agenda and clear goals of the charrette are needed.

    B. A strong facilitator needs to be flexible and have good listening skills.

    C. The facilitator should be biased.

    D. The charrette should only include the stakeholders and the architect.

    E. Charrettes are based on a linear process and discourage brainstorming and collaboration.

Q3.2 Which of the following can enhance an understanding of community issues and concerns? (Choose one)

    A. Team meetings

    B. Small task groups

    C. Stakeholder meetings

    D. An email from the architect to the town

    E. Permit review

Q3.3 Which of the following are not true concerning establishing goals for a project? (Choose two)

    A. Goals should reflect reasonable spatial scale and time horizons.

    B. Goals can be qualitative but not quantitative.

    C. Goals can be quantitative but not qualitative.

    D. Goals should include metrics and targets.

Q3.4 Which of the following strategies is not advised and will not help meet sustainability goals? (Choose one)

    A. Start the process early.

    B. Find the right team and process.

    C. Understand the systems across space and time.

    D. Set lofty goals.

    E. Follow an iterative process.

    F. Commit to continuous improvement.

Q3.5 Which of the following statements are true? (Choose two)

A. Design-bid-build projects encourage collaboration between design and construction teams during the design process.

B. Design-build projects encourage collaboration between design and construction teams during the design process.

C. Design-bid-build projects tend to award projects to the highest bidder.

D. Design-bid-build projects tend to award projects to the lowest bidder.

E. Design-build projects tend to award projects to the lowest bidder.

Q3.6 Which of the following statements are true? (Choose two)

A. Integrative projects typically have less design changes during the construction documents phase.

B. Integrative projects typically have more design changes during the construction documents phase.

C. Integrative projects typically have less change orders during construction.

D. Integrative projects typically have more change orders during construction.

Q3.7 Which of the following fields can best help provide an innovative approach to solving problems by following nature's patterns? (Choose two)

A. Architecture

B. Farming

C. Permaculture

D. Biomimicry

E. Construction

Q3.8 Which of the following are tools available to project teams to find synergies and increase efficiencies during the integrative design process? (Choose two)

A. RFIs

B. Energy modeling

C. BIM

D. RFPs

E. Value engineering

ONLINE RESOURCES

Visit Buildinggreen.com to learn more the benefits and challenges of the integrative design process: www2.buildinggreen.com/article/integrated-design-meets-real-world.

NOTES

1. USGBC®, *Green Building and LEED Core Concepts Guide,* 3rd ed. (2014), 30.
2. Ibid., p. 33.
3. Ibid.
4. Ibid., p. 34.
5. Ibid.
6. Ibid., p. 35.
7. Ibid.
8. Ibid., p. 39.
9. Ibid.
10. Ibid., p. 41.
11. Ibid.
12. Ibid., p. 30.
13. Ibid., p. 44.
14. Ibid., p. 45.
15. Ibid., p. 44.
16. Ibid., p. 30.
17. Ibid., p. 47.

CHAPTER 4

THIRD-PARTY VERIFICATION

WITH AN UNDERSTANDING OF THE COMPONENTS AND the benefits of sustainability and green building, it is now time to take the brief information provided in Chapter 1 a bit further. In Chapter 1, Leadership in Energy and Environmental Design (LEED®) was introduced along with U.S. Green Building Council (USGBC®). This chapter is intended to provide a thorough description of the different organizations associated with the rating systems. For the purposes of the LEED Green Associate™ exam, it is suggested to understand the following:

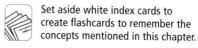 Set aside white index cards to create flashcards to remember the concepts mentioned in this chapter.

- The roles, missions, and primary responsibilities of USGBC and GBCI™
- How USGBC and GBCI operate
- The policies of USGBC and LEED

USGBC® AND GBCI™

USGBC, formed in 1992, is a member-based, nonprofit organization formed to transform the market toward green building through education, advocacy, and the LEED green building certification program. USGBC's mission statement is listed on their website as "to transform the way buildings and communities are designed, built and operated, enabling an environmentally and socially responsible, healthy, and prosperous environment that improves the quality of life."[1] USGBC created the Green Building Certification Institute (GBCI) in January 2008 to provide "independent oversight of professional credentialing and project certification programs related to green building," as indicated on the GBCI website.[2] GBCI's mission "is to be the premier organization independently recognizing excellence in green building performance and practice globally."[3]

USGBC released the first version of LEED in 2000, giving the design and construction industry a tool with which to measure performance and an outlet for third-party verification. They released only one type of rating system at the time but have now expanded the program to offer over 20 different types. At the time, the concepts and strategies of LEED were new to the industry but have since become common and well-known terms and technologies, ultimately changing the way we design, construct, and operate buildings. The support of the local, state, and federal governments has catapulted LEED into the forefront of any competition, such as Green Globes.

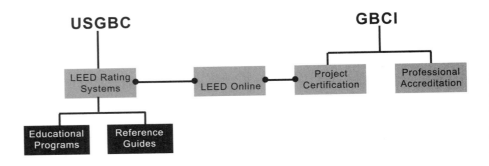

Figure 4.1 The roles of USGBC and GBCI.

Roles and Responsibilities

As indicated in Figure 4.1, USGBC is focused on developing the LEED green building certification program, as well as providing education and research programs. In order to develop the rating systems, USGBC created a LEED Steering Committee composed of six technical advisory groups (TAGs) to help the main categories evolve. Eight regional councils are also a part of USGBC to help with the regional components of the rating systems.

GBCI was created in order to separate the rating system development from the certification and credentialing process. Therefore, GBCI is responsible for administering the process for projects seeking LEED certification and for professionals seeking accreditation credentials. GBCI administers the LEED certification process for projects with the help of certification bodies. The certification bodies are responsible for managing the review process, determining a building's compliance with LEED standards, and establishing the level of certification for which they qualify. Because the certification bodies are an integral part of the certification process, they are responsible for answering and responding to **credit interpretation rulings** (CIRs). For a fee, team members of registered projects seeking LEED certification can submit a CIR for clarification about a credit or prerequisite within a LEED rating system. For the purposes of the exam, it is important to remember that CIRs are issued specific to one credit or prerequisite. Should a project team wish to set a precedent for the results to be applied to all future LEED projects, they can submit for an LEED Interpretation instead of a CIR. It is the same process but the fee is higher for an LEED Interpretation as compared to a CIR.

Although GBCI leaves CIRs to the certification bodies to respond to and manage, they remain responsible for administering the appeals process. Team members may appeal rulings made by the certification bodies during the certification process. Ultimately, GBCI is responsible for quality assurance during the certification and credentialing process.

The Policies of USGBC and GBCI

While preparing for the exam, it is important to remember two components about USGBC, GBCI, and LEED: the proper ways to speak about each of them and the proper ways to use the many logos (also referred to as marks). There are four types of logos to be aware of: organization (USGBC, GBCI), program (LEED rating system, Greenbuild International Conference and Expo), people

Make a flashcard to remember what a TAG is.

Create flashcards to remember the roles and responsibilities of USGBC and GBCI.

TIP **Study:** For those in the design and construction industry, it is helpful to think of a CIR like a request for information (RFI) as described in the previous chapter. Just like a contractor may issue an RFI to the design team for clarification about a detail to be constructed, a project team can issue a CIR to their assigned certification body.

TIP **Study:** CIRs and LEED Interpretations are further discussed in Chapter 6.

(accreditation earned), and project (certification level earned). For the purposes of the exam, it is important to remember the copyright and trademark uses for the marks, how the logos may be used, and how to properly use the terms in text. Although these guidelines are summarized here, it is advised to download the guidelines from both the USGBC and GBCI websites and review the documents.

When using any of the acronyms, it is important to define the term at the first mention. For example, in the Introduction of this guide "Leadership in Energy and Environmental Design" is mentioned for the first time and then followed by the acronym in parentheses (LEED). When using any of the logos, it is important to accompany the mark with a copyright or trademark symbol and an acknowledgment of ownership. For example, when LEED is mentioned for the first time in the introduction, it is followed by a registration symbol (®). This symbol is required only at the first mention for most publications. If the LEED logo is used, it must be followed by this statement of acknowledgment of ownership by USGBC: "'LEED' and related logo is a trademark owned by the U.S. Green Building Council and is used by permission."[4] The use of any of the logos is only allowed if:

- The logo is not the largest visual component of the publication (except for chapter use).
- The logo is not used to suggest any kind of USGBC or GBCI endorsement (see copyright page of this book, for example).
- The logo is not included on any sales contracts.
- The logo is not used on any material that reflects poorly on USGBC or GBCI.
- The logo is not distorted in proportion.
- The logo is not watermarked or placed behind text.
- The logo's color is not altered (except for LEED for Homes and LEED certification logos, as detailed below).
- The logo is not accompanied by any text wrapping.
- The logo is not reduced (no smaller than 20 percent) or enlarged (no bigger than 380 percent) of its original size.

The USGBC, LEED, or GBCI logos may not be used on any product packaging, and they cannot be associated with any text indicating a claim to earn points within the LEED rating systems. The term *LEED* may be used in manufacturers' literature, as long as the material is not indicating any sort of endorsement by USGBC or GBCI. The language must indicate a holistic approach and it is not just one product that can earn points, such as:

> Products are not reviewed or certified under the LEED rating system. LEED credit requirements cover the performance of materials in aggregate, not the performance of individual products or brands. For more information on LEED, visit www.usgbc.org/leed.[5]

It is acceptable for manufacturers to use either of the following statements: "Product A contributes toward satisfying Credit X under LEED" or "Product A [complies with] X requirements of Credit X under LEED" when referring to their products.[6]

It is critical to also remember proper use of the logos and terms after a person earns professional credentials (such as LEED Green Associate) and when a project registers and earns LEED certification. After passing the exam, professionals are allowed to add "LEED Green Associate" after their name, not "LEED GA." Although a statement of ownership is required when using the legacy LEED AP mark and any of the new credentials, it is not required on business cards. In terms of projects, after registering with GBCI to indicate a project seeking LEED certification, it would be improper to indicate the level of certification when referring to the project. For example, it is unacceptable to print, "This project is LEED Silver Registered," but it is acceptable to print, "This project is registered under the LEED Green Building Rating System." Remember also, a logo or mark does not exist for registered projects, so it is unacceptable to use one. When a project earns a level of LEED certification, team members are allowed to use the certification mark in conjunction with marketing materials for the LEED-certified project. Again, the ownership acknowledgment statement must be accompanied by the logo. Be sure to note the correct ways to refer to a certified project:

- "LEED certification" with a lowercase "c" is used to describe the certification process.

- "LEED certified" with a lowercase "c" is used to describe a project that has been certified.

- "LEED Certified" with a capital "C" is used to describe a project that has been certified to the base level: Certified. When a project is certified, the correct wording is "project A is LEED Silver" or "project A is LEED certified to the Silver level" or "project A is LEED Silver certified." Due to repetition, the wording "project A is LEED Certified certified" is not recommended. "Certified" to reference both certification and level is sufficient.[7]

Finally, how the terms are used in text is another component that could be tested on the exam. As displayed throughout this book, the terms *USGBC* and *GBCI* do not include the word *the* prior to them, except if they are used as an adjective, such as "the USGBC website ..." Be sure to note the following *unacceptable* ways to refer to USGBC:

- U.S.G.B.C.

- U.S. GBC

- United States Green Building Council

- US Green Building Council

- GBC[8]

In any case, it is advised that you receive proper permission before using any logos or statements about USGBC, GBCI, and LEED before printing or publishing any material, including websites.

QUIZ TIME!

These questions are formatted just as they would be on the exam. Notice the question indicates how many answers to select. The proper number of correct answers is required on the exam, as partial credit is not awarded.

In an effort to present information to you in multiple ways and help you learn, you may find questions asking about information that is new to you, that you did not read about throughout the book.

Q4.1   Which of the following is an unacceptable way to refer to a registered project seeking LEED certification? (Choose one)

    A. "Registered with the certification goal of Silver"

    B. "Upon completion, this project will apply to become LEED certified"

    C. "This project is registered under the LEED NC rating system"

    D. "As a first step toward LEED Green Building certification, [organization name] has registered this project with the USGBC to achieve LEED certification"

    E. "This project is LEED Platinum Registered"

Q4.2   Which of the following is correct? (Choose one)

    A. U.S. GBC

    B. US GBC

    C. U.S.G.B.C.

    D. U.S. Green Building Council

    E. United States Green Building Council

Q4.3   Who is responsible for the appeals process? (Choose one)

    A. GBCI

    B. USGBC

    C. Certification bodies

    D. None of the above

Q4.4   Credit interpretation rulings (CIRs) provide which of the following? (Choose two)

    A. Responses to written requests for interpretation of credit requirements

    B. Determination of whether a particular strategy can be used to satisfy two different credits at once

    C. Clarification of one existing LEED credit or prerequisite

    D. Definitive assurance that a particular method or strategy permitted on a previous project will be applicable to other projects in the future

Q4.5   Which of the following statements are true in reference to certification bodies? (Choose two)

    A. Certification bodies are managed by USGBC.

    B. Certification bodies are accredited to ISO standard 17021.

    C. Certification bodies are assigned to a project once a project is registered.

    D. Certification bodies are responsible for the responding to appeals.

    E. Certification bodies help individuals prepare for their accreditation exams.

ONLINE RESOURCES

Download the USGBC Trademark Policy at www.usgbc.org/Docs/Archive/General/Docs3885.pdf for more information.

Download the GBCI Logo Guidelines at www.gbci.org/Files/gbci-logo-guidelines.pdf for more information.

NOTES

1. USGBC website, www.usgbc.org/about.
2. GBCI website, www.gbci.org/org-nav/about-gbci/about-gbci.aspx.
3. Ibid.
4. USGBC, USGBC Trademark Policy, 2011, p. 2.
5. Ibid., p. 20.
6. Ibid.
7. Ibid., p. 16.
8. Ibid., p. 6.

CHAPTER 5

THE LEED GREEN BUILDING CERTIFICATION PROGRAM

IN THE PREVIOUS CHAPTER, AN OVERVIEW OF U.S. Green Building Council (USGBC®) and Green Building Certification Institute (GBCI™) functions and roles was provided as a stepping-stone to understanding more about the Leadership in Energy and Environmental Design (LEED®) rating systems and the LEED certification process. In this chapter, a synopsis of the LEED building certification program will be discussed, including:

- The LEED rating systems
- The categories of LEED
- Prerequisites and credits
- Credit weightings

Remember, the LEED building certification program was developed by USGBC as a tool to measure a building's performance. "LEED is a framework for identifying implementing, and measuring green building and neighborhood design, construction, operations, and maintenance."[1] The seven goals of the LEED building certification program include the following:[2]

 Set aside white index cards to create flashcards to remember the LEED green building certification program information presented in this chapter.

- To reverse contribution to global **climate change**
- To enhance individual **human health** and well-being
- To protect and restore **water resources**
- To protect, enhance, and restore **biodiversity** and ecosystem services
- To promote sustainable and regenerative **material resources** cycles
- To build a **greener economy**
- To enhance social equity, environmental justice, **community health,** and quality of life

When LEED was originally released, there was only one generic type of rating system, whereas now there are quite a few to choose from for specific project types such as retail, core and shell developments, and schools. Most of the rating systems have a correlating credential under the LEED AP with specialty, as mentioned in Chapter 1. The following information is summarized in Appendix A.

USGBC has released the following five reference guides containing the multitude of rating systems now available:

- LEED for Building Design and Construction (BD+C)
- LEED for Interior Design and Construction (ID+C)
- LEED for Buildings Operations and Maintenance (O+M)
- LEED for Neighborhood Development (ND)
- LEED for Homes Design and Construction

Project teams seeking guidance on which rating system is best suited for their project are encouraged to refer to the *Rating System Selection Guidance*. "The entire gross floor area of a LEED project must be certified under a single rating system and is subject to all prerequisites and attempted credits in that rating system, regardless of mixed construction or space usage type."[3] The document stipulates a 40/60 rule to help a project team choose between rating systems. The rule suggests that if the rating system does not apply to at least 40 percent of the gross floor area, it should not be used, and if it applies for more than 60 percent, it should be used. The rule has a gray area between 40 and 60 percent where it is up to the team to decide which rating system is most appropriate.

LEED FOR BUILDING DESIGN AND CONSTRUCTION (BD+C)

LEED for New Construction and Major Renovations™

The LEED for New Construction and Major Renovations (LEED for New Construction) rating system applies to most project types, although it was developed primarily for commercial office buildings. Other project types can include highrise residential buildings (9+ stories), government buildings, and institutional buildings (such as libraries and churches). It does not include K–12 schools, retail, data centers, warehouses and distribution centers, hospitality, or healthcare facilities.

This rating system can also be applied to major renovation work, including heating, ventilation, and air conditioning (HVAC) or interior rehabilitations or significant envelope modifications. With the LEED for New Construction rating system, the owner must occupy and complete more than 60 percent of the leasable square footage. For projects at existing facilities with a smaller scope, the LEED for Existing Buildings: Operations & Maintenance™ (LEED for Existing Buildings: O&M) rating system would be more appropriate (discussed later in the chapter). As with any LEED rating system, it is up to the project team to determine which system is best suited to their project.

LEED for Schools™

The LEED for Schools rating system applies best to the design and construction of new schools and ancillary learning spaces, as well as existing schools undergoing major renovations. This rating system is geared toward K–12 school types and can include any nonacademic project situated on the grounds of K–12 schools, such as administrative buildings, maintenance facilities, or dormitories. LEED

Make a flashcard for each of the rating systems to remember what project types are best suited for each.

Make another flashcard to remember that most of the BD+C rating systems require at least 60 percent of the project's gross floor area be complete by the time of certification (except core and shell).

TIP **V3V4:** LEED 2009 considered highrise residential buildings with 4 or more stories appropriate to use the LEED for New Construction and Major Renovations rating system, whereas V4 indicates the building must be more than nine stories now that the LEED for Multifamily Midrise rating system is available.

for Schools uses the LEED for New Construction rating system as a starting point and adds classroom acoustics, master planning, mold prevention, and environmental site assessment evaluation components. For postsecondary or prekindergarten projects, the project team can determine if LEED for New Construction or LEED for Schools is more appropriate. Existing academic buildings can look to the LEED for Existing Schools rating system.

LEED for Healthcare™

LEED for Healthcare was developed for healthcare projects including in-patient care facilities, licensed outpatient care facilities, and licensed long-term care facilities that operate seven days a week, 24 hours per day. The rating system addresses specific medical issues, such as sensitivity to chemicals and pollutants and other issues such as transportation from parking facilities and access to natural environments. Other types of medical facilities can look to this rating system, such as inpatient medical care for acute and long-term treatment, assisted-living facilities, medical offices, and research centers.

LEED for Core & Shell™

The owner must occupy more than 60 percent of the leasable square footage for LEED for New Construction projects and less than 40 percent for LEED for Core & Shell projects.

LEED for Core & Shell was developed for the speculative development market where project teams are not responsible for all of the building's design and construction. For example, a developer may wish to build a new building but is not yet sure who will lease the interior space. Without knowing who the tenant will be, it is difficult to determine how the interior spaces will be finished and utilized. Similar to LEED for New Construction, this rating system can be applied to commercial office buildings, medical office buildings, retail centers, warehouses, and lab facilities. The key difference between LEED for New Construction and LEED for Core & Shell relates specifically to occupancy. Remember, LEED for New Construction requires the owner to occupy more than 60 percent of the leasable square footage, where the LEED for Core & Shell rating system requires the owner to occupy less than 40 percent. Since the project team is left in the dark about the tenant(s), the rating system provides tools for guidance, such as default occupancy counts and energy modeling guidelines (specific for core and shell projects). The rating system appendix also includes tenant lease and sales agreement information specific to certification implications and LEED for Core & Shell precertification guidelines.

Precertification is available only within the LEED for Core & Shell rating system and is therefore unique. Remember, the rating system is aimed at the speculative development market, where a marketing tool is desired and beneficial. For an additional flat rate fee, project teams are allowed to submit for a precertification review based on declared environmental goals. Precertification is awarded based on the intentions of the project, not actual achievement of the stated goals. The review process is intended to take less than one month but can be expedited for an additional fee. Note that the precertification review fee does not include registration or regular certification review fees.

 V3V4: LEED 2009 required that an owner occupy no more than 50 percent of the gross floor area in order to pursue certification under the LEED for Core & Shell rating system whereas V4 stipulates a 40 percent threshold.

 Study: Remember, USGBC members pay a reduced rate for registration and certification, including precertification for LEED for Core & Shell projects.

LEED for Retail: New Construction™

LEED for Retail was developed in two different capacities depending on the type of space seeking certification: LEED for Retail: New Construction, and LEED for Retail: Commercial Interiors™. LEED for Retail: New Construction is geared toward whole-building certification for freestanding projects, while LEED for Retail: Commercial Interiors is aimed at tenants of shopping centers and malls. Existing, freestanding retail buildings can look to the LEED for Existing Buildings: Operations & Maintenance rating system.

LEED for Data Centers™

LEED for Data Centers was created for those buildings that house "high density computing equipment such as server racks, used for data storage and processing."[4]

LEED for Warehouses and Distribution Centers™

LEED for Warehouses and Distribution Centers was created for those buildings that "store goods, manufactured products, merchandise, raw materials, or personal belongings, such as self storage."[5]

LEED for Hospitality™

"Hotels, motels, inns, or other businesses within the service industry that provide transitional or short term lodging, with or without food"[6] can pursue certification under the LEED for Hospitality rating system.

LEED FOR HOMES

LEED for Homes: Homes and Multifamily Lowrise™ and LEED for HOMES: Multifamily Midrise™

LEED for HOMES: Homes and Multifamily Lowrise is aimed at the residential market for dwelling units (up to three stories) with a cooking area and a bathroom. Single-family homes and multifamily residential buildings apply. The LEED for Homes: Multifamily Midrise rating system applies to "multifamily residential buildings of 4 to 8 occupiable stories above grade."[7] Figure 5.1 provides a visual reference to help depict which rating system to use.

The LEED for Homes certification process also involves different team members than previously mentioned. Besides an architect, developer, engineers, and contractor, the rating system also requires a LEED for Homes provider to help kick off the project and a green rater to perform inspections and verification during construction. The provider reviews the green rater's work and submits the documentation for review, with his or her approval. The registration and certification fees are structured differently, too, as single-family homes and multifamily housing units are priced differently.

TIP **Study:** "Projects 3 to 5 stories may choose the Homes rating system that corresponds to the ENERGY STAR program in which they are participating."[8]

 TIP **Study:** LEED for Homes is the only rating system that addresses sizing a project appropriately using the Home Size Adjustment. Points are credited and deducted according to the number of bedrooms and the size of the house.

 TIP **Study:** Remember, units with nine or more habitable stories should use the LEED for New Construction rating system, but the LEED for Multifamily Midrise rating system should be used for buildings of four to eight stories and any residential structure with one to three stories is encouraged to use the LEED for Homes and Multifamily Lowrise rating system.

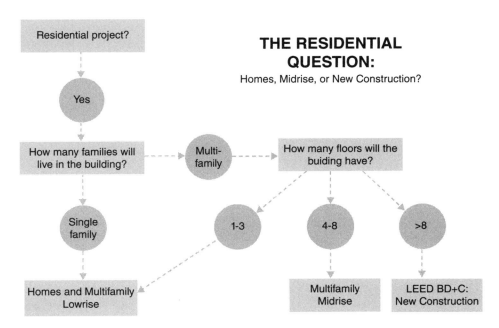

Figure 5.1 When to use the LEED for Homes rating system.[9]

LEED FOR INTERIOR DESIGN AND CONSTRUCTION (ID+C)

LEED for Commercial Interiors™

The LEED for Commercial Interiors rating system was developed to work hand-in-hand with LEED for Core & Shell. This rating system was designed for tenants who do not occupy the entire building and therefore do not have control over the design of the building systems, including the envelope and the core mechanical, electrical, and plumbing units.

As part of the LEED building certification program, two additional LEED for Commercial Interiors rating systems are also available:

1. LEED for Retail: Commercial Interiors™
2. LEED for Commercial Interiors: Hospitality™

LEED FOR BUILDING OPERATIONS AND MAINTENANCE (O+M)

LEED for Existing Buildings: Operations & Maintenance

The LEED for Existing Buildings: O&M rating system was developed for all commercial and institutional buildings and residential buildings of four or more habitable stories. This includes offices, services establishments, libraries, museums, and religious facilities. The rating system is aimed at single, whole buildings, whether multitenanted or single owner occupied. In addition to the components of the other rating systems, LEED for Existing Buildings: O&M also encourages buildings to

Create a flashcard to remember the five differences of LEED for Existing Buildings: O&M, such as cleaning programs and purchasing policies.

evaluate their exterior site maintenance programs, purchasing policies for environmentally preferred services and products, cleaning programs and policies, waste stream, and ongoing indoor environmental quality. LEED for Existing Buildings: O&M is the only certification that can expire, and therefore the only rating system that can be recertified. The program can be applicable to projects seeking certification for the first time or can apply to projects that were previously certified under another rating system, such as LEED for New Construction or LEED for Schools.

The following are additional rating systems available within the *LEED for Buildings Operations and Maintenance Reference Guide:*

- LEED for Existing Buildings: Retail™
- LEED for Existing Buildings: Schools™
- LEED for Existing Buildings: Hospitality™
- LEED for Existing Buildings: Data Centers™
- LEED for Existing Buildings: Warehouses and Distribution Centers™

TIP   **Study:** First-time LEED for Existing Buildings: O&M certifications are considered initial, and therefore projects would then need to be recertified.

Just as precertification is available only to LEED for Core & Shell projects, recertification is available only within the LEED for Existing Buildings: O&M rating system, and therefore is also unique. LEED for Existing Buildings: O&M certification can be awarded to existing buildings never certified under any rating system, existing buildings previously awarded under a different rating system, or existing buildings previously awarded certification within any of the LEED for Existing Buildings rating systems. LEED for Existing Buildings certifications are valid for five years, and therefore must be reapplied for and evaluated. Project teams must recertify all prerequisites but can decide to drop previously awarded credits or add new ones. Project teams also have the opportunity to decide to remain with the version of the LEED for Existing Buildings rating system originally pursued or to opt to use a newer version of the rating system for the recertification.

LEED FOR NEIGHBORHOOD DEVELOPMENT (ND)

LEED for Neighborhood Development: Plan™ and LEED for Neighborhood Development: Built Project™

The LEED for Neighborhood Development rating systems focus on the elements for smart growth, new urbanism principles, and sustainable building. This rating system was developed for projects including any portion of a neighborhood's design, including buildings (commercial and residential), infrastructure, street design, and open space. At least 50 percent of the total building floor area should be newly constructed or consist of a major renovation.

THE CATEGORIES OF LEED

TIP   **V3V4:** The IP and LT categories are new to LEED and did not exist in the LEED 2009 version of the rating systems.

As mentioned earlier, LEED began as just one rating system: LEED for New Construction. As most of the other rating systems were developed, they used this original rating system as a base and therefore include the same categories. With the release of LEED V4, all of the LEED rating systems have the following categories:

- Integrative Process (IP)
- Location and Transportation (LT)

- Sustainable Sites (SS)
- Water Efficiency (WE)
- Energy and Atmosphere (EA)
- Materials and Resources (MR)
- Indoor Environmental Quality (EQ)

The rating systems also include two other categories that act like bonus components: Innovation and Regional Priority (RP). As mentioned previously, LEED for Neighborhood Development is structured differently and therefore has only five categories, although two should look familiar:

- Smart Location and Linkage
- Neighborhood Pattern and Design
- Green Infrastructure and Buildings
- Innovation
- Regional Priority

PREREQUISITES AND CREDITS

As shown in Figure 5.2, within each category of each of the rating systems, there are prerequisites and credits. (MPRs will be discussed in the next chapter.) It is critical to remember that prerequisites are absolutely required, while credits are optional. Not all categories contain prerequisites, but all of the categories have credits. All of the prerequisites of each category, required by the majority of the rating systems, are noted in the following list. These minimum performance features will be discussed in Part II, within each chapter broken out by category. It does not matter if a project intends to pursue credits in every category—*all* prerequisites are required and are mandatory within the rating system the project is working within.

 Make a flashcard to remember the differences between credits and prerequisites. Be sure to include the following: credits are optional components that earn points, while prerequisites are mandatory, are not worth any points, and address minimum performance features.

 TIP **V3V4:** In LEED 2009, there was only one prerequisite covering indoor water usage reduction; in V4, there are three total prerequisites in the WE category.

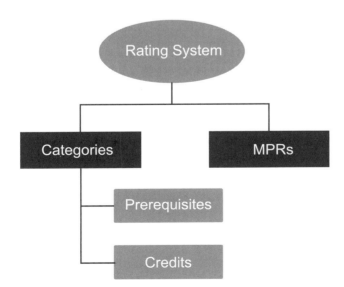

Figure 5.2 The components of a rating system.

The standard prerequisites covered in the LEED rating systems sorted by category:

Sustainable Sites

Construction Activity Pollution Prevention

Water Efficiency

Outdoor Water Use Reduction

Indoor Water Use Reduction

Building-Level Water Metering

Energy and Atmosphere

Fundamental Commissioning of Building Energy Systems

Minimum Energy Performance

Building-Level Energy Metering

Fundamental Refrigerant Management

Materials and Resources

Storage and Collection of Recyclables

Construction and Demolition Waste Management Planning

Indoor Environmental Quality

Minimum Indoor Air Quality Performance

Environmental Tobacco Smoke (ETS) Control

Each prerequisite and credit is structured the same and both include the same components.

> **TIP**
>
> **V3V4:** LEED 2009 did not include a prerequisite for metering or construction and demolition waste management planning. These are new requirements unique to V4.

The components of prerequisites and credits:

- Intent—describes the main goal or benefit for each credit or prerequisite.

- Requirements—details the elements to fulfill the prerequisite or credit. Some credits have a selection of options to choose from to earn point(s).

- Behind the intent—discusses the triple bottom line values to the credit or prerequisite as related to the defined intent.

- Step-by-step guidance—suggests strategies and technologies to comply with the requirements of the credit or prerequisite; includes examples.

- Further explanation—provides more information for special circumstances and project types; could include a Campus section and/or an International Tips section.

- Required Documentation—describes the necessary documentation requirements to be submitted electronically for certification review.

- Related credit tips—indicates the trade-offs and synergies of credits and prerequisites.

- Changes from LEED 2009—details the changes from the previous version of the rating system specific to a credit or prerequisite.

- Referenced standards—lists the standard referenced for establishing the requirements of the credit or prerequisite.

- Exemplary performance—think of these as bonus points for achieving the next incremental level of performance.

- Definitions—provides clarification for general and unique terms presented.

Credit Weightings

Since prerequisites are required, they are not worth any points. All credits, however, are worth a minimum of one point. Credits are always positive whole numbers, never fractions or negative values. All credits and prerequisites are tallied on scorecards (also referred to as checklists) specific to each rating system.

Any project seeking certification must earn a minimum of 40 points, but this does not mean 40 credits must be awarded as well because different credits are weighted differently and not worth only one point. At the beginning of the chapter, the goals of LEED were presented. The credits are independently weighted depending on how effective the credit addresses the seven impact categories (goals). The impact categories themselves are also weighted based on "scale, scope, severity and relative contribution of the built environment to the impact."[10] After the categories were clearly defined and weighted, three association factors were established in which to measure and scale the credits against the impact categories: relative efficacy, duration, and control.

As a result of this weighting exercise, LEED values those strategies that reduce the impacts on climate change and those with the greatest benefit for indoor environmental quality, focusing on energy efficiency and carbon dioxide (CO_2) reduction strategies. For example, transportation is a very important element within LEED, and therefore any credits associated with getting to and from the project site are weighted more. Water is an invaluable natural resource, and therefore water efficiency and consumption reduction is weighted appropriately to encourage project teams to design accordingly to use less. Providing renewable energy on a project's site will lessen the burden on fossil fuels, and therefore is also suitably weighted.

In summary, USGBC created a simplified, 100-base-point scale for the four different certification levels.

- ▪ Certified: 40–49 points
- ▪ Silver: 50–59 points
- ▪ Gold: 60–79 points
- ▪ Platinum: 80 and higher

The 100 base points are totaled from the main categories: IP, LT, SS, WE, EA, MR, and EQ. The last two categories make up 10 bonus points, for a total of 110 available points.

TIP **Study:** Refer to the sample LEED scorecard in Appendix F for a visual representation of how each category is composed of credits and prerequisites and the allocation of points.

TIP **V3V4:** To determine each credit's weight in LEED 2009 rating systems, USGBC referred to the U.S. Environmental Protection Agency's 13 Tools for the Reduction and Assessment of Chemical and Other Environmental Impacts (TRACI) categories for environmental and health concerns. Once the categories of impact were determined and prioritized, USGBC referred to the National Institute of Standards and Technology (NIST) for their research to determine a value for each of the credits by comparing each of the strategies to mitigate each of the impacts.

Make a flashcard so you can quiz yourself of the certification levels and coordinating point range.

QUIZ TIME!

These questions are formatted just as they would be on the exam. Notice the question indicates how many answers to select. The proper number of correct answers is required on the exam, as partial credit is not awarded.

In an effort to present information to you in multiple ways and help you learn, you may find questions asking about information that is new to you, that you did not read about throughout the book.

Q5.1   A project's LEED certification can expire. True or false?

    A. True

    B. False

Q5.2   Which type of project is best suited for the LEED for Commercial Interiors rating system? (Choose one)

    A. An existing hotel renovating their HVAC system

    B. A ground-up, new construction of a school

    C. A tenant improvement project within an existing commercial building

    D. A renovation project focusing on walls, HVAC, and finishes with a 40,000-square-foot new addition

Q5.3   A developer in Phoenix is seeking LEED Gold for a new lab facility to be built in the spring. They plan on occupying 32 percent of the facility. Which rating system should they register for? (Choose one)

    A. LEED for New Construction and Major Renovations

    B. LEED for Commercial Interiors

    C. LEED for Existing Buildings: Operations & Maintenance

    D. LEED for Core & Shell

Q5.4   Which categories are specific to the LEED for Neighborhood Development rating system and not available in the other rating systems? (Choose two)

    A. Sustainable Sites

    B. Smart Location and Linkage

    C. Innovation

    D. Green Infrastructure and Buildings

    E. Regional Priority

Q5.5   Which rating system addresses the appropriate sizing of a project? (Choose one)

    A. LEED for Homes

    B. LEED for New Construction and Major Renovations

    C. LEED for Core & Shell

    D. LEED for Neighborhood Development

Q5.6   Prerequisites are optional, depending on which categories and credits the project is pursuing. True or false?

    A. True

    B. False

Q5.7   A law firm occupying a 50-year-old office building is replacing the mechanical systems to improve energy performance and implementing green procurement and operations policies. Which LEED rating system best applies to this project? (Choose one)

    A. LEED for Commercial Interiors

    B. LEED for Existing Buildings: O&M

    C. LEED for Core & Shell

D. LEED for New Construction and Major Renovations

E. LEED for Neighborhood Development

Q5.8 Which of the following statements are true in regard to credit weightings? (Choose three)

A. USGBC consulted with NIST and the U.S. EPA's TRACI tool to determine the credit weightings.

B. Three association factors were used as a means to measure and scale each credit.

C. All of the LEED rating systems are based on a 100-point scale.

D. Seven impact categories were defined, with climate change most heavily weighted

E. All credits are worth two points within the LEED for New Construction, but only one point within LEED for Core & Shell.

Q5.9 If a university wishes to build a new administration building on their campus, they could look to LEED for New Construction and Major Renovations or LEED for Schools rating systems and determine which one is more applicable. (Choose one)

A. True, but only if the mechanical systems are on one loop.

B. False, administration buildings cannot be certified under LEED for New Construction.

C. True, the project team will need to determine which rating system is best suited to the project.

D. False, the university would need to look at the LEED for Universities rating system.

Q5.10 Which reference guide would you look to for information about the LEED for Schools rating system for a new, ground-up construction project you are working on? (Choose one)

A. LEED Reference Guide for Interior Design and Construction (ID+C)

B. LEED Reference Guide for Building Operations and Maintenance (O+M)

C. LEED Reference Guide for Homes Design and Construction

D. LEED Reference Guide for LEED for Neighborhood Development

E. LEED Reference Guide for Building Design and Construction (BD+C)

Q5.11 Which of the following answers the question: "What should a LEED project enhance?"? (Choose two)

A. Sustainable Sites

B. Community

C. Energy and Atmosphere

D. Human Health

Q5.12 Incorporating green building strategies, such as high-efficiency mechanical systems, onsite photovoltaic systems, and an indoor water wall to help with the indoor air quality and air conditioning, plays a role in what type of cost implications? (Choose two)

A. Increased life-cycle costs

B. Increased first costs

C. Reduced construction costs

D. Increased soft costs

E. Reduced soft costs

Q5.13 If a project plans on earning Silver certification under the LEED for Existing Buildings: Operations & Maintenance rating system, which point range would they aim for? (Choose one)

A. 50–59

B. 20–30

C. 40–49

D. 60–69

E. 30–39

Q5.14 Which of the following project types is applicable to the LEED for New Construction and Major Renovations rating system? (Choose one)

A. Healthcare facilities

B. Hospitality

C. Data center

D. Government facility

E. Warehouses and distribution centers

Q5.15 Which of the following is an association factor that was established to measure and scale the credits against the impact categories? (Choose two)

A. Water efficiency

B. Relative efficacy

C. Duration

D. Water metering

E. Biodiversity

ONLINE RESOURCES

Visit www.usgbc.org/sites/default/files/RatingSystemSelection_01272014.pdf for the Rating System Selection Guidance.

NOTES

1. USGBC website, www.usgbc.org/guide/bdc#cc_overview.

2. Ibid.

3. USGBC website, www.usgbc.org/certification.

4. USGBC, *LEED Reference Guide for Green Building Design and Construction* (2014), 34.

5. Ibid.

6. Ibid.

7. Ibid.

8. See note 4.

9. USGBC website, www.usgbc.org/articles/residential-question-homes-mid-rise-or-new-construction

10. LEED v4 Impact Category and Point Allocation Development Process, U.S. Green Building Council (2013), 6.

CHAPTER **6**

ESSENTIAL LEED® CONCEPTS

IN THE PREVIOUS CHAPTER, THE LEADERSHIP IN Energy and Environmental Design (LEED®) green building certification program was introduced, including the categories, prerequisites, and credits as a starting point to understanding the process during design and construction. In this chapter, a summary of the LEED project certification process will be discussed, focusing on:

■ LEED-Online

■ Minimum program requirements

■ The steps to certification

■ Special projects

LEED-ONLINE

Set aside white index cards to create flashcards to remember the essential concepts of LEED mentioned throughout this chapter.

In Chapter 2, the typical project team members were defined and listed, but one component was not included: the LEED project administrator. The LEED project administrator is responsible for coordination between all of the disciplines on the project team, by managing the documentation process once a project is registered with Green Building Certification Institute (GBCI™) until certification is awarded. The LEED project administrator can be one of the team members previously mentioned in Chapter 2 and therefore would serve a dual-purpose role, or he or she can be an addition to the team. The administrator is typically responsible for registering a project and granting access for each of the team members to LEED-Online, the online project management system.

LEED-Online is a web-based tool used to manage a project seeking LEED certification. It is the starting point to register a project with GBCI and communicate with the certification bodies, and is used to review the documentation submitted for both prerequisites and credits during design and construction. All projects seeking certification are required to utilize LEED-Online to complete the online credit templates and upload any required supporting documentation, such as drawings, contracts, and policies for review by GBCI. Project teams receive reviewer feedback, can check the status of application reviews, submit appeals, and learn the certification level earned for their project through LEED-Online. Credit interpretation requests are processed through LEED-Online on the LEED Formal Inquiries page.

When team members are invited to a project on LEED-Online, they need to log in to the LEED-Online website to gain access. Once signed in, they are greeted with the "My Projects" page to see a list of active projects they are assigned to. After selecting one of the projects, the "Project Dashboard" page appears. This Dashboard serves as a project's home page, looks very similar to the U.S. Green Building Council (USGBC®) website, and gives access to:

- The project's scorecard—shows which credits the team is pursuing and their status.

- Interpretations.

- LEED credit templates—think of these as the "cover pages" for each credit and prerequisite. Each of these templates summarizes how the project team has satisfied the requirements for the specific credit or prerequisite. There is a credit template for every prerequisite and credit, which must be submitted through LEED-Online. If a calculation is needed to show compliance, the template contains a spreadsheet to complete and automatically completes the calculation after the required data is inputted, according to the requirements described in the reference guides.

- Timeline—where a project administrator would submit for certification review.

- Postcertification—links to purchase plaques, certificates, and the like.

MINIMUM PROGRAM REQUIREMENTS

Just as there are prerequisites that must be achieved in each rating system, there are three minimum program requirements (MPRs) that must be met as well, in order for a project to receive certification. MPRs pertain to all the rating systems and are critical components that are not listed on a project scorecard, but instead are confirmed on LEED-Online. Should noncompliance with any of the three mandated MPRs be found at any time, a project could risk losing its certification, including any fees paid for registration and certification.

The USGBC website details the three MPRs as follows.[1]

MPR 1. Must Be in a Permanent Location on Existing Land

Intent

The LEED rating system is designed to evaluate buildings, spaces, and neighborhoods in the context of their surroundings. A significant portion of LEED requirements are dependent on the project's location; therefore, it is important that LEED projects are evaluated as permanent structures. Locating projects on existing land is important to avoid artificial land masses that have the potential to displace and disrupt ecosystems.

Requirements

All LEED projects must be constructed and operated on a permanent location on existing land. No project that is designed to move at any point in its lifetime may pursue LEED certification. This requirement applies to all land within the LEED project.

TIP **Study:** Remember, only invited team members can see a project's LEED-Online page, after a project is registered.

TIP **Study:** Be sure to check out Appendix B for an MPR summary chart.

TIP **V3V4:** LEED 2009 had seven MPRs while V4 only has three.

TIP **Study:** Movable buildings are not eligible to pursue certification. This includes boats and mobile homes.

MPR 2. Must Use Reasonable LEED Boundaries[2]

Intent

The LEED rating system is designed to evaluate buildings, spaces, or neighborhoods, and all environmental impacts associated with those projects. Defining a reasonable LEED boundary ensures that project is accurately evaluated.

Requirements

The LEED project boundary must include all contiguous land that is associated with the project and supports its typical operations. This includes land altered as a result of construction and features used primarily by the project's occupants, such as hardscape (parking and sidewalks), septic or rainwater treatment equipment, and landscaping. The LEED boundary may not unreasonably exclude portions of the building, space, or site to give the project an advantage in complying with credit requirements. The LEED project must accurately communicate the scope of the certifying project in all promotional and descriptive materials and distinguish it from any noncertifying space.

MPR 3. Must Comply with Project Size Requirements[3]

Intent

The LEED rating system is designed to evaluate buildings, spaces, or neighborhoods of a certain size. The LEED requirements do not accurately assess the performance of projects outside of these size requirements.

For LEED BD+C and O+M Rating Systems

A minimum of 1,000 square feet of gross floor area must be included in the scope of work.

For LEED ID+C Rating Systems

A minimum of 250 square feet of gross floor area must be included in the scope of work.

For LEED for Neighborhood Development Rating Systems

The LEED project should contain at least two habitable buildings and be no larger than 1,500 acres.

For LEED for Homes Rating Systems

The LEED project must be defined as a "dwelling unit" by all applicable codes. This requirement includes, but is not limited to, the International Residential Code stipulation that a dwelling unit must include "permanent provisions for living, sleeping, eating, cooking, and sanitation."

Boundary Types

MPR 2 refers to the LEED project boundary. There are three types of boundaries to be aware of for the purposes of LEED: property boundary line, LEED

 TIP **Study:** Buildings to be located on existing docks, piers, or other manufactured structures in or above water are eligible to pursue LEED certification.

TIP **Study:** Remember, all MPRs must be met in order to certify a project and to keep the certification once earned.

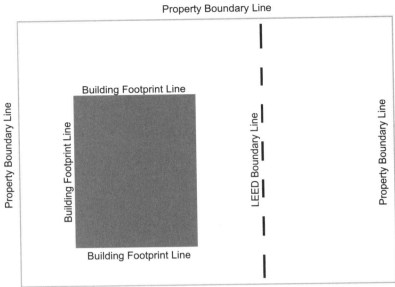

Figure 6.1 The different types of boundaries for a LEED project.

project boundary line, and the building footprint (Figure 6.1). The property boundary line refers to the land owned according to a plot plan or legal property deed. The LEED project boundary line may or may not be the same as the property boundary. For example, a university may own acres of land but may wish to develop only a portion of it for one academic building. Therefore, the LEED project boundary line sets the limits for the scope of work to be included in the documents for certification. The building footprint is the amount of land on which the building resides.

Local municipalities are responsible for establishing and determining sections of their town for different uses and therefore different zones, such as commercial, residential, and industrial zones. These sections of land are regulated based on:

Make a flashcard to remember the three types of boundaries associated with LEED projects.

- Building type (commercial, residential, mixed-use, etc.)
- Building height
- Footprint (impervious vs. pervious)

Project teams should be mindful of local regulations for land and the allowable uses. For the purposes of the exam, it is important to remember that although many credits may reference zoning, LEED will never override local, state, or federal requirements.

THE STEPS TO CERTIFICATION

Devising a LEED Work Plan[4]

Study: Remember, USGBC members pay a reduced fee for project registration and certification.

Step 1. Initiate discovery phase.

Step 2. Select LEED rating system.

Study: Chapter 3 described the discovery phase.

Step 3. Check minimum program requirements.

Step 4. Establish project goals. Once the goals are established at the goal-setting workshop, project teams will be able to select appropriate strategies and associated LEED credits to meet the goals.

Step 5. Define LEED project scope and boundary. Project teams are encouraged to investigate the Volume Program or the Campus Program. If the project owner is planning multiple similar buildings in different locations, the Volume Program may be useful to streamline certification. The Campus Program may be appropriate if the project includes multiple buildings in a single location.

Step 6. Develop LEED scorecard using the project goals and establish a target LEED certification level. Be sure to remember the concepts of systems thinking and integrative principles to avoid chasing points that might not fit the intentions and goals of the project.

Step 7. Continue discovery phase and reassemble the team occasionally to discuss synergies across disciplines and new opportunities.

Step 8. Continue iterative process until the solutions satisfy the project team and owner.

Step 9. Assign roles and responsibilities. Project teams should select one team member to take primary responsibility for leading the group through the LEED application and documentation process. This administrative leadership role may change from the design to the construction phase, but if it does, both leaders should be involved throughout the entire certification process to ensure an integrative approach.

Step 10. Develop consistent documentation during both design and construction phases.

Step 11. Perform quality assurance review and submit for certification.

The Certification Process

The LEED certification process for projects begins with project registration (see Figure 6.2). To register a project, the team administrator would sign in to LEED-Online and click on the "Create New Project" button and follow the instructions provided. The registration process requires entering basic project details, including project name, start and end dates, gross area, owner organization and contact information, and project address (geographic location). The next step involves requires the acceptance of the GBCI certification agreement. The third step includes payment, and then the registration information is confirmed with a receipt. The project administrator, the team member registering the project, is then awarded access to the project's LEED-Online page through the "My Projects" tab.

After a project is registered, the project administrator invites the other team members to the project's LEED-Online site and assigns members the coordinating prerequisites and credits they will be responsible for, ultimately granting them access to sign the credit templates. This means each prerequisite and credit has one responsible party assigned to it, and that person will generate and upload the required documentation specific to each prerequisite and credit. When a team member is assigned a credit or prerequisite, he or she becomes the **declarant** to sign the credit template. Remember, all prerequisites and credits

 Study: Ideally, the project administrator has past LEED project experience and is a LEED AP but it is not required.

 V3V4: In the older version of LEED-Online, the registration process required compliance with the MPRs related to the rating system under which the project was pursuing certification, whereas project teams registering under a V4 rating system will enjoy a more streamlined process.

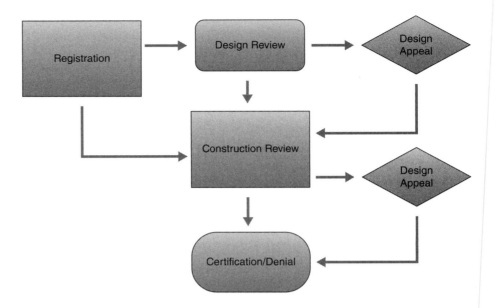

Figure 6.2 The certification process.

Make a flashcard to remember LPE!

TIP **Study:** One team member can be assigned to more than one credit or prerequisite. Additional team members can be invited to LEED-Online and not be assigned any credit or prerequisite.

Make a flashcard to remember the details of a CIR.

require a credit template, and some may require additional documentation. The additional documentation may be exempt if the design team opts to use the licensed-professional exemption (LPE) path. This optional path is determined on the credit template.

Credit interpretation rulings (CIRs, introduced in Chapter 4) can be submitted any time after a project is registered. The USGBC website contains a database of previously issued and precedent-setting interpretations for teams to query for more information before submitting a new one, although it should be noted LEED 2009 changed the CIR process. In the past, CIRs were posted online for all to use, whereas LEED 2009 presented a choice to project teams to determine the applicability of the formal inquiry they plan on issuing. Project teams could issue a Project CIR or a LEED Interpretation (See Table 6.1 for the differences between the two) depending on whether or not they wish to set a precedent (Figure 6.3).

Note that CIR rulings are not considered final, and therefore project teams are encouraged to upload their ruling with the coordinating credit or prerequisite when submitting for a certification review with LEED-Online.

Once the design team moves through the design phase and completes the construction documents, they are allowed to submit an application for a design review, although this is optional and not required. Split reviews provide the

Table 6.1 Project CIRs versus LEED Interpretations[6]

Project CIR	LEED Interpretation
Applicable to only one project	Applicable to multiple projects
Not published	Published in online Addenda database
Three- to four-week turnaround time	Three- to six-month turnaround time
Reviewed by GBCI	Reviewed by USGBC
Initial fee	Additional fee

The Project CIR and LEED Interpretation Processes

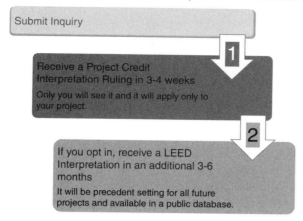

Figure 6.3 Submitting a formal inquiry.[5]

team with a preliminary certification status to see where the project stands with point-earning potential (at least from a design prerequisite and credit standpoint). If the team decides not to pursue this preliminary review at the end of design, they would wait to submit their documentation until after substantial completion. In summary, a project team can choose a split review for two certification reviews (one at the end of the design phase and another at the end of construction) or submit all documentation for a construction review after substantial completion.

At the time of a review submission, the LEED project administrator will need to pay a fee for certification review. This certification fee is based on the rating system the project is seeking certification with, the project's square footage, and if the project was registered under a corporate membership account with USGBC. The project administrator will be required to submit a short project narrative to provide the certification body a background of the project, the intended use of the project, the location and surrounding areas, and any other details deemed appropriate. Project photographs or renderings, elevations, floor plans, and any details should also be uploaded to LEED-Online.

Make a flashcard to remember the three factors a project's certification fees are based on.

LEED for Existing Buildings: Operations & Maintenance™

Although projects registered under the LEED for Existing Buildings: Operations & Maintenance (LEED for Existing Buildings: O&M) rating system use LEED-Online just like most other LEED registered projects, there is a key difference with the process for certification. When a project is pursuing certification under the rating systems in the BD+C or ID+C reference guides, the project is ultimately certified for the design and construction of a green building. Existing building projects, however, are certified for a particular snapshot in time (Figure 6.4). This **performance period** is a continuous period of time in which a building or facility's performance is measured. Since design-side and construction-side prerequisites and credits do not exist within the LEED for Existing Buildings: O&M rating system, as opposed to most of the other rating systems, there is not an opportunity for design and construction reviews by the GBCI certification body. LEED for Existing Buildings: O&M projects are submitted for certification review only after the performance period is completed.

Figure 6.4 The Wyndham Worldwide corporate headquarters in Parsippany, New Jersey, earned LEED Silver certification under both the LEED for Commercial Interiors™ and LEED for Existing Buildings: O&M rating systems. While pursuing their initial LEED for Existing Buildings: O&M certification, Wyndham started its performance period about two years after occupancy.

The Time Frames of Certification Reviews

Table 6.2 outlines the schedule associated with the submission and review times during the LEED certification review process. Bear in mind that the time frames listed apply to both design reviews and construction reviews. Once a project team submits for either type of review, they must then wait 25 business days to hear back from their assigned certification body. The certification body updates LEED-Online to indicate whether a credit or prerequisite is "anticipated" or "denied," or will issue clarification requests to the team specific to any credits or prerequisites in question. The team then has 25 business days to respond with more information to explain how they satisfy the requirements of the credit or prerequisite requiring clarification. At that time, the team must wait 15 business days to receive indication whether the credit or prerequisite clarified is either "anticipated" or "denied." If the team submitted for a design review, they would repeat the steps listed earlier at the end of substantial completion in order to submit for a construction review. It is not until this review process that the final decision to award or deny credits and prerequisites takes place.

Table 6.2 Certification Review Schedule

Process	Days
Preliminary design review or construction review	25 business days
Team reply	25 business days
Final review	15 business days
Appeal (if necessary)	25 business days
Appeal review (if necessary)	25 business days
Certification awarded	

Should the team receive a "denied" status, they can issue an appeal to GBCI for a fee within 25 business days. GBCI would then have 25 business days to review the appeal and issue a ruling to the project team. Once the appeal process ends, certification is awarded.

 TIP **Study:** Remember, GBCI is responsible for the appeals process!

SPECIAL PROJECTS

Project teams must document information consistently across credits but may encounter a few challenges depending on the project's intended use and scope of work. Even with all of the different LEED V4 rating systems available, some projects do not fit perfectly under the umbrella of just one. Chapter 5 introduced the 40/60 rule to help select a rating system but after the rating system has been selected, project teams can refer to the following for additional guidance as related to special projects.

Resources are available throughout the different reference guides for mixed use, multitenant complexes, and other unique project types. For example, a mixed-use project pursuing certification under the LEED for New Construction and Major Renovations™ rating system include a retail space, the project team may wish to refer to LEED for Retail™ for guidance for that space. Project teams working on a project that includes incomplete spaces might need guidance on how to comply. For these types of projects, the owner must commit to completing the space(s) to meet the prerequisites and credits being pursued by the project; or the owner must provide the tenant with design and construction guidelines to encourage them to follow suit with the rest of the building (whomever is responsible for finishing the spaces). Project teams may also be faced with multiple buildings within the LEED project boundary where a Campus approach may not be appropriate. In this case, project teams must analyze the project as a whole across all prerequisites and credits and they must be consistent across all credits in terms land and building floor areas.

QUIZ TIME!

These questions are formatted just as they would be on the exam. Notice the question indicates how many answers to select. The proper number of correct answers is required on the exam, as partial credit is not awarded.

In an effort to present information to you in multiple ways and help you learn, you may find questions asking about information that is new to you, that you did not read about throughout the book.

Q6.1 Which of the following meets the MPR regarding minimum gross floor area for the LEED for Existing Buildings: Operations & Maintenance rating system? (Choose one)

    A. 250 square feet

    B. 500 square feet

    C. 1,000 square feet

    D. 2,500 square feet

Q6.2 Which rating system can be precertified? (Choose one)

A. LEED for Commercial Interiors

B. LEED for New Construction

C. LEED for Existing Buildings: O&M

D. LEED for Core & Shell™

Q6.3 Which of the following rating systems are not eligible to pursue a split certification review? (Choose two)

A. LEED for Commercial Interiors

B. LEED for New Construction

C. LEED for Existing Buildings: O&M

D. LEED for Core & Shell

E. LEED for Neighborhood Development: Plan™

Q6.4 Which of the following statements are true in reference to minimum floor area requirements? (Choose two)

A. LEED BD+C projects must include a minimum of 1,000 square feet of gross floor area, while LEED ID+C projects are required to have a minimum of 250 square feet of gross floor area.

B. LEED for Schools™ projects must include a minimum of 2,000 square feet of gross floor area, while LEED ID+C projects are required to have a minimum of 550 square feet of gross floor area.

C. LEED for Retail: New Construction™ projects must include a minimum of 5,000 square feet of gross floor area while LEED O+M projects are required to have a minimum of 1,000 square feet of gross floor area.

D. LEED for Healthcare™ projects must include a minimum of 1,000 square feet of gross floor area, while LEED O+M projects are required to have a minimum of 10,000 square feet of gross floor area.

E. LEED for Schools must include a minimum of 1,000 square feet of gross floor area.

Q6.5 How many MPRs exist in the LEED V4 green building certification program? (Choose one)

A. Seven

B. Three

C. Six

D. One

E. Five

Q6.6 Which of the following statements are true? (Choose two)

A. Appeals are mailed to GBCI.

B. Appeals can be submitted 25 business days after final certification review.

C. Appeals are free.

D. Appeals can pertain only to credits, not prerequisites or MPRs.

E. Appeals are submitted through LEED-Online.

Q6.7 Which of the following statements are true? (Choose two)

A. Minimum program requirements do not exist for LEED for Homes projects.

B. Credit interpretations requests are reviewed by GBCI.

C. Project team members must create different passwords for each project they wish to register on LEED-Online.

D. LEED Interpretations are reviewed by USGBC.

Q6.8 Design reviews can prove to be a beneficial option for a team to pursue since the project can be awarded points before construction begins. True or false?

A. True

B. False

Q6.9 LEED project registration provides which of the following? (Choose two)

A. Three credit interpretation requests (CIRs)

B. One preapplication USGBC review of project submittals and documentation

C. One point toward LEED certification for registration prior to the development of construction documents

D. Access to online LEED credit templates for the project

E. Establishment of contact with GBCI and the assigned certification body

Q6.10 An application for LEED certification must contain which of the following? (Choose two)

A. Project summary information, including project contact, project type, project cost, project size, number of occupants, estimated date of occupancy, etc.

B. A list of all members of the design and construction team, including contact information, documented green building industry experience, and indication of all LEED Accredited Professionals

C. Completed LEED credit templates for all prerequisites and attempted credits, plus any documentation specifically required to support those templates

D. Detailed documentation for all credits pursued, including full-sized plans and drawings, photocopies of invoices for all purchased materials, records of tipping fees, all energy modeling inputs and assumptions, and evidence of all calculations performed in support of LEED credits

Q6.11 When should the construction credits and prerequisites be submitted for final certification review? (Choose one)

    A. Beginning of construction

    B. One year after occupancy

    C. After substantial completion

    D. Once permit is obtained

    E. Six months after occupancy

Q6.12 Regarding the application process for LEED certification, which of the following is a correct statement? (Choose one)

    A. LEED credit templates and documentation may be submitted only after occupancy.

    B. All LEED credit templates and documentation must be submitted prior to construction.

    C. Prerequisites and credits marked as "Design" may be submitted and reviewed at the end of the design phase.

    D. The optional design-phase submittal allows projects to secure points for specified LEED credits, for which a preliminary certification will be awarded, if the project has earned a sufficient number of points.

Q6.13 How long does a project team have to submit an appeal after receiving certification review comments back from GBCI? (Choose one)

    A. 15 business days

    B. 25 business days

    C. 45 business days

    D. 1 week

    E. 1 month

Q6.14 Which of the following correctly characterize credit interpretation requests (CIRs)? (Choose three)

    A. Can be viewed only by the primary contact for a registered project

    B. Can be submitted any time after a project is registered

    C. Can be requested online

    D. Can be requested only in a written request mailed to GBCI

    E. Can address more than one credit or prerequisite

    F. Are relevant to one specific project

Q6.15 A LEED Accredited Professional is presented with a project that was started without sustainable design or LEED certification in mind and is about to enter the construction documents phase. However, neither the owner nor any of the design team members involved thus far have significant experience with either LEED or sustainable design. Given this situation, which of the following would tend to have the most influence on the effectiveness of the sustainable design process for a project aimed at LEED certification? (Choose three)

A. Starting the sustainable design process and consideration of LEED-related goals as soon as possible

B. Extensive research, evaluation, and life-cycle assessment for intended material and technology options

C. Aggressive value engineering of individual line items to ensure that the budget is not exceeded

D. Collectively delegating responsibility for specific target LEED credits and associated strategies to appropriate team members

E. Establishing means of collaborative, interdisciplinary communication among team members as a departure from a conventionally more segmented design process

ONLINE RESOURCES

To learn more about LEED Online, be sure to check out the demo video at https://www.youtube.com/watch?v=9bKqhFpg-YI.

LEED 2009 uses a different version of LEED Online found at www.leedonline.com. V4 projects are registered at www.ugbc.org/leedonline.new/.

To learn more about submitting a formal inquiry on LEED Online, visit https://www.leedonline.com/formalinquiries/.

For Rating System Selection Guidance, download this document www.usgbc.org/resources/rating-system-selection-guidance.

For more information about the change of the CIR process, visit www.gbci.org/Certification/Resources/cirs.aspx.

To learn more about LEED Interpretations, visit www.usgbc.org/leed/tools/interpretations.

For a list of current LEED Interpretations, visit www.usgbc.org/leed-interpretations.

NOTES

1. USGBC website, www.usgbc.org/node/2742910?return=/credits/new-construction/v4/minimum-program-requirements.

2. USGBC website, www.usgbc.org/node/2742911?return=/credits/new-construction/v4/minimum-program-requirements.

3. USGBC website, www.usgbc.org/node/2742912?return=/credits/new-construction/v4/minimum-program-requirements.

4. USGBC website, www.usgbc.org/guide/bdc#cc_overview.

5. LEED Online website, www.leedonline.com/formalinquiries/start.

6. LEED Online website, www.leedonline.com/irj/go/km/docs/documents/usgbc/leed/config/common/LOv3Help/default.htm?formal_inquiries.

PART II

DIVING IN: THE STRATEGIES AND TECHNOLOGIES OF LEED®

CHAPTER **7**

LOCATION AND TRANSPORTATION

THIS CHAPTER BEGINS THE DETAILED STUDY OF the strategies and technologies described within each of the Leadership in Energy and Environmental Design (LEED®) categories, starting with Location & Transportation (LT). The main topics include the factors applicable to site selection and location. As with making any other decision while working on a green building project, all components within the LT category, such as compact development, alternative methods of transportation, and community connectivity, are weighed on the triple bottom line values of environmental, economic, and community aspects.

Location is an extremely important aspect of sustainable design. Where a project is located and how it is developed can have multiple impacts on the ecosystem and water resources required during the life of a building. The site location can impact a building's energy performance with respect to orientation; it also could impact rainwater runoff rates or light pollution levels. How does the site fit into the existing infrastructure, such as water, electricity, sewage, and gas utility services? Was it previously developed? Is the site contaminated, and can it be remediated for redevelopment? Are there wetlands or steep slopes? Is it a habitat for endangered species? Carbon emissions should be evaluated as well, as they could be impacted due to the transportation required to get to and from the site. Is there public transportation access available? How much parking is available for cars? Is the project site dependent on the use of cars, or are there existing pedestrian paths and bicycle networks? If so, are there incentives for carpools or vanpools? A project should also bring value to the community. Is it possible to connect the area where people live and work? These concepts and questions should trigger some of the important factors to consider when deciding on a particular site and its true sustainable value. These types of site selection strategies aid in the success of earning LEED certification, as proven by the project team for the Norman Hackerman Building at the University of Texas at Austin (Figure 7.1).

To help evaluate a potential project site, the LT category within the LEED rating systems is broken down into three factors:

1. Location
2. Transportation
3. Neighborhood pattern and design

LOCATION

According to the *Green Building and LEED Core Concepts Guide,* there are three factors of location:[1]

Dedicate one color index card for all your flashcards within the LT category. This way, anytime you see that color, you will associate that flashcard with LT concepts and strategies.

V3V4: LEED 2009 did not contain an LT category.

Make a flashcard to remember the three factors to address within the LT category. Appendix D summarizes all of the strategies to know for the LEED Green Associate™ exam.

Sustainable design criteria should be developed as soon as possible, thus impacting site selection.

Figure 7.1 The 300,000-square-foot Norman Hackerman Building at the University of Texas at Austin, by CO Architects, earned LEED Gold certification for addressing location and transportation strategies discussed in this chapter. *Photo courtesy of Tom Bonner*

 When comparing a building that is car dependent versus one that is accessible via public transportation, bicycles, or walking, the latter will typically have lower total emissions. One study concluded that an average U.S. office building expends 30 percent more energy for commuting occupants as compared to the energy needed for the building itself. Occupants of green buildings built in suburban locations demand twice as much energy for commuting to the building as the energy needed to operate the facility![2]

 Make a flashcard to remember the three factors of location.

- *Natural context*—think of everything given by Mother Nature: climate, soils, sun, wind, vegetation, and rain.
- *Infrastructural context*—this includes utilities and roadway access.
- *Social context*—think about the historic value of the site, local regulations including zoning, and connections to the community.

Determining the location of a green building project should be encouraged by previously developed locations to avoid sprawling development into the suburbs, where undeveloped (greenfield) sites would then be disturbed. The idea is to build *up* and not *out* to promote smart growth, to help increase density, and reduce the negative environmental impacts of building on existing, cohesive natural habitats, preserving open space and farmland. Some municipalities offer an increased **floor-to-area ratio** (FAR) incentive to encourage the development of green buildings within certain communities. Zoning departments typically define building setback development lines based on the use and location of a neighborhood or town. Developers with an increased FAR allowance can build more within the setback lines and then in turn can sell more space.

From an environmental perspective, the selection of a sustainable site would avoid the destruction of wildlife habitats to help lessen the threat of the ability to survive. The goal is to preserve land and therefore preserve plant and animal species. From an economic standpoint, avoiding sprawl development helps to lessen the burden of expanding infrastructure for both utilities and transportation. The social equity of the proper site selection could include the protection of the natural environment to be enjoyed and observed by future generations for ecological and recreational purposes.

Strategies

Green buildings are encouraged to incorporate the following six strategies for proper, sustainable site selections, according to the *Green Building and LEED Core Concepts Guide*:[3]

1. *Increase density.* Maximize square footage, minimize impacts on land (Figure 7.2). Building density evaluates a building's total floor area as compared to the total area of the site and is measured in square feet per acre.

2. *Choose redevelopment and infill development.* Opt to renovate existing buildings or develop sites between existing structures. Remediate **brownfield** sites to improve the quality of communities and neighborhoods (Figure 7.3). This strategy helps to "limit the amount of land covered by buildings, pavement, or infrastructure while also making more efficient use of the space within existing communities."[4]

3. *Locate near existing infrastructure.* Save the owner money by eliminating the need to bring utilities to a project site, avoid urban sprawl, and consolidate development (Figure 7.4).

4. *Protect habitat.* Preserve wildlife and open space with minimal **site disturbance.** There is no reason to remove vegetation and trees in areas not to be developed; these areas should be protected and not destroyed. Avoid

 Make a flashcard to remember the definition of *floor-to-area ratio:* the proportion of the total floor area of a building to the total land area the building can occupy.

 An increased FAR increases the density and therefore preserves open space.

 If less parking were provided due to urban redevelopment projects with access to public transportation, construction costs would be lower.

Figure 7.2 Urban development in downtown Miami, Florida.

Figure 7.3 Villa Montgomery Apartments, a remediation project in Redwood City, California, by Fisher-Friedman Associates, earned LEED Gold certification under the LEED NC rating system, for compliance with multiple Sustainable Sites strategies, including brownfield site selection and remediation. *Photo courtesy of FFA*

Figure 7.4 This redevelopment project in Miami takes advantage of existing infrastructure.

development on wetland areas and do not disrupt the habitats of endangered species.

5. *Increase diversity of uses.* Provide value in a community and connect people with the services they need for work and living.

6. *Encourage multiple modes of transportation.* Provide pedestrian paths and bicycle networks to integrate with public transportation.

TRANSPORTATION

Transportation is one of the key components addressed within the LEED green building certification program, as it accounted for 33 percent of total U.S. greenhouse gas emissions in 2008 and 13.5 percent of total carbon dioxide emissions globally.[6] As buildings traditionally have contributed to the need for transportation, green buildings have the opportunity to impact the statistics by reducing the "length and frequency of vehicle trips and encourage shifts to more sustainable modes of transportation."[7] The environmental benefits of sustainable strategies for transportation include a reduction in pollution, including vehicle emissions.

Vehicle emissions have a dramatic impact on climate change, smog, and acid rain, among other air quality problems, according to Wikipedia.[8] The economic benefits include the reduction of the need to build and maintain roadways. The social component to reducing transportation impacts includes an improvement of human health, by increasing the encouragement and accessibility of walking or biking from place to place.

The *Green Building and LEED Core Concepts Guide* indicates transportation is most impacted by four factors:

- *Land use*—length and frequency of trips
- *Vehicle technology*—quantity and types of energy and support systems needed to move people and goods to and from the site
- *Fuel*—environmental impact of vehicle operation
- *Human behavior*—a daily transportation decision combining the listed impacts[10]

Strategies

Project teams are encouraged to address the following three design and planning strategies to help reduce transportation impacts of their sites, according to the *Green Building and LEED Core Concepts Guide*:[11]

1. *Choose a site adjacent to mass transit.* Sustainable sites provide building occupants access to public transportation (Figure 7.5).

2. *Limit parking capacity.* Sustainable buildings do not have a surplus of parking, which directly reduces impervious surfaces and encourages the use of mass transit or bicycle commuting. Reducing the amount of parking also minimizes the amount of land to be developed, therefore lowering construction costs.

3. *Encourage bicycling.* Make it convenient and install bike racks (Figure 7.6) and showers.

Create a flashcard to remember the six strategies to address when selecting a site.

Make a flashcard to remember the definition of a *brownfield*: "real property, the expansion, redevelopment, or reuse of which may be complicated by the presence or potential presence of a hazardous substance, pollutant, or contaminant."[5] Cleaning up and reinvesting in these properties protects the environment, reduces blight, and takes development pressures off green spaces and working lands.

Vehicle technology, transportation fuels, and land use are the major contributors to transportation-contributed greenhouse gas emissions.

Land use is the ultimate contributor to the demands of transportation.

Make a flashcard to remember the four impacts of transportation.

Improvements in land-use patterns and investments in public transportation infrastructure alone could reduce greenhouse gas emissions from transportation in the United States by 9 to 15 percent by 2050.[9]

Make a flashcard to remember the three strategies to address transportation during design and planning.

Figure 7.5 Mass transit in New Jersey.
Photo courtesy of David Cardella

Project teams are encouraged to address the following three operations and maintenance strategies to help reduce transportation impacts of their sites, according to the *Green Building and LEED Core Concepts Guide*:[12]

1. *Encourage carpooling.* Incentivize occupants with reserved and preferred parking spaces or a reduction in parking rates for carpools and vanpools. If more occupants participated in a ride-share program, less parking would be needed (Figure 7.7).

Figure 7.6 The Florida town of Lauderdale-by-the-Sea encourages residents to bike to the beach by installing racks to secure their bicycles to.

Figure 7.7 Preferred parking for car/vanpool vehicles.

2. *Encourage or provide alternative fuel vehicles.* Building occupants should be encouraged to use low-emission vehicle types with reserved parking spaces as an incentive, or, better yet, the owners can provide hybrid or alternative fuel vehicles for occupant usage. Green buildings also have the opportunity to provide electric car recharging stations to further incentivize the use of alternative fuel vehicles (Figure 7.8).

Figure 7.8 Refueling station within a parking garage in Miami.

Make a flashcard to remember the four strategies to address transportation during operations and maintenance.

If more people carpooled, walked, or biked to work or school, there would be less pollution.

3. *Incentivize building users/employees.* These include reserved parking spaces or parking discounts for multioccupancy vehicles. Suppose your boss offered you cash for riding your bike to work and a place to safely store it. Would that incentivize you? What if parking rates were higher for single-occupancy vehicles—would that convince you to carpool?

4. *Support alternative transportation.* This could include vehicle sharing programs, a city-wide trolley system, or any alternative to reduce the number of single-occupant automobile commuters at the building or town level (Figure 7.9).

Documenting Transportation Strategies

Consistency across prerequisites and credits is imperative when documenting compliance with the different LEED category requirements. Understanding the terms to document compliance will help ensure consistency. Within the LT category, it is important for teams to calculate the following properly:

■ *Walking and bicycling distance.* The shortest path analysis is used to predict the use of amenities by taking into account "pedestrians' and bicyclists' access to amenities, taking into account safety, convenience, and obstructions to movement. When calculating the walking or bicycling distance, sum the continuous segments of the walking or bicycling route to determine the distance from origin to destination"[13] to ensure that the maximum allowable distance is not exceeded. For the purposes of the LEED Green Associate

Figure 7.9 The Car2Go program makes transportation flexible with its vehicle sharing offers.

exam, do not worry about what the maximum distances are, but instead how to calculate compliance.

- *Total vehicle parking capacity.* Parking capacity includes all off-street parking available to the project occupants and visitors. If the off-street available parking is meant to be shared among other projects, project teams are required to "determine the project's share of parking allocated to the project."[14]

- *Preferred parking.* Project teams can provide preferred parking to incentivize users to carpool or drive a green vehicle. Project teams must locate these preferred parking spaces closest to the building entrance outside of the spaces marked for people with disabilities. Should the project include a multilevel garage, the preferred parking spaces must be located on the level closest to the main entrance of the building.

NEIGHBORHOOD PATTERN AND DESIGN

Of the various LEED rating systems, LEED for Neighborhood Development™ (ND) has the largest ability to impact the mind-set of commuting and the behavior of travel and, therefore, the largest impact to reduce the transportation impacts associated with buildings (Figure 7.10). LEED ND project teams are encouraged to expand the three strategies of site selection as discussed earlier, to the scale of a neighborhood and not just one building's site. Since the rating system promotes pedestrian access and walking as a primary means of transportation, LEED ND project teams should evaluate a neighborhood's street grid density to determine a neighborhood's density and, therefore, how pedestrian friendly it is. The rating system further encourages this strategy by encouraging the **diversity of use** to promote walking and for the residents to become less dependent on cars. A diversity of businesses and community services allows an integration of uses to minimize the length of travel.

 TIP V3V4: LEED 2009 allowed project teams to draw a straight-line radius to document compliance with pedestrian distances to public transportation and other community resources. LEED V4 replaced this strategy with the shortest path analysis to ensure that the amenities are utilized.

 Create a flashcard to remember that pedestrian infrastructure not only includes sidewalks and crosswalks but all weather surface footpaths or equivalent pedestrian facilities.

 Create a flashcard to remember that bicycle infrastructure not only includes on-street bike lanes but also off-street bike paths and trails and streets with low vehicle speed limits.

Figure 7.10 Northwest Gardens in Fort Lauderdale, Florida, incorporates multiple bike and pedestrian paths throughout the community to encourage other methods of transportation in lieu of automobiles. *Photo courtesy of Scott Strawbridge of the Housing Authority of the City of Fort Lauderdale*

Figure 7.11 Designing walkable streets and appropriate building-to-street width ratios encourages pedestrian and bicyclist use. *Photo courtesy of Scott Strawbridge of the Housing Authority of the City of Fort Lauderdale*

Strategies

Project teams are encouraged to address the following eight strategies during design and planning to help reduce transportation impacts of their sites, according to the *Green Building and LEED Core Concepts Guide*:[15]

1. *Design walkable streets.* Make it appealing to pedestrians by limiting speed limits, design buildings to face wide sidewalks, and think about the building height-to-street-width ratio (Figure 7.11).

2. *Include pedestrian amenities,* such as shade, benches, and trees (Figure 7.12).

Figure 7.12 Northwest Gardens, a LEED Gold certified neighborhood, provides benches and shade from trees for pedestrian and resident use.

Figure 7.13 Northwest Gardens has multiple community gardens throughout the Gold certified neighborhood redevelopment project. *Photo courtesy of Scott Strawbridge of the Housing Authority of the City of Fort Lauderdale*

3. *Use compact development strategies.* Increase the number of residential units and commercial square footage by acre.

4. *Promote connectivity.* Limit culs-de-sac, and gated communities should be prohibited.

5. *Provide diverse land uses.* Sustainable communities include a variety of services, such as civic buildings, retail shops, and restaurants.

6. *Create a diverse community.* A diversity of housing types supports a variety of household types, ages, sizes, and income levels to cohabitate in the same neighborhood.

7. *Support access to sustainable food.* Community gardens and farmer's markets should be included in neighborhoods for residents to use (Figure 7.13).

8. *Ensure that all residents have easy access to grocery stores.* It is important that there are healthy resources available to residents and not just fast food establishments.

 Make a flashcard to remember the eight strategies to address sustainable neighborhood pattern and design.

 TIP **Career:** Did you enjoy learning about the location and transportation strategies within this chapter? Perhaps a career in urban and master planning might be for you. Planning professionals are typically involved in the development, revitalization, and preservation of communities, zoning administration, economic development, and geographic information systems (GIS).

QUIZ TIME!

These questions are formatted just as they would be on the exam. Notice the question indicates how many answers to select. The proper number of correct answers is required on the exam, as partial credit is not awarded.

In an effort to present information to you in multiple ways and help you learn, you may find questions asking about information that is new to you, that you did not read about throughout the book.

Q7.1 What is the foundation for sustainable design for individual buildings or entire neighborhoods? (Choose one)

    A. Carbon emissions

    B. Location

    C. Water use

    D. Orientation

    E. Energy use

Q7.2 Transportation accounted for ____ percent of total U.S. greenhouse gas emissions in 2008 and ____ percent of total carbon dioxide emissions globally. (Choose one)

    A. 13.5; 33

    B. 33; 13.5

    C. 20; 33

    D. 33; 20

Q7.3 Which of the following types of properties is best suited for a LEED project? (Choose two)

    A. Greenfields

    B. Floodplains

    C. Habitat for any endangered species

    D. Urban infill

    E. Site with existing infrastructure

    F. Previously developed site with steep slopes

Q7.4 Which of the following street grid density descriptions promotes a more pedestrian friendly community? (Choose one)

    A. A higher street grid density with narrow streets interconnecting

    B. A higher street grid density with wide streets interconnecting

    C. A lower street grid density with wide streets interconnecting

    D. A lower street grid density with narrow streets interconnecting

Q7.5 Which of the following represent the major factors that impact transportation effects on the environment? (Choose three)

    A. Vehicle technology

    B. Fuel

    C. Human behavior

    D. Quality of roads

    E. Suburban development

Q7.6 Which of the following are sustainable strategies that should be implemented on an auto-dependent green building? (Choose four)

    A. Provide priority parking for carpools/vanpools.

    B. Provide a mass transit discount program to employees.

    C. Supply alternative fuel vehicles and accessibility to recharging stations.

    D. Offer discounted parking rates for multioccupant vehicles.

    E. Incorporate basic services (such as a bank, gym, cleaners, or pharmacy) for occupant usage in the new building.

Q7.7 Which of the following are effective and sustainable strategies to address transportation for a LEED project? (Choose three)

    A. Choose a site near a bus stop.

    B. Limit parking.

    C. Encourage carpooling.

    D. Provide SUVs for all employees.

    E. Choose a greenfield site.

Q7.8 Which of the following are the results of developing greenfield sites? (Choose three)

    A. Increased total regional development footprint

    B. Decreased total regional development footprint

    C. Reduced land available for agricultural use

    D. Fragmented wildlife habitat

    E. Encouraged wildlife habitat

Q7.9 Which of the following are true? (Choose two)

    A. Brownfield sites are considered sensitive land and should not be developed.

    B. Brownfield sites can improve environmental performance.

    C. Sustainable communities include diverse uses and housing types.

    D. Infill development increases the amount of land covered by structures, pavement, and infrastructure components.

    E. Sites without access to public transportation are not eligible to earn LEED certification.

Q7.10 Integrating a building into a community does not offer which of the following? (Choose one)

    A. Reduced cost to owners

    B. Enhanced health

    C. Increased economic activity

    D. Enhanced productivity

    E. Encourage biodiversity

    F. Conserve undeveloped land

Q7.11 Which of the following types of spaces should not be included in total parking capacity calculations? (Choose three)

    A. Existing parking spaces

    B. On-street parking on public rights of way

    C. Off-street parking outside of the LEED project boundary available to the building's visitors

    D. Parking spaces for fleet vehicles

    E. Motorcycle parking

Q7.12 Shortest path analysis includes which of the following? (Choose three)

    A. Total vehicle parking capacity

    B. Preferred parking

    C. Convenience

    D. Safety

    E. Vehicle share programs

    F. Obstructions to movement

ONLINE RESOURCES

Check out this website for some fuel saving tips: www.epa.gov/greenvehicles/you/saving.htm.

NOTES

1. USGBC, *Green Building and LEED Core Concepts Guide,* 3rd ed. (2014), 12.

2. H. Levin. "Driving to Green Buildings: The Transportation Energy Intensity of Buildings." *Environmental Building News* 16(9) (2007), www.buildinggreen.com.

3. USGBC, *Green Building and LEED Core Concepts Guide,* p. 53.

4. Ibid.

5. EPA website, http://epa.gov/brownfields/overview/glossary.htm.

6. USGBC, *Green Building and LEED Core Concepts Guide,* p. 53.

7. Ibid., p. 54.

8. Wikipedia website, http://en.wikipedia.org/wiki/Vehicle_Emissions.

9. USGBC, Green Building and LEED Core Concepts Guide, p. 54.

10. USGBC website, www.usgbc.org/guide/bdc#cc_overview.

11. USGBC, *Green Building and LEED Core Concepts Guide,* p. 54.

12. Ibid.

13. USGBC website, www.usgbc.org/guide/bdc#cc_overview.

14. Ibid.

15. USGBC, *Green Building and LEED Core Concepts Guide,* p. 55.

CHAPTER 8

SUSTAINABLE SITES

THIS CHAPTER BEGINS THE DETAILED STUDY OF the strategies and technologies described within each of the Leadership in Energy and Environmental Design (LEED®) categories, starting with Sustainable Sites (SS). The main topics include the factors applicable to site design, construction, and maintenance. As with determining any other strategy while working on a green building project, all components within the SS category should be weighed on a project's triple bottom line values of environmental, economic, and community aspects.

Once a site is selected, the project team needs to assess the site's attributes and conditions to determine the most sustainable approach for development to integrate the building with local ecosystems and preserve biodiversity. What is the existing imperviousness? How much open space is near the project? What is the climate of the region? The answers to these types of questions can help a project team to decide on some of the important strategies to consider when developing a site and how it can contribute to a sustainable environment. They need to consider how much of the site will need to be developed and how much can be preserved/restored as open space. They need to work together to reduce the heat gain from the sun for the entire site, including rooftop areas. These types of site development strategies aid in the success of earning LEED certification, as proven by the project team for the Kohler Environmental Center (Figure 8.1).

 It's time to pick a different color for flashcards created for SS topics. If you do not have enough colors for each of the main categories, combine SS flashcards with the flashcards you made for the concepts identified in the Location and Transportation (LT) category.

 Study: Of those ecosystem services that have been assessed, about 60 percent are degraded or used unsustainably.[1] Ecosystems provide regenerative services and are therefore considered natural capital.

 Study: Between 1982 and 2001, approximately 34 million acres of open space (an area the size of Illinois) were lost to development—approximately 4 acres per minute or 6,000 acres a day.[2]

 V3V4: LEED 2009 addressed site selection and site development in just this category, whereas V4 separates the strategies into the LT and SS categories.

Figure 8.1 The Kohler Environmental Center in Wallingford, Connecticut, implemented site development and stormwater management, contributing to the achievement of earning LEED Platinum certification. *Photo courtesy of Kohler Co.*

Make a flashcard to remember the three factors to address within the SS category. Appendix D summarizes all of the strategies to know for the LEED Green Associate™ exam.

To help evaluate a potential project site, the SS category within the LEED rating systems is broken down into three factors:

1. Site design and management

2. Rainwater management

3. Heat island effect

SITE DESIGN AND MANAGEMENT

 Create two flashcards to remember each of the definitions for *native and adaptive plantings* and *potable water.*

Once a building's site is selected, site design and management become the next components to address when working on a green building project. Project teams are encouraged to utilize the concepts of sustainable landscaping techniques, including **native and/or adaptive plantings** and water-efficient irrigation systems. Native plantings refer to native vegetation that occurs naturally, while adaptive plantings are not natural but can adapt to their new surroundings; both can survive with little to no human interaction or resources. Project teams should select plants that will not only require less water and maintenance, but also improve the nutrients in the soil and deter pests at the same time. Implementing these measures reduces the amount of chemicals in the water infrastructure, and therefore improves the quality of surface water and saves building owners from purchasing fertilizers and pesticides. Avoiding or reducing the amount of **potable water** (drinking water supplied by municipalities or wells) used for irrigation, decreases the quantity of water required for building sites and therefore reduces maintenance costs as well.

 Create a flashcard to remember the definitions of *imperviousness*: surfaces that do not allow water to pass through them; and *perviousness*: surfaces that allow water to percolate or penetrate through them.

Sustainable sites should also address two other components: minimizing **impervious**, or hardscape, surfaces such as parking lots and paved walkways, and utilizing optimized exterior lighting schemes within their site designs. Impervious surfaces ultimately contribute to **stormwater runoff** and therefore decrease the quality of surface water and reduce groundwater recharge (Figure 8.2). In terms of site lighting, traditionally there has been little attention paid to the quality of the night sky and the effects on wildlife, or to the wasteful energy use approach for exterior lighting.

 Create another flashcard to remember the definition of *stormwater runoff*: rainwater that leaves a project site flowing along parking lots and roadways, traveling to sewer systems and water bodies.

It is inefficient to illuminate areas not used at night, light areas beyond a property's boundary, or overcompensate light levels. If light contrast levels are minimized, light pollution is reduced, dark night skies are preserved, and nocturnal animal habitats remain unaffected.

Project teams are encouraged to use low impact development (LID) and green infrastructure (GI) strategies to create natural, sustainable exterior environments that can be sustainably maintained to add to the economic, environmental, and social equity of their green building projects.

Strategies

There are five core strategies that address these site design concepts to be considered for implementation when designing a sustainable site[3]:

 Create another flashcard to remember the definition of *building/ development footprint*: the amount of land the building structure occupies not including landscape and hardscape surfaces such as parking lots, driveways, and walkways.

1. *Preserve open space and sensitive areas.* Reduce the size of a **building's footprint** (Figure 8.3), increase the FAR, and decrease the amount of land developed, and therefore maximize the amount of open space. If parking is required, use a tuck-under approach. Sensitive areas include wetlands, bodies of water, and habitats for endangered species.

Figure 8.2 Dick's Sporting Goods Corporate Headquarters in Pittsburgh, Pennsylvania, designed by Strada Architecture, LLC, incorporates roof water capture to reduce the stormwater runoff and reduce the need for potable water for irrigation. *Image courtesy of Strada Architecture LLC*

2. *Minimize hardscape.* These impervious surfaces contribute to stormwater runoff and therefore carry pollutants to the water stream, decreasing the quality of water (Figure 8.4).
3. *Use native landscaping.* In terms of site design, using native and adaptive vegetation and/or utilizing a high-efficient irrigation system reduces the amount

Figure 8.3 The high-efficiency Duke Law Star Commons project in Durham, North Carolina, by Shepley Bulfinch, obtained its LEED Certification by providing access to public transportation and reducing site disturbance and the heat island effect. *Photo courtesy of Kat Nania, Shepley Bulfinch*

Figure 8.4 Turfstone™ Open-Grid Pavers allow stormwater to pass through, in order to recharge groundwater and reduce runoff. *Photo courtesy of Pavers by Ideal*

 TIP **Study:** Light trespass is the unwanted light shining on another's property.

 Create a flashcard to remember the five site design strategies.

of water needed and can provide habitat for local birds and other species (Figure 8.5).

4. *Prevent light pollution.* Exterior light fixtures should project light down, not up toward the night sky (Figure 8.6). Minimal light levels should be maintained at night for safety for parking lots and walkways, but what about areas not occupied at night?

5. *Protect and restore habitat.* Dedicate protected areas for the life of the project. Create a conservation management plan to ensure that the open space is protected. Project teams might consider placing the protected areas in a land trust.

There following are three strategies for sustainable site operations and maintenance[4]:

1. *Develop a sustainable management plan.* Not only should an integrated pest management (IPM) plan be implemented by the maintenance team, but so

Figure 8.5 Using soil amendments, such as mulch, can help to reduce water loss and erosion, as well as naturally curb weeds and regulate soil temperatures. *Photo courtesy of Lee and Diane Wansor*

should a plan for cleaning the exterior surfaces. These plans should reduce or eliminate chemicals and waste that could flow into the water stream and therefore decrease the water quality. The plans should also address energy and water usage to avoid waste, as well as other pollution reduction methods.

2. *Implement conservation programs.* Protect species and habitat by working with local ecologists and nonprofit organizations.

3. *Maintain site lighting to prevent light pollution.* Whenever higher light levels are needed, put the fixtures on timers to shut off automatically after hours.

 Create a flashcard to remember the three strategies to address for site operations and maintenance.

Figure 8.6 The Utah Botanical Center's Wetland Discovery Point building at Utah State University in Kaysville was mindful of the nocturnal environment in which the center resides by providing very minimal exterior lighting and shielding any fixtures that would pollute the night sky. *Photo courtesy of Gary Neuenswander, Utah Agricultural Experiment Station*

TIP **V3V4:** LEED 2009 used the term stormwater management, whereas V4 uses rainwater management.

TIP **Study:** Nonpoint source pollutants are one of the biggest risks to the quality of surface water and aquatic life.

TIP **Study:** Think about the typical approach of rainwater management. Most projects remove rainwater from the area as quickly as possible. This strategy may prevent flooding but is threatening the function of the watershed. Now imagine if we instead mirrored the natural water flow system and increased infiltration into the ground. What if we captured and reused the water? What if we treated the water before it leaves the site?

TIP **Study:** A Washington State Department of Ecology study noted that rainwater runoff from roads, parking lots, and other hardscapes carries some 200,000 barrels of petroleum into the Puget Sound every year—more than half of what was spilled in the 1989 Exxon Valdez accident in Alaska.[5]

! Reducing the amount of impervious surfaces, and increasing pervious surfaces, helps to reduce rainwater runoff and therefore also helps to save the quality of water.

RAINWATER MANAGEMENT

In the previous section, strategies were presented to address while designing a sustainable site, including the importance to reduce the amount of impervious surfaces. One benefit of minimizing impervious surfaces, such as asphalt and concrete, is the reduction of rainwater runoff, which causes degradation of the quality of surface water and reduces groundwater recharge to the local aquifer. The reduction in surface-water quality is caused by both a filtration decrease and the increase of hardscape areas containing contaminants. The increase of impervious surfaces and rainwater runoff has put water quality, aquatic life, and recreational areas at risk.

Nonpoint source pollutants, such as oil leaked from cars or fertilizers from plantings, are one of the biggest risks to the quality of surface water and aquatic life. These pollutants typically contaminate rainwater flowing along impervious surfaces on the journey to sewer systems or water bodies, especially after a heavy rainfall. Once this rainwater is in the sewer system, it then contaminates the rest of the water and takes a toll on the process to purify it, or it contaminates the body of water into which it is dumped. These bodies of water also then suffer from soil erosion and sedimentation, deteriorating aquatic life and recreational opportunities. Therefore, allowing rainwater to percolate and penetrate through **pervious** surfaces, such as pervious concrete, porous pavement (Figure 8.7), or open-grid pavers, reduces the pollution of surface water and is less of a burden on our ecosystem. For projects located in urban areas where space is limited, oil separators can be utilized to remove oil, sediment, and floatables. Within an oil separator, heavier solid materials settle to the bottom while floatable oil and grease rise to the top.

Project sites could also include other strategies to reduce runoff including **wet** or **dry ponds.** Both of these approaches utilize excavated areas used to detain rainwater from leaving the site and therefore slow runoff. Two other options include on-site filtration methods. **Bioswales,** or engineered basins with vegetation, can be utilized to increase groundwater recharge and reduce peak rainwater runoff (Figure 8.8). The other option, **rain gardens,** functions to collect and filter runoff while reducing peak discharge rates. Rooftops also contribute to the pollution of surface water, so implementing a green, or vegetated, roof would also reduce stormwater runoff. The best environmental strategies include treating all surface water before allowing it to leave the site. For example, the Rivers Casino project team designed the site so that all surface water flows through a series of catchment areas that promote plant growth as a means to filter the water before it enters the riverbank (Figure 8.9).

The triple bottom line benefits of managing rainwater include preserving the natural ecological systems, such as wetlands that promote **biodiversity** and help manage rainwater (see Figure 8.10). If the natural environment is already able to manage rainwater, we could take advantage of the economic savings of not creating manmade structures to do it for us, as well as the costs to maintain the structures. There is also social equity in managing runoff and maintaining clean surface water: the preservation of aquatic life and the ability to enjoy recreational activities.

Strategies

For the purposes of the LEED Green Associate exam, it is important to remember the following three design strategies for managing rainwater[6]:

Figure 8.7 Installing pervious materials, such as pervious asphalt, helps to manage rainwater runoff. *Image courtesy of BASF Corporation*

1. *Minimize impervious areas.* Remember open-grid pavers, porous paving, pervious concrete, and green roofs to increase pervious surfaces (Figure 8.11).

2. *Control rainwater.* Remember rain gardens, dry ponds, and bioswales slow down runoff while allowing the natural environment to infiltrate and clean the water of pollutants.

3. *Incorporate rainwater management into site design.* Implement multipurpose features, such as streets with bioswales to collect and hold rainwater.

 Create a flashcard to remember the three design strategies to address rainwater management.

Figure 8.8 Bioswales, an onsite filtration strategy, can help to recharge the groundwater and reduce rainwater runoff. *Photo courtesy of Thomas M. Robinson, EDR*

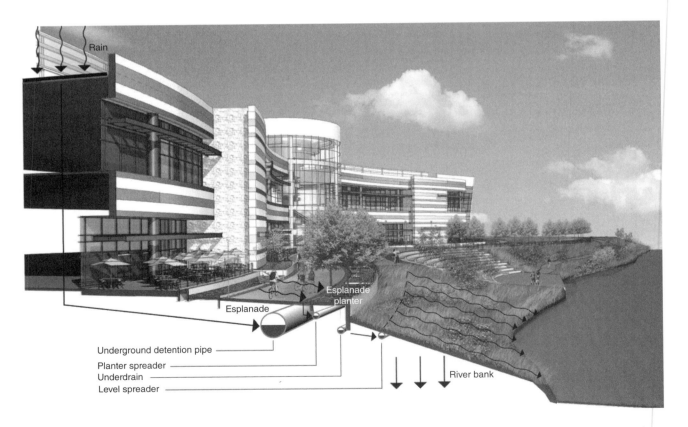

Figure 8.9 Rivers Casino Riverfront Park in Pittsburgh, Pennsylvania, addresses rainwater quantity and quality by incorporating filtration measures to capture and clean rainwater. *Image courtesy of Strada Architecture, LLC*

Figure 8.10 The Utah Botanical Center's Wetland Discovery Point project, at Utah State University in Kaysville, earned LEED Platinum certification for its efforts to create biodiversity. *Photo courtesy of Gary Neuenswander, Utah Agricultural Experiment Station*

There are two strategies for rainwater management in operations and maintenance[7]:

1. *Redirect rainwater* into rain gardens, bioswales, or other water-retaining landscape features.
2. *Harvest rainwater.* Collect it and use it later for nonpotable uses, such as irrigation, custodial uses, and flushing toilets and urinals, but be mindful of local rules and regulations (see Figure 8.12).

 TIP **Study:** Project teams are encouraged to research the regional environmental conditions when establishing a rainwater management strategy for a project. Rainwater collection maybe encouraged in one region while prohibited in others.

 Green roofs have many synergies, including maximizing open space, creating a habitat for wildlife, and reducing rainwater runoff and the heat island effect, but they also help to insulate a building and therefore reduce energy use. The trade-offs with green roofs include installation cost and maintenance.

 Create a flashcard to remember the two operations and maintenance strategies to address rainwater management.

 TIP **Career:** Rainwater management strategies are typically the responsibility of the civil engineer. Engaging a landscape architect is suggested to select the proper vegetation specific to a region to ensure that potable water is minimally used.

Figure 8.11 This vegetated roof at the Allegany County Human Resources Development Commission's community center in Cumberland, Maryland, minimizes impervious areas to reduce rainwater runoff. *Photo courtesy of Moshier Studio*

Figure 8.12 Rainwater is collected onsite and stored in cisterns at the Utah Botanical Center's Wetland Discovery Point building and used to flush toilets, as well as irrigate the site, therefore reducing the need for potable water. *Photo courtesy of Gary Neuenswander, Utah Agricultural Experiment Station*

 Tuck-under parking helps to reduce impervious surfaces, reduces the impacts of the urban heat island effect, reduces runoff, and helps to preserve open space for parking and nonparking uses.

 Besides low-SRI, nonreflective surface materials, car exhaust, air conditioners, and street equipment contribute to the heat island effect, while narrow streets and tall buildings can serve to further exacerbate the problem.

 An increase in energy demand is not the only consequence of heat island effect. Wildlife species may not be able to adapt to the higher temperatures and begin to decline.

 Create a flashcard to remember the definition of the heat island effect.

 Create a flashcard to remember the definition of solar reflectivity index (SRI).

HEAT ISLAND EFFECT

Although energy use will be discussed in more detail in Chapter 10, materials used for site design and rooftops can efficiently impact the use of energy for two reasons. Think of summertime at the grocery store parking lot and how you can see heat emitting from the black asphalt surface. The sun is attracted to darker surfaces, where heat is then retained. Multiply this effect in a downtown, urban area to understand the true impacts of urban **heat island effect**. By specifying and implementing materials with a high **solar reflectance (SR)** or **solar reflectivity index (SRI)**, green building projects can reduce the heat island effect and the overall temperature of an area. A material's SRI value is based on the material's ability to reflect or reject solar heat gain measured on a scale from 0 (dark, most absorptive) to 100 (light, most reflective).

If a lighter roofing material is used, the mechanical systems do not have to compensate for the heat gain to cool a building, therefore reducing the use of energy (Figure 8.13). If light-colored materials are used for surface paving, walkways, and rooftops, light can be distributed more efficiently at night to reduce the number of light fixtures required, which saves money during construction and, later, during operations (Figure 8.14).

Strategies

There are three strategies that aim to reduce the heat island effect[8]:

1. *Use reflective roof materials.* Using materials with high SRI can reduce the heat island effect (Figure 8.15) and spread light at night for a cost-effective approach to exterior lighting.

2. *Reduce the area of paved surfaces exposed to sunlight.* Start by reducing the amount of hardscape, then implement light colored paved areas and/or shade it with vegetation. Locate parking under ground to also minimize the exposure to sunlight.

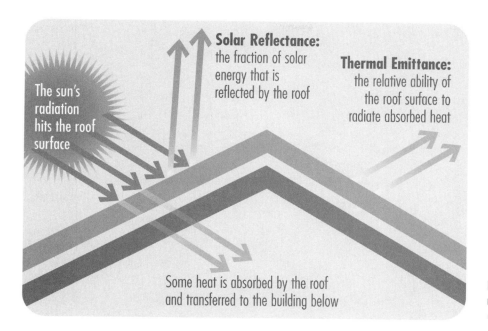

Figure 8.13 Diagram illustrating solar reflectance and thermal emittance. *Image courtesy of Cool Roof Rating Council, www.coolroofs.org*

Figure 8.14 The roof at Villa Montgomery Apartments in Redwood City, California, reduces the urban heat island effect by the installation of a combination of a high–solar reflectance index (SRI) roof material with photovoltaic systems (generating a portion of the electricity needed for operations), along with a green roof, including a playground that offers residents the opportunity to enjoy the outdoor environment. *Photo courtesy of FFA*

Figure 8.15 The Armstrong World Industries Corporate Headquarters in Lancaster, Pennsylvania, has a white roof, a strategy that helped the project earn Platinum certification under the LEED for Existing Buildings rating system. *Photo courtesy of Armstrong Ceiling and Wall Systems*

 It is the collective strategies that have the biggest reduction of building-associated environmental impacts, such as tuck-under parking with reserved spaces for low-emitting fuel types and carpools/vanpools. Remember the synergies of green building strategies.

 Create a flashcard to remember an important strategy for projects in arid climates: evapotranspiration, the return of water to the atmosphere after evaporating from plants' leaves.[9]

 Create a flashcard to remember the three strategies to reduce the heat island effect.

 Career: Heat island effect strategies are typically the responsibility of the architect for roofing selections. A structural engineer and landscape architect is encouraged for a vegetated roof design. A civil engineer typically works with the architect and landscape architect for planning the site and selecting hardscape materials.

3. *Plan an urban forest or a green roof.* Think about walking down the streets of your favorite downtown neighborhood with the street trees, shrubs, and other landscaping used to reduce the heat island effect by evapotranspiration and shading.

QUIZ TIME!

These questions are formatted just as they would be on the exam. Notice the question indicates how many answers to select. The proper number of correct answers is required on the exam, as partial credit is not awarded.

In an effort to present information to you in multiple ways and help you learn, you may find questions asking about information that is new to you, that you did not read about throughout the book.

Q8.1 Which of the following is the best landscape design strategy to implement to reduce heat island effects? (Choose one)

    A. Absorption

    B. Xeriscaping

    C. Increased SRI

    D. Deciduous trees

    E. Increased imperviousness

Q8.2 The owner of a two-story office project has suggested that he is interested in the installation of a vegetated roof system and would like the design team to evaluate it as an option. Which set of team members best represents all of those who might offer meaningful input to this evaluation? (Choose one)

A. Architect, landscape architect, and civil engineer

B. Architect, contractor, and structural engineer

C. Landscape architect, contractor, civil engineer, and structural engineer

D. Architect, structural engineer, landscape architect, and civil engineer

E. Architect, structural engineer, landscape architect, civil engineer, and mechanical engineer

F. Architect, structural engineer, landscape architect, civil engineer, mechanical engineer, and contractor

Q8.3 Emissivity is an indication of which of the following material properties? (Choose one)

A. Ability to reflect light from light sources

B. Ability of a transparent or translucent material to admit solar gain

C. Ability of a material to absorb heat across the entire solar spectrum, including all nonvisible wavelengths

D. Ability of a material to give up heat in the form of long-wave radiation

Q8.4 The design team has attempted to address 50 percent of the hardscape surfaces on the project's site to meet the requirements to reduce the heat island effect for LEED compliance. Which of the following strategies should the LEED Accredited Professional discuss with the design team? (Choose three)

A. Effective tree-shaded area of hardscape features

B. Solar reflectance index for all nonstandard paving materials proposed

C. Percentage of perviousness for proposed open-grid paving materials

D. Emissivity of all low-SRI hardscape features in the design

E. Runoff coefficients for impervious paving materials selected

Q8.5 Which of the following are strategies to reduce rainwater runoff? (Choose three)

A. Green roofs

B. Impervious asphalt

C. Pervious pavers

D. Bioswales

E. Decrease open space

Q8.6 A vegetated roof system using native and adapted plant species has the opportunity to contribute to earning which three strategies? (Choose three)

A. Community connectivity

B. Rainwater management

C. Heat island effect

D. Prevent light pollution

E. Restore habitat

Q8.7 Which of the following are LEED concepts that are *most* significantly influenced by site selection prior to design of the project? (Choose two)

A. Heat island effect

B. Green vehicles

C. Public transportation access

D. Minimize water usage

E. Brownfield redevelopment

Q8.8 What material options would be best to comply with the LEED rating systems for roofing materials? (Choose two)

A. Gray asphalt with an SRI of 22

B. Aluminum coating with an SRI of 50

C. Red clay tile with an SRI of 36

D. White ethylene propylene diene monomer (EPDM) with an SRI of 84

E. White cement tile with an SRI of 90

F. Light gravel on built-up roof with an SRI of 37

Q8.9 Which of the following are examples of impervious surfaces? (Choose three)

A. Asphalt

B. Sealed surfaces

C. Turf grass

D. Concrete

E. Porous pavers

Q8.10 Which of the following are true? (Choose three)

A. LID methods minimize heat island effects.

B. LID methods increase light pollution.

C. SRI values are relative to roofs while SR values are intended for nonroof hardscape materials.

D. Rainwater runoff can contribute to eutrophication.

E. Uplighting is not considered light pollution.

F. Project teams are encouraged to use impervious paving systems for parking lots and other hardscape areas to help manage rainwater runoff.

ONLINE RESOURCES

For a funny study break, check out this light pollution dispute between neighbors: www.quickmeme.com/p/3vrw3r.

NOTES

1. UN Environment Programme, State and Trends of the Environment 1987–2001, Section B, Chapter 5, www.unep.org/geo/geo4/report/05_ Biodiversity.pdf, 161.

2. U.S. Forest Service website, www.fs.fed.us/projects/four-threats/facts/open-space.shtml.

3. USGBC, *Green Building and LEED Core Concepts Guide,* 3rd ed. (2014), 57.

4. Ibid., p. 58.

5. USGBC website, www.usgbc.org/guide/bdc#cc_overview.

6. USGBC, *Green Building and LEED Core Concepts Guide,* p. 59.

7. Ibid.

8. Ibid., p. 60.

9. Ibid., p. 57.

CHAPTER 9

WATER EFFICIENCY

THIS CHAPTER FOCUSES ON THE STRATEGIES AND technologies described within the Water Efficiency (WE) category of the Leadership in Energy and Environmental Design (LEED®) rating systems, including methods to reduce the consumption of water, our most precious resource that is often taken for granted. As the demand for water continues to increase and supplies are decreasing, it is challenging for municipalities to keep up. "In 60 percent of European cities with more than 100,000 people, groundwater is being used faster than it can be replenished."[1]

The U.S. Geological Survey estimates that buildings account for 12 percent of total water use in the United States. Potable water that is delivered to buildings and homes is first pulled from local bodies of water, treated, and then delivered. This water is typically used for toilets, urinals, sinks, showers, drinking, irrigation, and for equipment uses, such as mechanical systems, dishwashing, and washing machines. Once the wastewater leaves the building or home, it is treated and then delivered back to the body of water. When the influx supersedes the capacity of the wastewater treatment facilities, overflow will result. This overflow can pollute and contaminate nearby water bodies, the sources of potable water, therefore causing the need for more treatment facilities to be built. Therefore, it is critical to understand how to reduce the amount of water we consume, to reduce the burden on the entire cycle, especially as we are threatened with shortages in the near future.

Green building project teams are encouraged to start with an "efficiency first" approach when designing a water conservation strategy, including the specification of efficient fixtures, equipment, and appliances that require less water. "Understanding how water is being used allows teams to identify where they should focus conservation efforts."[2] They should then implement rainwater-harvesting technologies to capture nonpotable water to use for multiple applications inside and out. In order to capture rainwater, runoff is collected from a roof and stored in a cistern on site (Figure 9.1). Each of the three uses of water detailed in this chapter include strategies for nonpotable water uses to reduce consumption.

Building and site designs can help to reduce the amount of water that is required for operations and the amount of wastewater that leaves a site. Water efficiency for green buildings is addressed in two components:

1. Indoor water use

2. Outdoor water use

Water efficiency helps to reduce energy and therefore costs by reducing the amount of water that must be treated, heated, cooled, and distributed. This strategy is important to grasp, as the energy required to treat and transport water is not captured by a utility meter.

 Remember to pick a new color for flashcards created for the Water Efficiency category topics.

 TIP Create a flashcard to remember the two types of water uses described in the Water Efficiency category. Remember, Appendix D summarizes all of the strategies of each category to remember for the exam.

Figure 9.1 Capturing and storing rainwater to use for irrigation reduces the need for potable water. *Photo courtesy of Rainwater HOG, LLC*

TIP **Study:** A study by California's Energy Commission determined that about 19 percent of the state's electricity, 30 percent of its natural gas, and over 80 billion gallons of diesel fuel is consumed by water treatment and pumping each year.[3]

Once these efficiency strategies are implemented to reduce the amount of water required, it is also important to monitor consumption and note any inefficient occurrences, such as leaks.

Similar to the strategies discussed within the Location and Transportation (LT) and the Sustainable Sites (SS) categories, there are triple bottom line values to water-efficient strategies. From an environmental standpoint, the more we build with impervious surfaces, the harder it is for the groundwater to recharge naturally. From an economic viewpoint, the more we contribute to sprawl, the more we increase the demand for more facilities and additional distribution systems to be built at a cost to the public. In addition, the energy required to heat water is in direct comparison to the amount of water used; use less hot water, use less energy, save money. Although the social equity of water is drastically understated, as its economic value does not reflect its importance, maintaining

Figure 9.2 The Utah Botanical Center's Wetland Discovery Point project is located within a natural habitat requiring the team to address environmental impacts as a result of the new construction, such as water quality. In order to earn its Platinum certification the team utilized a trombe wall as a thermal mass to capture the heat from the sun during the day and release it at night for heating. *Photo courtesy of Gary Neuenswander, Utah Agricultural Experiment Station*

clean sources of water is imperative to future generations. The Utah Botanical Center's Wetland Discovery Point project earned Platinum level certification for addressing each of the triple bottom line components for the project (Figure 9.2).

When approaching the strategies to reduce water for a project seeking LEED certification, it is necessary for the project teams to calculate a **baseline** for water usage versus what the project is intended to require. The WE prerequisite and each of the credits utilizes the Energy Policy Act of 1992 (EPAct 1992) for flow and flush rates associated with conventional and efficient fixtures (see Table 9.1). Project teams should also reference the Energy Policy Act (EPAct) of 2005, as it became U.S. law in August 2005.

Once the fixture water consumption is determined, project teams need to account for the occupant usage to calculate how much water is required for the building.

The full-time equivalent (FTE) occupancy is an estimation of actual building occupancy in terms of hours occupied per day and is used to determine the number of occupants for the building that will use the fixtures. FTE is calculated by dividing the total number of occupant hours spent in the building (each full-time employee is assumed to be in the building for eight hours) divided by

 Create a flashcard to remember the Energy Policy Act of 1992 (EPAct 1992) as the standard for the WE prerequisite and credits. Project teams are encouraged to select EPA WaterSense and ENERGY STAR products.

 Create a flashcard to remember baseline versus design: the amount of water a conventional project would use as compared to the design case.

 TIP **Study:** Notice that FTE is the acronym for *full-time* equivalent and not *full-time employee*. Make sure you account for part-time and transient occupants as well!

 A low-flow water closet uses 30 percent less water than a conventional water closet.

Table 9.1 Water Consumption Assumptions According to EPAct 1992

Fixture Type	Gallons per Flush (gpf)
Conventional water closet (for baseline calculations)	1.6
Low-flow water closet	1.1
Ultra-low-flow water closet	0.8
Composting toilet	0.0
Conventional urinal (for baseline calculations)	1.0
Waterless urinal	0.0

eight. Therefore, full-time employees have a value of one. Part-time employees must also be considered in the calculations, if they work four hours a day, they have a value of 0.5. If a building has 100 occupants, 50 of whom work full time and 50 of whom work part time, the FTE for the project is 75. It is also important to remember to include transient occupants in occupancy calculations. For example, if a project team were designing a library, they would need to account for the visitors to the library, as well as the staff and employees. These visitors are thought of as transient occupants for the purposes of LEED.

INDOOR WATER USE

TIP **Study:** Wastewater from toilets and urinals is considered *blackwater*. Kitchen sink, shower, and bathtub wastewater is also considered a source of blackwater. Remember, it's not the source that matters, but what could be in it! For example, washing machine wastewater could be considered blackwater, as it is used to wash cloth diapers.

Indoor water use typically includes the water used for water closets, urinals, lavatories, and showers. Break room or kitchen sinks are also included in the calculations for indoor water use. For the purposes of the exam, it is important to understand and remember the differences between a flush fixture and a flow fixture and how their consumption is measured. Flush fixtures, such as toilets and urinals, are measured in **gallons per flush** (gpf). Flow fixtures, such as sink faucets, showerheads, and aerators, are measured in **gallons per minute** (gpm).

Create flashcards to remember flow and flush fixture types and how they are measured.

The LEED rating systems define potable water use as an important component that green buildings should address and therefore require a reduction in consumption as a minimal performance feature. This importance is characterized by the means of a prerequisite within the WE category. Therefore, LEED-certified projects must demand at least 20 percent or less indoor water as compared to conventionally designed buildings.

Process Water

Create a flashcard to remember the uses for process water.

The types of water use reduction intentions previously described may be more obvious strategies for green buildings as opposed to the third type: process water.

Water used for building systems, such as heat and cooling air, is considered process water. Process water is used for industrial purposes, such as chillers, cooling towers, and boilers, and also includes water used for business operations, such as washing machines, ice machines, and dishwashers.

TIP **Study:** A cooling tower "uses water to absorb heat from air-conditioning systems and regulate air temperature in a facility."[4]

Building managers and owners should be aware where water is required and how much is consumed at those specific locations. Green building design teams know efficient building systems require less water. Taking advantage of closed-loop systems allows buildings to extend the use of water in a contaminant-free environment. Installing meters to understand the demands of water for building systems and how much is consumed could help economically, specifically in terms of cooling tower makeup water. This water is evaporated during the operation of a cooling tower and, if metered, could be an opportunity for credit from the utility company, as it does not enter the sewer system, which would then need to be treated.

ENERGY STAR-certified appliances, such as washing machines and dishwashers, are energy efficient and require less process water.

Water efficiency strategies incorporated into site design, such as collecting rainwater onsite, can help to reduce the demand for indoor water for flush fixtures.

Strategies

Keeping within the lines of the basic concept to use less water, efficient indoor water strategies help to change the typically traditional, wasteful behavior of occupants. Project teams should conduct life-cycle cost assessments for determining the best solution for their projects. For example, waterless urinals might cost less to install, as they do not require wastewater piping, but their maintenance costs might be higher than a conventional fixture. Overall, most of these strategies will not be noticeable, but will substantially reduce water consumption. The following three strategies are listed in the *Green Building and LEED Core Concepts Guide:*[5]

1. *Install efficient plumbing fixtures* such as low-flow toilets, showerheads, and faucets (Figure 9.3). Some teams go a step further and install waterless fixtures, such as toilets and urinals (Figure 9.4). Automatic faucet sensors and metering controls should also be considered. When existing fixtures cannot be replaced, buildings should employ flow restrictors and sensors on flow fixtures.

2. *Use nonpotable water* for flush functions for toilets and urinals, including captured rainwater (Figure 9.5), **graywater**, and municipal reclaimed water.

3. *Install submeters* to track consumption and monitor for leakage.

Create a flashcard to remember the three strategies for indoor water use.

Create a flashcard to remember the definition of *graywater:* wastewater from showers, bathtubs, lavatories, and washing machines. This water has not come into contact with toilet waste according to the International Plumbing Code (IPC).

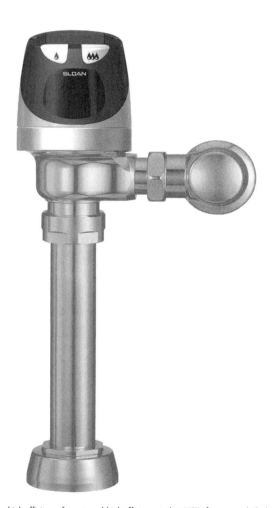

Figure 9.3 Using high-efficiency faucets and high-efficiency toilet (HET) fixtures and Flushometers, which use 1.28 gpf or less, helps to achieve the water reduction prerequisite of 20 percent. *Photo courtesy of Sloan Valve Company*

Figure 9.4 Waterless urinals help to reduce the indoor water consumption. *Photo courtesy of SmithGroup, Inc.*

Figure 9.5 Rainwater is collected for reuse to reduce the need for potable water at the Natural Resources Defense Council's Robert Redford Building in Santa Monica, California. *Photo courtesy of Grey Crawford*

OUTDOOR WATER

Water used for irrigating landscaping accounts for the primary use of outdoor water usage, and is therefore a component to be addressed and reduced in green buildings. Remembering the concepts discussed in the previous chapter, site design including native and adaptive plants can drastically reduce the amount of water required for irrigation, if not eliminate the need for irrigation all together (Figure 9.6). If irrigation is required, implementing a high-efficiency system can also substantially reduce the amount of water required over conventional designs. Green building projects might also implement other sustainable options, including capturing rainwater to use for irrigation and indoor water flush functions.

Chapter 8 introduced the heat island effect and how it is responsible for an overall temperature increase of an area. Combining the impacts of greenhouse

 Remember, both composting and mulching optimize soil conditions to add to the efficiencies of native and adaptive plantings and high-efficiency irrigation systems.

 Study: The amount of water delivered by sprinkler heads is measured in gallons per minute (gpm).

Figure 9.6 Native and noninvasive plantings do not require irrigation or fertilizers.

gas emissions, the heat island effect, and increased impervious surfaces from sprawling developments, water is thus evaporating at quicker rates and not getting delivered to plants and vegetation. Project teams need to be aware of these conditions and plan accordingly, efficiently, and sustainably. To calculate the amount of water actually delivered to vegetation by the proposed irrigation system and not blown away or evaporated, a project team determines the **irrigation efficiency** of the proposed system. For the purposes of the exam, it is important to remember what the team members need to consider as part of the calculations, not necessarily how they calculate factors, such as irrigation efficiency.

Strategies

Pulling together the concepts and strategies from the Sustainable Sites (SS) category, such as native planting and xeriscaping, and repeating a couple from indoor water use, the outdoor water use strategies include:[6]

1. *Implement native and adapted plants*—requires little to no maintenance. Drought-resistant plants are the *best* environmental option! Can also provide habitat for native wildlife.

2. *Use xeriscaping,* combining native planting with soil improvements and efficient irrigation systems (Figure 9.7).

 Remember the strategies discussed in the previous chapter. Proper site design will help to reduce water consumption for landscaping needs. Reducing water demands affects both the SS and WE categories.

 Career: Interested in landscaping and design? Landscape architects typically work with architects and civil engineers when designing the exterior environment and selecting the various types of vegetation. LEED project teams depend on the landscape architect to select locally adapted plants to save water for irrigation.

 Study: Xeriscaping can also be used as a sustainable landscaping strategy, as it uses drought-adaptable and minimal-water plant types along with soil covers, such as composts and mulches, to reduce evaporation.

Figure 9.7 Xeriscaping helps to reduce the need for potable water for irrigation.

Figure 9.8 Collecting and storing rainwater for reuse helps to reduce the burden on the local municipality. *Photo courtesy of Rainwater HOG, LLC*

3. *Specify high-efficiency irrigation systems*—moisture sensors included! Types include surface drip, underground, and bubbler systems.

4. *Use nonpotable water,* specifically for irrigation. Includes captured rainwater, graywater, and municipal reclaimed water (Figure 9.8).

5. *Install submeters* to track consumption and monitor for leakage.

 Remember the sources of nonpotable water, including capturing rainwater, to reduce the demands for the many outdoor, indoor, and process water uses. See the end of the book for flashcard examples.

 Create a flashcard to remember the five strategies for outdoor water use.

QUIZ TIME!

These questions are formatted just as they would be on the exam. Notice the question indicates how many answers to select. The proper number of correct answers is required on the exam, as partial credit is not awarded.

In an effort to present information to you in multiple ways and help you learn, you may find questions asking about information that is new to you, that you did not read about throughout the book.

Q9.1 If an existing building seeks water efficiency strategies but has a limited budget, installing which of the following would be economically viable options? (Choose two)

    A. Aerators

    B. Low-flow toilets

    C. Waterless urinals

    D. Capturing rainwater for irrigation

    E. Flush valves

Q9.2 Which of the following products are not examples of a flow fixture? (Choose two)

    A. Lavatory faucets

    B. Toilets

    C. Sprinkler heads

    D. Aerators

    E. Showerheads

    F. Urinals

Q9.3 Which of the following strategies might contribute to water-efficient landscaping? (Choose three)

    A. Planting of hardwood trees to provide shade

    B. Planting native or adapted plant species

    C. Installing turf grass

    D. Reducing amount of pervious surface area

    E. Combining vegetated swales and cisterns to capture rainwater

Q9.4 A previously developed site is undergoing a major renovation. The plans include avoiding undeveloped areas and planting more than half of the site area with native and adapted vegetation. Retention ponds and bioswales will also be implemented with native vegetation. Which of the following LEED concepts might these design strategies contribute? (Choose four)

    A. Heat island effect

    B. Rainwater runoff reduction

    C. Site disturbance

D. Water-efficient landscaping

E. Increase density

Q9.5 The major renovation of a four-story, 40,000-square-foot building in Florida includes repaving existing parking areas along the entire length of the south and west facades of the building. The building and parking areas compose the entire site to its boundaries, not leaving any green space. The common afternoon rain showers have led the design team to select open-grid paving with vegetated cells equivalent to 50 percent of its surface in lieu of a lower-first-cost solution, such as black asphalt. Based on the information provided, which of the following benefits and LEED strategies might the open-grid paving strategy contribute? (Choose three)

A. Reduced site disturbance

B. Water-efficient landscaping

C. Heat island effect

D. Rainwater management

E. Optimize energy performance

F. Water use reduction

Q9.6 Which of the following are types of process water uses? (Choose three)

A. Cooling towers

B. Boilers

C. Washing machines

D. Cisterns

E. Toilets

Q9.7 Which of the following are potential sources of nonpotable water? (Choose three)

A. Blackwater

B. Municipally supplied reclaimed water

C. Captured rainwater

D. Wastewater from a toilet

E. Graywater

Q9.8 Which of the following uses are best described and suitable for nonpotable water? (Choose two)

A. Drinking water

B. Irrigation

C. Clothes washing

D. Process water

E. Dishwashing

F. Showers

Q9.9 Which of the following are true? (Choose two)

A. Building meters account for the energy to treat and transport water.

B. Some municipalities do not allow rainwater to be captured and reused.

C. LEED recommends for project teams to develop alternative water sources first and then select high-efficiency fixtures when strategizing for water reduction.

D. Graywater is suitable for drinking.

E. Green building projects are rewarded for reducing demand and reusing water for both indoor and outdoor water demands.

Q9.10 Which of the following is not true concerning locally adapted plants? (Choose one)

A. Provides habitat for native wildlife.

B. Requires the same amount of water as native plants.

C. Require more water.

D. Require less water.

ONLINE RESOURCES

Interested in more green building facts? Visit www.usgbc.org/articles/green-building-facts for more information on the top 10 states in the United States for LEED and other market impact statistics.

NOTES

1. USGBC, *Green Building and LEED Core Concepts Guide*, 3rd ed. (2014), 62.

2. UN Water's website, www.unwater.org/downloads/Water_facts_and_trends.pdf, p. 8.

3. California Energy Commission's website, http://energy.ca.gov/2005publications/CEC-700-2005-011/CEC-700-2005-011-SF.PDF, p. 7.

4. USGBC (2008). *LEED for Existing Buildings: Operations + Maintenance Reference Guide*, Glossary, p. 493.

5. USGBC, *Green Building and LEED Core Concepts Guide*, 3rd ed., p. 65.

6. Ibid.

CHAPTER **10**

ENERGY AND ATMOSPHERE

This chapter focuses on the strategies and technologies to address energy use and consumption as described in the Energy and Atmosphere (EA) category of the Leadership in Energy and Environmental Design (LEED®) rating systems. By now, we all understand the environmental impacts of using fossil fuels to generate electricity.

According to the International Energy Agency, oil, coal, and natural gas are the primary energy sources for the world.[1] Neither of these resources is renewable, quantities are limited, and they have detrimental environmental impacts. Each step of the electricity production process harms the environment and ecosystem in one way or another. For example, the burning of coal releases harmful pollutants and greenhouse gases that contribute to global warming and climate change, reducing air quality on a global scale. Given the fact the built environment consumes a large portion of the energy used on a daily basis, it is imperative we look to alternative energy sources. Remember from Chapter 2, buildings account for 39 percent of primary energy use, 72 percent of electricity consumption, and 38 percent of carbon dioxide (CO_2) emissions.[2] Therefore, the LEED rating systems put the most emphasis on the EA category by offering the largest opportunity to earn points, as an attempt to reduce the electrical consumption and corresponding CO_2 emissions of certified buildings.

Remember from Chapter 4, the EA category includes four prerequisites to set the minimum performance requirements to be achieved, thereby requiring any projects seeking certification to reduce demand at a minimum level. Beginning with an understanding of the requirements of these three prerequisites helps to comprehend the concepts of the EA category. These prerequisites are as follows:

- Fundamental Commissioning of Building Energy Systems
- Minimum Energy Performance
- Building-Level Energy Monitoring
- Fundamental Refrigerant Management

COMMISSIONING

The first prerequisite of the EA category requires a new building to be commissioned by a commissioning agent (CxA). "Commissioning is the process of verifying and documenting that a building and all its systems and assemblies are planned, designed, installed, tested, operated, and maintained to meet the owner's project requirements" (OPR).[3] The OPR, developed early in the design process

 It's time to pick a different color for flashcards created for EA category topics.

 Study: Burning coal releases the following harmful pollutants into the atmosphere: carbon dioxide, sulfur dioxide, nitrogen oxide, and mercury.

 V3V4: Remember, LEED 2009 did not include the Building-Level Energy Metering prerequisite.

 Career: Commissioning agents typically have a mechanical engineering background.

 Study: Remember, it is best to assess and implement green building strategies as early as possible in the design process, including commissioning.

Create a flashcard to remember HVAC&R stands for heating, ventilation, air conditioning, and refrigeration.

Study: The terms *commissioning agent* and *commissioning authority* can be used interchangeably.

Study: Commissioning of new buildings has an average payback of 4.8 years and typically costs about $1 per square foot, according to a study conducted by Lawrence Berkley National Laboratory.[4]

Study: Retro-commissioning applies to the commissioning of existing buildings with an average simple payback of 0.7 years with a median cost of $0.27 per square foot, according to a study conducted by Lawrence Berkley National Laboratory.[5]

Create a flashcard to remember the benefits of a CxA:
1. Minimize or eliminate design flaws.
2. Avoid construction defects.
3. Avoid equipment malfunctions.
4. Ensure preventative maintenance is implemented during operations.

Create a flashcard to remember ASHRAE 90.1-2010, as the baseline standard for energy performance.

Study: The International Green Construction Code (IGCC) includes ASHRAE 189.1 as an alternative compliance path. You may want to make a note on your cheat sheet to keep track of the reference standards.

Study: A study by New Buildings Institute LEED Certified buildings use 24% less energy.[6]

Study: Building envelope refers to the system of walls, roofs, windows, and floor that form the exterior of a building.

by the owner and the CxA, includes the environmental goals of the project and is issued to the design team to develop a basis of design (BOD) for the major building systems, such as lighting; domestic hot water; heating, ventilation, air conditioning, and refrigeration (HVAC&R); and any renewable energy generated on-site.

The commissioning process continues prior to the development of construction documents, as the CxA is required to review the design drawings and specifications to avoid design flaws and ensure that the environmental goals are included, such as water and energy use reductions. The CxA works diligently during construction to ensure that the building system equipment is installed, calibrated, and performs appropriately and efficiently to avoid construction defects and equipment malfunctions. Before the building is occupied, the CxA helps to educate the facility management teams on the operation and maintenance strategies specific to the building. Within one year after occupancy, the CxA returns to the site to ensure that the building systems are working accordingly and address any needed adjustments.

MINIMUM ENERGY PERFORMANCE

Besides the Fundamental Commissioning prerequisite, the LEED rating systems also require buildings to perform to a minimum energy standard. Similar to the reference standard EPAct 1992 in the Water Efficiency (WE) category, which is used to create a baseline for comparison to the design case, a baseline is needed within the EA category to evaluate energy use reduction percentages of a project. Therefore, LEED references American Society of Heating, Refrigerating, and Air-Conditioning Engineers (ASHRAE) Standard 90.1-2010 to determine the minimum energy performance requirement for buildings seeking LEED certification.

The integrative design process is critical within all the LEED categories, but is essential within the EA category, especially when evaluating energy use (Figure 10.1). Energy performance, demands, and requirements are affected by multiple components, including:

- Site conditions, such as heat island reduction, can reduce energy demand as equipment will not need to compensate for heat gain from surrounding and adjacent areas.

- Building orientation can affect the amount of energy needed for artificial heating, cooling, and lighting needs by taking advantage of passive design strategies, such as daylighting and natural ventilation.

- How much water needs to be heated or cooled? If building system equipment and fixtures require less water, less energy is therefore required. If all of the building equipment is sized appropriately and works efficiently, then less energy is demanded (Figures 10.2 and 10.3).

- Roof design can impact how much energy is required for heating and cooling by implementing a green roof or a roof with high solar reflective index (SRI) value.

- Building envelope thermal performance, including window selections, can reduce mechanical system sizing and energy demands by ensuring a thermal break between the interior and exterior environments.

Figure 10.1 The Pennsylvania Department of Conservation and Natural Resources' Penn Nursery project incorporates radiant heat flooring to optimize its energy consumption. *Photo courtesy of Moshier Studio*

- Light fixture types and the lamps/bulbs they require can reduce energy use by providing more light per square foot, but require fewer kilowatts per hour and therefore optimize lighting power density.

- Generating onsite renewable energy can reduce the amount of energy needed from the municipally supplied grid (Figure 10.4).

- Commissioning a building ensures that the equipment and systems are performing as they were intended, to maintain consistent and minimal energy demands (Figure 10.5).

- Educating occupants and operations and maintenance teams on how a building is intended to perform, what the environmental goals are, and providing them with the tools to monitor the performance will help to keep energy use to a minimum.

The preceding bullet points describe the importance and need for project team members to work in a cohesive and integrative fashion to optimize the performance of a building and its site, ultimately reducing the amount of energy required for operations. Project teams are encouraged to take advantage of energy modeling and simulation software to study and evaluate how their specific project will function. Teams that utilize building information modeling (BIM) software have an advantage to determine synergistic opportunities for their projects to add efficiencies. Both of these design phase studies also contribute to whole-building life-cycle cost assessments to determine trade-offs between up-front costs and long-term savings.

Process Energy versus Regulated Energy

When a project team prepares and creates an energy simulation model (Figure 10.6), they should differentiate between **regulated** and **process**

 Study: Any time you see ASHRAE 90.1, think ENERGY!

 Career: Interested in minimizing energy demand through proper building system design? You may be suited for a career in mechanical or electrical engineering. Lighting designers also impact energy demand with fixture and lamp selections.

 Study: Minimize solar gain in the summer and maximize it in the winter with the help of passive design strategies! Passive designs capitalize on the four natural thermal processes: radiation, conduction, absorption, and convection.

 Study: Remember, SRI is the acronym for solar reflective index and is synonymous with albedo. Do you remember the scale used for SRI? Is it better to have a higher or lower score?

 Study: The key to energy modeling and simulation is whole-building evaluation, not individual component assessments. How do all of the systems work together?

Figure 10.2 High-efficiency boilers can help to achieve energy performance and savings goals. *Photo courtesy of SmithGroup, Inc.*

 Create a flashcard to remember the uses of regulated energy.

energy. LEED minimum energy performance criteria address only regulated energy, as process energy is not included or calculated. Regulated energy uses include the following:

- Lighting—interior and exterior applications (parking garages, facades, site lighting)
- HVAC—space heating, cooling, fans, pumps, toilet exhaust, ventilation for parking garages
- Service water for domestic and space heating purposes

Figure 10.3 Installing high-efficiency chillers can help to achieve energy performance and savings goals. *Photo courtesy of SmithGroup, Inc.*

Process energy uses include computers, office equipment, kitchen refrigeration and cooking, washing and drying machines, and elevators and escalators. Miscellaneous items, such as waterfall pumps and lighting that is exempt from lighting power allowance calculations such as lighting integrated into equipment, are also categorized as process energy uses. For the purposes of the LEED Green

 Create a flashcard to remember the uses of process energy.

Figure 10.4 This LEED Gold certified BMW dealership in Beijing installed wind turbines onsite to help generate electricity needed for operations, reducing the demand from the grid. *Photo courtesy of Urban Green Energy*

Figure 10.5 Load bank testing is part of the commissioning process. *Photo courtesy of Jerry Adessa*

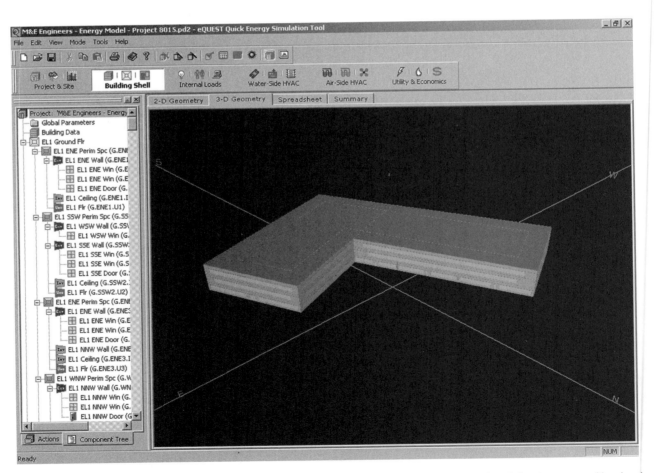

Figure 10.6 Modeling a proposed building can help project teams identify synergies to increase a building's performance and to calculate the energy saved based on those strategies. *Photo courtesy of M&E Engineers, Inc.*

Associate exam, it is important to remember the different process energy uses to understand what is included in the calculations for minimum and optimized energy performance requirements.

REFRIGERANTS

Besides commissioning and minimum energy performance prerequisites, the LEED rating systems also require buildings to manage refrigerants appropriately. Refrigerants enable the transfer of thermal energy and are therefore a critical component of air-conditioning and refrigeration equipment. Although they are cost effective, refrigerants have environmental trade-offs, as they contribute to ozone depletion and global warming. Therefore, project teams need to be mindful of the **ozone-depleting potential (ODP)** and **global warming potential (GWP)** of each refrigerant to determine the impact of the trade-offs, as an environmentally perfect refrigerant does not yet exist.

To comply with the Fundamental Refrigerant Management prerequisite, teams should refer to the Montreal Protocol when determining which refrigerants to use for their projects. The Montreal Protocol bans **chlorofluorocarbons** (CFCs) and requires **hydrochlorofluorocarbons** (HCFCs) to be phased out as they have the biggest impact on ozone depletion. CFC-based refrigerants are highest in ODP, more than HCFCs. Hydrofluorocarbon (HFC)-based refrigerants have no ODP but have GWP. Although other options exist that are not as harmful to the ozone, they have bigger and greater contributions to the production of greenhouse gases.

These alternative options are also not as efficient as CFCs and HCFCs, and in turn, cause cooling systems to be less efficient by using more energy per unit of cooling output.

 TIP Study: Remember, chlorofluorocarbons (CFCs) are not allowed, and hydrochlorofluorocarbons (HCFCs) are to be phased out according to the Montreal Protocol.

 Create a flashcard to remember that refrigerants should be evaluated based on ODP and GWP impacts and what these acronyms stand for.

 The ozone molecules found in the upper stratospheric atmosphere absorb harmful ultraviolet radiation and therefore help to protect the environment and human health. Refrigerants that deplete the ozone layer therefore contribute to climate change.

EXISTING BUILDINGS

As previously described, new construction and major renovation projects use ASHRAE 90.1-2010 as the baseline standard for energy performance. Existing buildings seeking LEED certification utilize a different resource, the Environmental Protection Agency's (EPA's) ENERGY STAR Portfolio Manager, as a benchmarking system for energy use (Figure 10.7). Portfolio Manager is a free online, web-based tool in which users enter electricity and natural gas consumption data to be evaluated against the performance of buildings with similar characteristics.

For existing buildings where converting or replacing systems containing CFCs is not feasible, buildings must commit to phasing out the CFC-based refrigerants within five years from the end of the project's performance period.

 TIP Study: An ENERGY STAR rating from Portfolio Manager of 50, indicates the average energy performance of a building. A study by New Buildings Institute discovered LEED-certified projects have an overall average score of 68.[7]

 Create a flashcard to remember that CFC refrigerants must be phased out for existing building projects.

STRATEGIES TO SATISFY EA PREREQUISITES AND CREDITS

Project teams are encouraged to focus on the following four components in order to address the goals and intentions of the EA category to help reduce greenhouse gas emissions:

1. Energy Demand
2. Energy Efficiency

 TIP Study: Remember, prerequisites are absolutely required, do not contribute to earning points, and ensure that certified buildings meet minimum performance criteria.

Figure 10.7 Facility managers and owners are encouraged to use the Environmental Protection Agency's (EPA's) ENERGY STAR Portfolio Manager tool to benchmark a building's performance. The Wyndham Worldwide Headquarters in Parsippany, New Jersey, had a score of 92 at the time they earned Silver certification under the LEED for Existing Buildings: Operations & Maintenance rating system.

 Create a flashcard to remember the four components of the EA category. Be sure to refer to Appendix D for a summary of all of the strategies to remember for the exam.

 Study: Remember from the Study Tip listed in Chapter 4, LEED for Homes™ is the only rating system that addresses sizing a project appropriately using the Home Size Adjustment and offers an adjustment in the certification level thresholds for projects with fewer square feet.

 Create a flashcard to remember California's Title 24 as another energy standard.

 Study: Remember, adjacent buildings can be used as shade to help reduce cooling needs.

 Remember, green roofs help to insulate a building, therefore help to reduce energy demands. Can you name another benefit of a green roof?

 Create a flashcard to remember the four strategies to address energy demand.

3. Renewable Energy

4. Ongoing Energy Performance

Energy Demand

The following four strategies, as listed in the *Green Building and LEED Core Concepts Guide*, address the energy demand of green buildings to help to save energy and therefore help to reduce greenhouse gas emissions and save money[8]:

1. *Establish design and energy goals.* Use standards such as ASHRAE 90.1 and California's Title 24, building codes such as the International Green Construction Code (IGCC), as well as benchmarks such as EPA's ENERGY STAR Portfolio Manager.

2. *Size the building appropriately.* Excessive and unnecessary vertical or horizontal square footage is wasteful and inefficient. Buildings should be designed to meet and not exceed the needs of the owner and occupants.

3. *Use free energy.* Natural resources should be explored early in the design process to meet the heating, cooling, ventilation, and lighting needs of a project (Figures 10.8, 10.9, and 10.10).

4. *Insulate* (Figure 10.11). High-performance building envelopes help to reduce the size of HVAC systems, thus help to use less energy.

Demand Response

"Demand response (DR) strategies encourage electricity customers to reduce their usage during peak demand times, helping utilities optimize their supply-side energy generation and delivery systems."[9] Utility companies are offering different programs with varying incentives such as tiered electricity pricing. Another

Figure 10.8 The Wetland Discovery Point building at Utah State University in Kaysville utilized a ground-source heat pump to exchange heating and cooling loads between the building and the earth to reduce their energy consumption by 30 percent. *Photo courtesy of Gary Neuenswander, Utah Agricultural Experiment Station*

option rewards commercial accounts that change their usage patterns when they receive an alert from the utility company announcing a DR event.

"By reducing overall demand for electricity, DR helps utilities avoid building additional power generation facilities, transmission lines, and distribution stations, thereby avoiding some of the environmental effects of energy infrastructure and consumption."[10]

 V3V4: Once a pilot credit offered as part of LEED 2009, Demand Response is now a credit opportunity in LEED V4.

 Study: A DR event is also sometimes referred to as a curtailment event.

Figure 10.9 Concord Hospital in Concord, New Hampshire, designed by Shepley Bulfinch, incorporates a green roof to optimize the energy performance of the building and skylights to allow daylighting to the interior environment, to further reduce the energy demand by reducing the need for artificial lighting. *Photo courtesy of Kat Nania, Shepley Bulfinch*

 Remember the intentions of the SS and WE credits and prerequisites along with the requirements of the EA credits and prerequisites. Reducing water demands affects the SS, WE, and EA categories.

 Create a flashcard to remember the units of measurement for energy: electricity is measured in kilowatts per hour, natural gas in therms, and liquid fuel in gallons.

Energy Efficiency

Addressing the energy demands listed earlier is the first step of reducing required energy for building operations. Using energy efficiently builds off of the energy demand reduction strategies proposed and implemented. The goal to energy efficiency is to optimize **energy use intensity,** or to get the most out of a unit of energy. Energy use intensity is measured in **British thermal units per square foot per year (kBtus/sf/yr)** or **kilowatt hours per square foot per year (kWh/sf/yr).** Project teams assess the *energy use per square foot* when working with the majority of LEED rating systems and *use per capita* when working on a LEED for Neighborhood Development™ project.

Figure 10.10 The Wetland Discovery Point building at Utah State University utilizes a trombe wall to capture heat from the sun, as well as radiant heat flooring to increase the energy efficiencies of the project. *Photo courtesy of Gary Neuenswander, Utah Agricultural Experiment Station*

Figure 10.11 Spray foam insulation helps to seal any leaks of conditioned air to the exterior environment, therefore optimizing energy use. *Photo courtesy of Rhino Linings*

Considering that the majority of a building's energy use is dedicated to space heating and lighting, addressing the efficiency for both is encouraged by the LEED rating systems. Evaluating the performance of the envelope and the efficiency of the building systems can reduce space-heating needs. When improving the efficiencies of lighting, project teams should tackle lighting strategies from a few different angles. First, the fixture type and count should be determined and calculated with the coordinating lamp or bulb type, with consideration for the use of each space. Remember, the goal is to meet the needs of the occupants, yet require minimal energy usage. For example, compact fluorescent lamps (CFLs) last longer and use less energy than conventional incandescent lamps, but deliver appropriate light levels. Using more energy, the incandescent fixtures emit more heat, in turn causing the mechanical system to work harder to cool a space. Finally, color schemes of interior spaces should also be considered when designing lighting plans. Lightly colored walls, workstations, and other interior elements tend to reflect more light than darker surfaces, allowing interior design decisions to stretch the efficiencies of light even further to possibly reduce the amount of required fixtures or lamps.

The *Green Building and LEED Core Concepts Guide* describes the following six strategies to use energy more efficiently[11]:

1. *Address the envelope.* Remember to incorporate high-performance glazing to avoid unwanted heat gain or loss, properly insulate the exterior walls and roof (Figure 10.12), and weatherize the building.

2. *Install high-performance mechanical systems and appliances* (Figures 10.13, 10.14, and 10.15). Determine the trade-offs of the up-front costs versus the operating costs by conducting a life-cycle cost analysis.

3. *Use high-efficient infrastructure* (Figure 10.16) *and traffic signals.* Think about the consistent and long-term use of these fixtures to understand the value of longer life and cost savings from less energy required for operation.

 Passive design strategies include maintaining a warm building in the winter, a cool building in the summer, and taking advantage of natural daylighting opportunities.

TIP **Study**: The environmental impacts of HVAC systems should be evaluated based on energy performance and the expected life of the equipment.

Figure 10.12 Selecting insulated concrete forms (ICFs) as a building envelope material increases the energy performance of a building. *Photo courtesy of Moshier Studio*

Figure 10.13 Incorporating cooling towers can help to remove process waste heat by the means of water evaporation. *Photo courtesy of SmithGroup, Inc.*

4. *Capture efficiencies of scale* (Figure 10.17). Think about large universities or corporate campuses that use district systems to thermally condition multiple buildings on a single loop.

5. *Use energy simulation.* Model the *whole building* with regulated energy uses to optimize synergies (Figure 10.18).

6. *Monitor and verify performance.* Commissioning, implementing building automation systems, and retro-commissioning all help to ensure energy efficiency.

 Create a flashcard to remember the six strategies to use energy more efficiently.

Figure 10.14 Utilizing a heat exchange system can help to reduce energy demands and save an owner operating costs. *Photo courtesy of SmithGroup, Inc.*

Figure 10.15 Project teams are encouraged to specify ENERGY STAR appliances to reduce plug load demands. *Image courtesy of U.S. EPA*

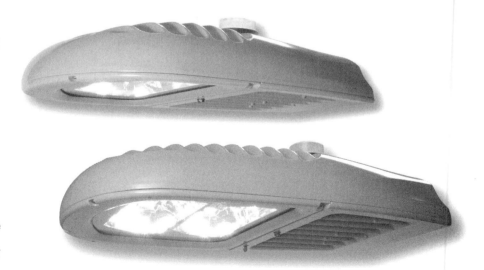

Figure 10.16 Installing light-emitting diode (LED) streetlight fixtures can help to decrease the energy demand for neighborhoods. *Photo courtesy of General Electric Company*

Figure 10.17 The large hydroelectric generators at the Hoover Dam help to capture efficiencies of scale. *Photo courtesy of the Fischetti family*

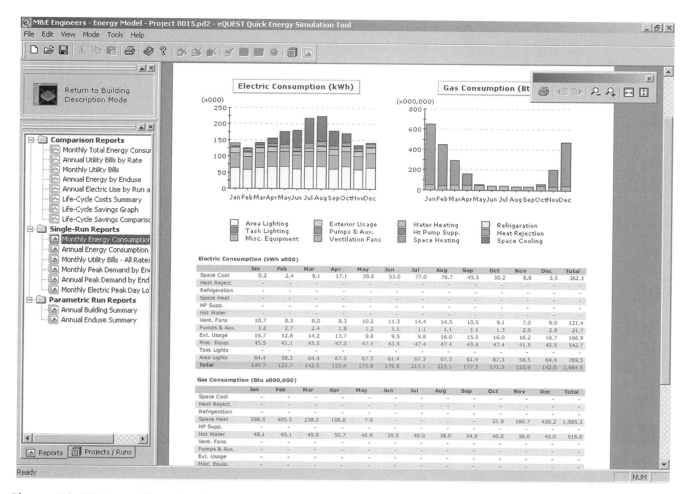

Figure 10.18 Energy modeling tools, such as eQUEST, assist project teams to determine energy consumptions. *Image courtesy of M&E Engineers, Inc.*

Create a flashcard to remember the six types of qualifying renewable energy sources.

Create a flashcard to remember the two strategies to incorporate renewable energy.

Create a flashcard to remember the meaning of the acronym REC.

Create another flashcard to remember the two strategies to implement renewable energy into a green building project.

Renewable Energy

Keeping with the same goals previously discussed, implementing renewable energy technologies into a green building project can reduce the need to produce and consume coal, nuclear power, oil, and natural gases for energy, therefore reducing pollutants and emissions, as well as increasing air quality. For the purposes of LEED, eligible renewable energy sources include solar, wind, wave, biomass, geothermal power (Figure 10.19), and low-impact hydropower. The *Green Building and LEED Core Concepts Guide* describes the following two strategies to incorporate renewable energy and reduce the use of fossil fuels:[12]

1. *Generate on-site renewable energy.* Clean electricity must be generated onsite by photovoltaic panels (Figure 10.20), wind turbines, geothermal, biomass, or low-impact hydropower. Think solar hot water heaters!

2. *Purchase green power or renewable energy credits (RECs).* Generated offsite (Figure 10.21) and not associated with supplying power to a specific project site seeking LEED certification. Think tradable commodities!

Ongoing Energy Performance

The benefits of commissioning new buildings and retro-commissioning existing buildings include monitoring building system demands during operations. Tracking the performance of a green building ensures that the building operates as it was designed and intended. The *Green Building and LEED Core Concepts Guide* describes the following four strategies to ensure optimal performance[13]:

1. *Adhere to the OPR.* Remember, this is the first part of the commissioning process that takes place as early as possible in the design process. This helps to communicate the environmental goals of the project to the design team, to be incorporated into the drawings and specifications.

2. *Provide staff training.* The building occupants should be aware of how to use less energy, such as turning off lights and computers after hours. Operations and maintenance staff should also be aware how to operate their facility and the way it was designed to function (Figure 10.22).

Figure 10.19 Sherman Hospital in Elgin, Illinois, utilizes geothermal energy to minimize energy demands from the grid. *Photo courtesy of Kat Nania, Shepley Bulfinch*

Figure 10.20 Stoller Vineyards in Dayton, Oregon, generates electricity onsite by the means of photovoltaic panels mounted on the roof. *Photo courtesy of Mike Haverkate, Stoller Vineyards*

Figure 10.21 Cedar Creek Wind Farm in Colorado helps to produce clean, renewable energy. *Photo courtesy of Brian Stanback*

Project teams should follow four sequential steps to reduce energy use within their projects:
1. Reduce demand.
2. Employ means to use energy efficiently, such as high-performance equipment.
3. Assess renewable energy opportunities on and off site.
4. Monitor use to ensure that the building is operating and maintained accordingly.

Create a flashcard to remember the four ways to ensure optimal performance of a LEED-certified project.

3. *Conduct preventative maintenance.* It typically costs less to be proactive than reactive. Scheduled maintenance keeps the building and its systems operating efficiently.

4. *Create incentives for occupants and tenants.* Provide feedback to occupants on energy usage to achieve and exceed the project's goals.

Figure 10.22 Inspecting building systems and educating the operations and maintenance staff on how the systems are intended to operate helps to ensure a building performs the way it was designed.
Photo courtesy of Rainwater HOG, LLC

QUIZ TIME!

These questions are formatted just as they would be on the exam. Notice the question indicates how many answers to select. The proper number of correct answers is required on the exam, as partial credit is not awarded.

In an effort to present information to you in multiple ways and help you learn, you may find questions asking about information that is new to you, that you did not read about throughout the book.

Q10.1 Which of the following are not subject to LEED minimum energy requirements? (Choose three)

    A. Office equipment

    B. Elevators

    C. Chillers

    D. Process energy

    E. Regulated energy

Q10.2 When addressing refrigerants for a project and to comply with the Fundamental Refrigerant Management prerequisite, which of the following should be considered? (Choose three)

    A. Fan motors and variable-frequency drives for ventilation air handlers

    B. Base building air-conditioning systems

    C. Boilers for heating systems

D. Reuse of existing HVAC&R systems

E. Elimination of substances with high ozone-depleting potential from use in air-conditioning and refrigeration systems

Q10.3 ASHRAE Standard 90.1-2010 is primarily concerned with which of the following? (Choose one)

A. Lighting design

B. Ventilation effectiveness

C. Energy consumption

D. Ozone depletion

Q10.4 Which of the following are categorized as regulated energy? (Choose three)

A. Computers

B. Space heating

C. Refrigeration

D. Service hot water

E. Lighting

Q10.5 Which of the following can balance the contribution of renewable energy sources? (Choose one)

A. CFCs

B. RECs

C. Demand response

D. Commissioning

Q10.6 Which of the following are appropriate statements with regard to commissioning in the context of green building? (Choose two)

A. The CxA should be a primary member of the design team who is directly responsible for the project design or construction management.

B. The CxA should be separate and independent from those individuals who are directly responsible for project design or construction management (preferably from a separate firm).

C. The CxA is indirectly responsible for verifying the performance of building systems and equipment prior to installation, calibration, and operations.

D. The CxA is responsible for verifying the performance of building systems and equipment after installation.

Q10.7 Which energy demand reduction strategy is missing from the list? (Choose one from the following list)

Establish energy design and energy goals.

Use free energy.

Insulate.

    A. Size the building appropriately.

    B. Use thermal storage.

    C. Use energy simulation.

    D. Purchase off-site renewable energy.

Q10.8 Which of the following could contribute to earning the On-site Renewable Energy credit? (Choose three)

    A. Passive solar design concept that captures winter heat from the sun

    B. Photovoltaic panels that provide electricity to the building

    C. A wind farm located within 500 miles of the project and operated by the local utility company

    D. A ground-source heat pump that takes heat from the ground

    E. Solar hot water system

    F. An onsite electric generator powered by geothermal energy

    G. A solar farm adjacent to the project site providing clean power to the grid

Q10.9 What is the primary intent of the Green Power credit? (Choose one)

    A. To comply with the Montreal Protocol

    B. To encourage more solar farms in the United States and avoid carbon trading

    C. To encourage the development and use of renewable clean energy that is connected to the utility grid

    D. To minimize production of greenhouse gases by generating onsite renewable energy

Q10.10 Which of the following is not a measurement for energy use in the United States? (Choose one)

    A. Kilowatt-hours for electricity

    B. Liters for liquid fuel

    C. Therms for natural gas

    D. Gallons for liquid fuel

Q10.11 The engineer working on a new corporate building project seeking LEED for Core & Shell™ certification has proposed a cogeneration system that provides electricity cooling, heating, hot water, and dehumidification of outside air. The waste heat from the gas turbine–powered electric generator exhaust is designed and intended to drive an absorption chiller for cooling the building, therefore not using any CFCs or HCFCs. To which of the following LEED credits might these strategies contribute? (Choose two)

A. Commissioning

B. On-Site Renewable Energy

C. Enhanced Refrigerant Management

D. Green Power

E. Optimize Energy Performance

Q10.12 What is the overall average ENERGY STAR Portfolio Manager score of LEED-certified buildings according to the New Buildings Institute? (Choose one)

A. 50

B. 68

C. 75

D. 100

Q10.13 When should the OPR be prepared? (Choose one)

A. Schematic design

B. Construction documents

C. Design development

D. Beginning of construction

E. After substantial completion

Q10.14 What are the three largest energy sources according to the International Energy Audit? (Choose three)

A. Coal

B. Solar

C. Oil

D. Natural gas

E. Photovoltaic

F. Hydrofluorocarbon

Q10.15 Which of the following are true? (Choose two)

A. CFCs and HCFCs help to protect the ozone layer.

B. There is a strong correlation between square footage and energy consumption.

C. A curtailment event is also known as a DR event.

D. The commissioning process starts after construction documents are issued for permit review.

E. Project teams looking to purchase RECs should look to the Montreal Protocol.

ONLINE RESOURCES

Visit www.energystar.gov/portfoliomanager for more information about the Portfolio Manager benchmarking tool.

NOTES

1. International Energy Agency website, www.iea.org/publications/ freepublications/publication/kwes.pdf, p. 6.

2. USGBC, *Green Building and LEED Core Concepts Guide*, 3rd ed. (2014), 3.

3. Ibid., p. 11.

4. Ibid. p. 69.

5. Ibid.

6. Ibid. p. 64.

7. New Buildings Institute's website, http://newbuildings.org/sites/default/files/ Energy_Performance_of_LEED-NC_Buildings-Final_3-4-08b.pdf, p. 7.

8. USGBC, *Green Building and LEED Core Concepts Guide*, 3rd ed.

9. Ibid., p. 66.

10. Ibid.

11. Ibid., p. 68.

12. Ibid., p. 69.

13. Ibid., p. 70.

CHAPTER 11

MATERIALS AND RESOURCES

AS THE PREVIOUS CHAPTERS POINTED OUT, THE built environment can be quite tolling on the natural environment. This book has so far presented means of minimizing impacts from the project site and reducing water and energy demands, while this chapter details strategies to minimize the environmental impacts of building materials as depicted in the Materials & Resources (MR) category in the Leadership in Energy and Environmental Design (LEED®) green building certification program (Figure 11.1). This chapter details how to assess and select materials and what to do with them after their useful life, two critical elements for the environment and the building industry, as buildings are a large consumer of natural resources. The LEED V4 changes encourage project teams to focus on minimizing the embodied energy and other impacts associated with the extraction, production, transportation, consumption, maintenance, and disposal of building materials through life-cycle assessment fostering resource efficiency.

According to the *LEED Reference Guide for Building Design and Construction* unmanaged extraction practices of our natural resources "can cause not

Figure 11.1 Wyndham Worldwide earned Silver certification by specifying green materials, such as those with recycled content and that are locally extracted, processed, and manufactured, to reduce the detrimental impacts of the construction of their new campus in Parsippany, New Jersey. *Photo courtesy of Office Furniture Partnership*

only deforestation but also degradation of water sources, habitat loss, threats to rare and endangered species, releases of toxic chemicals, and the infringement of indigenous peoples' rights."[1] More specifically, one report conducted in 2011 suggests, "construction and demolition waste constitutes about 40 percent of the total solid waste in the United States and about 25% of the total waste stream in the European Union."[2] As a result, green building project team members are advised to evaluate the environmental impact of their materials and product specifications.

Project teams may then find themselves asking, "Where does steel come from? What kinds of materials are used to make green building products? How far did the raw material for the windows have to travel to the manufacturing plant? How far is the manufacturing plant from the project site? What happens to the leftover gypsum wallboard scraps? Is it better to use local wood products or bio-based products manufactured and procured from all over the country? How long will this material perform for and what happens to it after its useful life? How can we eliminate waste? What are the environmental preferable attributes of carpet?"

To help answer these types of questions, this chapter addresses two components for consideration as related to material and resource selection and disposal[3]:

1. Conservation of materials

2. Environmentally, socially, and locally preferable materials

3. Waste management and reduction

It's time to pick a different color for flashcards created for MR topics.

Create a flashcard to remember the three components to address within the MR category.

CONSERVATION OF MATERIALS

Implementing sustainable building materials impacts a project's triple bottom line, just as with site selection and energy and water demands. The idea is to eliminate the need for new materials, with a focus on material reuse, the highest form of material conservation. Beside conservation natural resources, material reuse can "also retains the cultural value and the contextual relevancy."[4]

Strategies

The following five strategies, as listed in the *Green Building and LEED Core Concepts Guide,* are intended to conserve materials throughout a project's life cycle:[5]

■ *Reuse existing buildings and salvaged materials* (Figure 11.2)—consider adaptive reuse strategies to find significantly different uses for existing structures to not only avoids extracting materials for a new building, disposing waste in landfills, and converting greenfield sites into development.

■ *Plan for smaller, more compact communities*—to prevent urban sprawl and reduce the new for new infrastructure, such as roads and utilities.

■ *Design smaller, more flexible homes and buildings*—implement more dual-purpose spaces and eliminate unused spaces.

■ *Use efficient framing techniques*—Space studs at 24 inches (instead of 16 inches) (Figure 11.3) and use structural insulated panels (SIPs) (Figure 11.4) strategies that increases performance while using less material.

Create a flashcard to remember the five strategies to conserve materials throughout a project's life cycle.

■ *Promote source reduction in operations*—encourage employees to reuse office supplies and implement a minimal print and double sided print policy.

Figure 11.2 Finding new uses for existing buildings helps to extend the life of the existing building stock and avoids demolition and waste. *Photo Courtesy of SmithGroup, Inc*

ENVIRONMENTALLY PREFERABLE MATERIALS

The LEED green building certification program not only helps to define the parameters of green building products, but also helps to identify environmentally responsible procurement strategies during both construction and operations, as the first strategy to reduce the life cycle impacts of the products used at a project site. As previously mentioned, architects need to specify materials

 Create a flashcard to remember rapidly renewable fiber or animal materials (excluding leather and other animal hides) must be grown or raised in 10 years or less and meet the Sustainable Agriculture Standard.

 Create a flashcard to remember the difference between preconsumer and postconsumer recycled contents. Products made with material left over from the manufacturing process are considered to have preconsumer waste, whereas materials made with manufactured products at the end of their useful life are considered to have postconsumer waste.

TIP **Study:** ISO 14021-1999—Environmental Label and Declarations is the referenced standard that declares a material having postconsumer/preconsumer recycled content.

 Create a flashcard to remember the regional materials must be extracted, processed, *and* manufactured within 100 miles of the project site to be considered local.

Figure 11.3 Using efficient framing strategies helps to reduce waste and save money. *Photo courtesy of Anastasia Harrison, AIA, LEED AP BD+C*

Figure 11.4 The second floor and roof of the BASF donated Near-Zero Energy Home in Paterson, New Jersey, is constructed using SIPs, covered with an additional one-inch-thick layer of EPS. The SIPs form a solid thermal envelope around the structure using less dimensional lumber for wood studs, sills, and headers than typical stick frame construction, substantially reducing air infiltration compared with conventional construction techniques. The solid core of insulation also eliminates the convection looping that can occur in typical stick frame construction as a result of gaps and spaces within batt insulation placed between studs. The resulting energy efficiency allows heating and cooling equipment to be downsized, reducing initial capital costs and operating costs. *Photo courtesy of BASF Corporation*

 Create a flashcard to remember that sustainably grown and harvested FSC wood requires chain-of-custody documentation, tracking a product from harvest/extraction to the installation location, including processing, manufacturing, and distribution.

appropriately to provide contractors the guidelines for the types of building materials they should purchase and install during construction. During operations, building owners and facility managers should address the products they are purchasing by also implementing sustainable procurement policies. As the LEED for Existing Buildings: Operations & Maintenance™ (LEED for Existing Buildings: O&M) rating system dictates, these policies can address the goals and thresholds for purchasing ongoing consumables, such as lamp types, food, cleaning products, and paper products; and durable goods, such as electronics and furniture.

The following eight characteristics, as listed in the *Green Building and LEED Core Concepts Guide,* are intended to guide material and product selection to conserve materials throughout a project's life cycle[6]:

- Support local economy (Figure 11.5)
- Sustainably grown and harvested (Figure 11.6)
- Have intended end-of-life scenarios that avoid landfill (Figure 11.7)
- Contain recycled content from industrial or consumer resources (Figure 11.8)
- Made of bio-based material
- Free of toxins
- Long lasting, durable and reusable
- Made in factories that support human health and workers' rights

With the awareness, interest, and demand of green products, unfortunately misleading and incorrect information has presented itself, confusing consumers and specifiers. Greenwashing can imply a product is more sustainable than it actually is but also is the result of the inability to compare products with different environmental attributes.

 Create a flashcard to remember the eight environmentally preferable attributes of materials and products.

 Create a flashcard to remember what greenwashing is.

Figure 11.5 Purchasing materials that are extracted, processed, and manufactured within 100 miles helps to reduce the transportation impacts associated with building materials. *Photo courtesy of Gary Neuenswander, Utah Agricultural Experiment Station*

When the LEED green building certification program was originally introduced, a demand was created for environmentally preferable products causing a transformation of the market. The LEED V4 changes increasing that demand and creates a platform in which to compare products with different sustainable characteristics: **life-cycle assessment (LCA)**.

With this market transformation, project teams are encouraged to seek more information about building materials and products in order to better understand a material's environmental impact and aid in the selection process. LCA, as introduced in Chapter 2, is a tool available to project teams offering a more thorough snapshot of different building materials and products, thus promoting

TIP **V3V4:** LEED V3 suggested LCAs as a design tool but V4 offers credit opportunities to earn points to projects that utilize transparency tools.

Figure 11.6 Purchasing wood from sustainable and responsible forests helps to ensure resources for future generations. *Photo courtesy of Gary Neuenswander, Utah Agricultural Experiment Station*

Figure 11.7 Sustainable procurement choices, such as cradle-to-cradle (C2C) certified task chairs composed of recycled content, helps to avoid landfills and the need for virgin materials. *Photo courtesy of Steelcase, Inc.*

improvement and innovation from the manufacturing community. An LCA includes the evaluation of **embodied energy,** such as the extraction location of raw materials, the manufacturing process and location, the impact on construction workers and building occupants, the expected term of use during operations, the disposal options available, and the energy contained within the product itself. A product that is no longer useful or cannot be recycled at the end of its life is considered to be a **cradle-to-grave** product, whereas if a product can be

Figure 11.8 Permeable pavers made with recycled content not only help to recharge the groundwater, but also help to reduce the need for virgin materials. *Photo courtesy of AZEK Pavers*

Figure 11.9 Products can be certified within five categories and at five levels of certification by the Cradle to Cradle Product Innovation Institute. The evaluation criterion includes material health, material reutilization, renewable energy and carbon management, water stewardship, and social fairness. *Image courtesy of Cradle to Cradle Products Innovation Institute*

recycled or reused at the end of its useful life, it is considered **cradle-to-cradle** (Figure 11.9). With the evaluation of these components, the results of an LCA will help to determine the material selections to include in the construction purchasing policy to help guide the contractor.

LCAs are just one type of transparency tools to help project teams make informed decisions concerning material selection. Environmental Product Declarations (EPDs) and material ingredient disclosures also provide a comprehensive understanding of materials and products.

Strategies

Although LEED for Existing Buildings: O&M is the only rating system that includes a sustainable purchasing policy *prerequisite*, each of the rating systems offer other opportunities to earn points for projects that implement similar policies. The LEED green building certification program offers the following strategies to promote sustainable purchasing during design and operations to ultimately reduce the impacts of materials and products on the environment[7]:

1. *Identify local sources of environmentally preferable products.*

2. *Develop a sustainable materials policy.* Define goals, thresholds, and procedures for purchasing ongoing consumables and durable goods, such as furniture and equipment. Materials should be evaluated based on their upstream and downstream impacts. Lastly, policies should be monitored for compliance and effectiveness.

3. *Specify green materials and equipment.* Remember the eight environmental attributes presented previously in this chapter (Figure 11.10). Green Seal and Forest Stewardship Council (FSC) are third-party certifications to also look for when selecting materials. Remember ENERGY STAR equipment and appliances from the EA category? It is another third-party certification to look for when purchasing equipment and appliances (Figure 11.11).

4. *Specify green custodial products.* Look for Green Seal, Environmental Choice, or EPA standards when purchasing green cleaning products and materials (Figure 11.12).

 Create a flashcard to remember the four strategies to promote sustainable purchasing during design and operations.

Figure 11.10 Installing CRI Green Label Plus Program carpet tiles avoids the contamination of the indoor air. *Photo courtesy of Beaulieu Commercial*

Calculating Green Building Products for LEED

Although the LEED Green Associate™ exam is meant to test for a basic understanding of green building and operation strategies, there can be questions related specifically to LEED requirements. As related to the MR category, questions could be related to the following:

■ *Required products and materials.* When documenting compliance with MR category prerequisites and credits, project teams are required to include the portions of the projects that are being constructed or renovated. If portions

Figure 11.11 Look for the ENERGY STAR logo when selecting electronic equipment and appliances.

are excluded from the contractual scope-of-work, those portions are excluded from complying with LEED.

■ *Qualifying products and exclusions.* Project teams must include all permanently installed building materials and products when documenting compliance within the MR category, including all of the materials that fall into Constructions

Figure 11.12 Tork Xpressnap napkins have 100 percent recycled content and are Eco-logo certified with Environmental Choice. Choosing these types of products help to reduce environmental damage.

V3V4: LEED V3 did not allow MEP products to be included in MR calculations but LEED V4 offers some flexibility for project teams to opt to include items such as piping, plumbing fixtures, and/or ducts.

Make a flashcard to remember what types of products are required to be included in credit compliance documentation and other products that must be excluded, such as elevators, escalators, and fire suppression systems.

Specifications Institute (CSI) MasterFormat Divisions 3-10, 31, and 32. Project teams have the option whether or not to include furniture but if they do, the furniture must be applied consistently throughout the category's cost-based credits. Project teams also have the choice to include mechanical, electrical, or plumbing (MEP) products in credit calculations. However, they do not need to include all of the products if there are some that do not comply. With this approach teams are able to include the products that help them but exclude the ones that do not contribute toward earning the credit(s). All special equipment must be excluded from credit calculations.

■ *Product definitions.* Within the MR category, compliance is based on either the number of products or product cost. Products are defined whether or not they arrive to the project site ready for installation or if they are a site-assembled product (Figure 11.13). In addition, the products are identified by the functions of its components. For example, drywall is composed of three items: gypsum, backing, and a binder characterized as one product: drywall. Concrete is different although still composed of three products: aggregate, admixtures, and cement. With concrete being a site-assembled product, these three products are considered separate products. Furthermore, similar products from the same manufacturer may serve different functions, such as flat versus egg shell paints (Figure 11.14) or desk chair (Figure 11.15) versus a side chair.

■ *Determining product cost.* Project teams are confronted with two types of costs to calculate within the MR category: individual material cost and project cost. Individual material costs do not include labor or installation equipment but is required to include all taxes and expenses to deliver the product to the site. When calculating project cost, project teams have two options to choose between: actual material costs or default material costs.

Figure 11.13 Concrete is a site-assembled product with each of its components serving different functions.

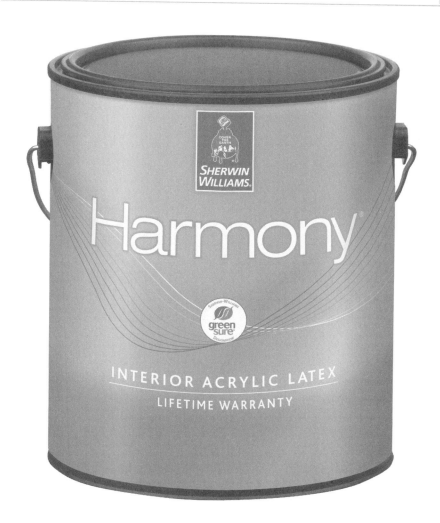

Figure 11.14 Sherwin-Williams offers different types of paints and coatings. Each of the products must be calculated separately within the MR category. *Photo courtesy of Sherwin-Williams.*

Figure 11.15 Steelcase offers different types of chairs. Depending on the function of the chair, each of the products must be calculated separately within the MR category. *Photo courtesy of Steelcase, Inc.*

Figure 11.16 Demountable partitions are considered to be an assembled product and therefore must be calculated accordingly. *Photo courtesy of Office Furniture Partnership*

TIP **V3V4:** LEED V3 included MR Credit 5: Regional Materials to allow teams to pursue points for purchasing material extracted, processed, and manufactured within 500 miles of the project site. LEED V4 addresses regional procurement by the location valuation factor within several credits in the MR category. Be sure to remember V4 differs and sets 100 miles as the threshold.

! Do you remember what form the contractor would fill in to upload to LEED-Online to show compliance with the MR credits?

TIP **Study:** Landfills require sunlight, moisture, and oxygen in order to decompose material; quite a challenging feat for a dark, enclosed environment, don't you think?

Actual material cost includes all taxes and delivery fees but does not include labor. Default material cost allows for project teams to calculate 45 percent of the total construction cost for the project. The total construction cost must include any optional products as discussed previously, such as furniture and MEP items.

■ *Location valuation factor.* To incentivize and reward project teams for purchasing locally produced products and materials, several credits within the MR category value regional products and materials at 200 percent. To qualify, a product must be extracted, manufactured, and purchased within 100 miles of the project site and must meet at least one of the sustainable criteria defined within the particular credit. Sustainable criteria can include recycled content, rapidly renewable, and/or FSC certification. If a product does not meet at least one of the sustainable criterions, it is simply valued at 100 percent.

■ *Determining material contributions of an assembly.* Some building materials are homogenous (i.e., ceiling tiles, rubber base) while others are fastened together, or assembled (i.e., demountable partitions, office chairs) (Figure 11.16). To calculate an assembly, the material cost is multiplied by the percent compliant by weight by the percent of the product that meets the sustainable criteria. For example, a premade window assembly valued at $2,250 with a post consumer recycled content of 12 percent for 80 percent of the assembly (by weight) has a contributing value of $216.

WASTE MANAGEMENT

Construction processes and building operations must be addressed to minimize environmental impacts from disposal and waste. When waste is collected and hauled from a construction site or an existing facility, it is typically brought to a landfill or an incineration facility, both of which contribute to greenhouse gas emissions. Landfills produce and then leak methane, a potent greenhouse gas, and incineration facilities processes produce carbon dioxide. As another environmental detriment, think about the potential for landfills to contaminate groundwater sources. As a result, green building project teams and facility managers are encouraged to address **waste diversion** strategies for new and existing buildings to avoid landfills and incineration facilities.

Since the inception of LEED, certified projects have diverted more than 80 million tons of waste from landfills with this volume expected to grow to 540 million tons by 2030.[8] To keep the momentum going, the LEED green building certification program requires projects to address the solid waste management strategies as defined by the EPA: source reduction, reuse, recycling, and waste to energy.

Construction waste management plans should address whether waste will be separated on-site into individually labeled waste containers or collected in a **commingled** fashion in one container and sorted off-site. As with many of the components addressed within the LEED green building certification program, there are trade-offs to address when deciding between the two options. Commingled collection reduces the amount of space needed onsite, while onsite collection may require additional labor to manage the sorting effort. In either case, land clearing debris and soil should not be included in the calculations, but metals, concrete, and asphalt should all be collected for recycling and accounted for (Figure 11.17). Recycling options for paper, cardboard, plastics, and wood varies by region.

The LEED green building certification program includes a prerequisite to address waste management policies during operations for the collection and storage of recyclables. At a minimum, LEED projects must recycle paper, corrugated cardboard, glass, plastics, and metals. LEED for Existing Buildings: O&M offers point opportunities for auditing waste streams and implementing waste management policies for ongoing consumables (such as soap, batteries, and paper goods) and durable goods (such as furniture and electronics). Think about the potential for air and water contamination from batteries and fluorescent light bulbs, if they were not recycled.

The new version of the LEED green building certification program now includes a prerequisite for construction and demolition waste management planning. Teams are required to develop and implement a plan identifying at least materials to be diverted. The material types and total amount diverted is also required to comply. Project teams can pursue points under the credit for surpassing a minimum threshold of percentage of waste diverted and therefore keeping materials in active use longer.

Strategies to Reduce Waste during Construction[9]

1. *Design buildings that produce less waste.* Installing prefabricated products and material efficient framing produce less waste.

2. *Develop a construction waste management policy.* The policy should identify a goal, such as a 50 percent diversion to direct the contractor.

3. *Establish a tracking system.* Require the contractor to provide waste hauler reports and monitor for compliance.

Create a flashcard to remember the EPA statistic for current recycling rates of 32 percent.

Create a flashcard to remember the four preferred strategies, as defined by the EPA, for reducing waste in landfills.

Create a flashcard to remember the minimum types of items to be recycled during operations to meet the requirements of the MR prerequisite: paper, corrugated cardboard, glass, plastics, and metals.

TIP **Study:** Do you remember the three prerequisites in the MR category as mentioned in Chapter 5?

Do you remember the benefits of mulching discussed in Chapter 8?

Study: Waste is calculated in volume or weight (tons).

Create a flashcard to remember the three strategies to reduce waste during construction.

Figure 11.17 Dedicated waste container for masonry to be collected for recycling.

Strategies to Reduce Waste during Operations and Maintenance[10]

1. *Develop a solid waste management policy.* The policy should identify a goal and identify procedures.

2. *Conduct a waste stream audit.* Audits of the entire consumables waste stream can help to improve recycling rates by raising awareness.

3. *Maintain a recycling program.* Make it easy and convenient for occupants and users to recycle (Figure 11.18).

4. *Monitor, track, and report.* Track performance with hauler reports and provide feedback to improve diversion rates.

5. *Compost.* Use landscaping and food debris as mulch (Figure 11.19).

6. *Provide recycling for durable goods.* Durable goods to be donated, reused, or recycled include furniture and e-waste.

 Create a flashcard to remember the six strategies to reduce waste.

Figure 11.18 The Pennsylvania Convention Center made recycling easy at the Greenbuild International Conference and Expo in Philadelphia.

Figure 11.19 Using a compost bin to dispose of food and landscaping debris helps to generate mulch to use onsite for landscaping. *Photo courtesy of the Fischetti family*

QUIZ TIME!

These questions are formatted just as they would be on the exam. Notice the question indicates how many answers to select. The proper number of correct answers is required on the exam, as partial credit is not awarded.

In an effort to present information to you in multiple ways and help you learn, you may find questions asking about information that is new to you, that you did not read about throughout the book.

Q11.1 Which of the following materials qualify as preconsumer recycled content? (Choose three)

    A. Metal stud manufacturing scrap sent back into the same manufacturing process

    B. Paper towels manufactured from cardboard used for packaging

    C. Medium-density fiberboard panels manufactured with sawdust generated by the manufacturing of structural insulated panels

    D. Concrete made with fly ash collected from coal-burning power plants

    E. Carpet padding manufactured with waste fiber collected from textile manufacturing plants

Q11.2 The percentage calculation for rapidly renewable materials accounts for which of the following? (Choose two)

    A. Cost of rapidly renewable materials

    B. Volume of rapidly renewable materials

    C. Combined weight for all rapidly renewable materials

    D. Total materials cost for the project

Q11.3 Which of the following is not an example of rapidly renewable materials? (Choose one)

    A. Strawboard

    B. Oak wood flooring

    C. Cotton insulation

    D. Cork flooring

    E. Wheatboard

Q11.4 A library is to be constructed with wood posts and beams salvaged from barns in the region, and purchased FSC Certified Wood for doors and trim. The owner is interested in determining whether the project meets the requirements of certified wood for LEED. The qualification of products and determination of their contribution to certified wood requires keeping track of which of the following? (Choose two)

    A. Cost of certified wood products as a percentage of the total material cost of the project

    B. Cost of certified wood products as a percentage of the total cost for wood products purchased for the project

    C. Weight of certified wood products as a percentage of all new wood products used on the project

    D. Chain-of-custody documentation for all FSC certified wood products

E. Chain-of-custody documentation for all new wood products purchased for the project

Q11.5 Which of the following resources should a facility manager consult in reference to finding more information about sustainable purchasing options? (Choose three)

A. Green Seal

B. ENERGY STAR Portfolio Manager

C. ENERGY STAR

D. EPA

E. FSC

Q11.6 Which of the following greenhouse gases is a by-product of landfills? (Choose one)

A. Carbon monoxide

B. Methane

C. Sulfur dioxide

D. Nitrous oxide

Q11.7 Which of the following statements are not true about green building materials? (Choose two)

A. Rapidly renewable materials are harvested within ten years.

B. Cradle-to-grave materials can be recycled.

C. Products with postconsumer recycled content can contribute to earning LEED credits while products with preconsumer recycled content cannot.

D. Cotton insulation can be considered a type of rapidly renewable material.

Q11.8 Which of the following would the contractor upload to LEED-Online? (Choose two)

A. Rainwater management plan

B. Total amount of waste diverted from a landfill

C. The total material cost of the project and the percentage containing recycled content

D. Energy modeling calculations to show expected energy savings

Q11.9 When addressing materials and resources, a project team should incorporate which of the following to comply with the credits and prerequisites of the MR category? (Choose three)

A. The SRI value of the roof

B. Location of manufacturing plant of steel

C. The type of car the CEO drives

D. Postconsumer recycled content of a chair

E. Extraction location of silica

Q11.10 Which of the following are examples of permanently installed building products? (Choose three)

A. Doors

B. Casework

C. Concrete forms

D. Furniture

E. Framing

Q11.11 Which of the following is not considered an ongoing consumable product? (Choose one)

A. Soap

B. Batteries

C. Furniture

D. Paper towels

E. Lamp bulbs

Q11.12 How is waste hauled from a construction site calculated for the purposes of LEED? (Choose one)

A. As a percentage of total material cost of a project

B. As a percentage of the total material volume or weight

C. As a percentage of total cost of a project

D. In tons

Q11.13 What is the most common way to divert waste from landfills? (Choose one)

A. Source reduction, such as prefabrication

B. Waste to energy

C. Reuse of existing materials

D. Recycling

Q11.14 Which of the following avoids environmental harms from the supply chain through to end of life? (Choose one)

A. Source reduction

B. Waste to energy

C. Reuse of existing materials

D. Recycling

Q11.15 Which of the following are considered separate products when calculating compliance with MR credits? (Choose two)

A. Different colored flat paints with the same VOC

B. Carpet with different pile heights by the same manufacturer

C. Different colored carpets with the same pile heights by the same manufacturer

D. Gypsum wallboard with varying thicknesses by the same manufacturer

Q11.16 Which of the following are strategies to reduce the demand of new materials? (Choose two)

    A. Reuse existing buildings

    B. Design denser, mixed-use neighborhoods

    C. Densely spaced framing members

    D. Specifying FSC certified wood

Q11.17 What is the value of brick pavers, with 32 percent preconsumer content, that were processed 87 miles and manufactured 99 away from a project site? (Choose one)

    A. 100 percent

    B. 132 percent

    C. 32 percent

    D. 150 percent

    E. 200 percent

Q11.18 What are the components to determine contributions of an assembled product? (Choose three)

    A. Total construction cost

    B. Total material cost

    C. Total product cost

    D. Percent compliant by weight

    E. Default material cost

    F. Percent compliant with the sustainable criteria

Q11.19 Which of the following statements are true? (Choose two)

    A. Project teams have the option to include furniture in MR credit calculations.

    B. Project teams must include furniture in MR credit calculations.

    C. Escalators and other process equipment are required to be included in MR credit calculations.

    D. Escalators and other process equipment are not to be included in MR credit calculations.

Q11.20 Which of the following statements are true? (Choose two)

    A. Project teams have the option to include concrete formwork and other temporarily used products in calculations.

    B. Project teams must include concrete formwork and other temporarily used products in calculations.

    C. Project teams must exclude concrete formwork and other temporarily used products in calculations.

    D. Project teams have the option to include MEP items in MR credit calculations

    E. Project teams must include MEP items in MR credit calculations.

ONLINE RESOURCES

For an example of an EPD, visit www.kalzip.com/PDF/eur/Kalzip_EPDsECO.pdf.
If you have never watched *The Story of Stuff*, I encourage you to do so. Go to
http://storyofstuff.org/.

NOTES

1. USGBC, *LEED Reference Guide for Green Building Design and Construction* (2014), 527.

2. European Commission Service Contract on Management of Construction and Demolition Waste, Final Report, www.eu-smr.eu/cdw/docs/BIO_Construction%20and%20Demolition%20Waste_Final%20report_09022011.pdf (accessed April 2014).

3. USGBC, *Green Building and LEED Core Concepts Guide*, 3rd ed. (2014), 71.

4. Ibid.

5. Ibid., p. 72.

6. Ibid.

7. Ibid., p. 73.

8. USGBC, *LEED Reference Guide for Green Building Design and Construction*, p. 468.

9. USGBC, *Green Building and LEED Core Concepts Guide*, 3rd ed., 74.

10. Ibid., p. 75.

CHAPTER 12

INDOOR ENVIRONMENTAL QUALITY

THIS CHAPTER FOCUSES ON THE ELEMENTS ENCOMPASSED in the indoor environment, such as thermal conditions and acoustics, as detailed in the Indoor Environmental Quality (EQ) category of the Leadership in Energy and Environmental Design (LEED®) green building certification program (Figure 12.1). Remember that Chapter 2 introduced the importance of indoor environments, since Americans typically spend about 90 percent of their time indoors, according to the Environmental Protection Agency (EPA). This chapter will identify ways to "enhance the lives building occupants, increase the resale value of the building, and reduce liability for building owners"[1] and designers.

The *LEED Core Concepts Guide* indicates "occupants of green buildings are typically exposed to far lower levels of indoor pollutants and have significantly greater satisfaction with air quality and lighting than occupants of conventional buildings."[2] Because employee salaries and benefits are the biggest cost for a business, larger than operating costs for facilities, such as utilities, the satisfaction and health of the occupants should be a high priority. Retaining employees in order to avoid the additional costs of training new hires can help to add efficiencies to the economic bottom line for businesses. Research studies have found "a 2% to 16% increase in workers' and students' productivity"[3] according to Carnegie Mellon. Reducing absenteeism due to health impacts increases productivity and reduces liability of inadequate indoor environmental quality. "Even small increases in productivity can dramatically increase the value of a building."[4]

The LEED green building certification program offers the following strategies to improve indoor environments:

1. Indoor Air Quality
2. Lighting
3. Acoustics
4. Occupant Experience

It's time to pick a different color for flashcards created for Indoor Environmental Quality topics.

Create a flashcard to remember the four components of the EQ category. Take note—occupant experience includes thermal comfort, views, and ergonomics. Lighting includes both artificial and daylighting.

Figure 12.1 Businesses, such as Haworth, will enjoy a return on their investment for increasing their employee satisfaction by providing a comfortable work environment. Addressing such factors as daylighting, views, and low-emitting material selections helps to bring value to the indoor environmental quality. *Photo courtesy of Haworth Inc.*

INDOOR AIR QUALITY

With all of the supporting evidence of indoor environmental quality, understanding the common sources of air contaminants is the first step to establish the proper strategies to be implemented on a project[5]:

- Tobacco smoke
- Building materials that emit **volatile organic compounds** (VOCs)
- Combustion processes in heating, ventilating, and air conditioning (HVAC) equipment; fireplaces and stoves; and vehicles in garages or near entrances
- Mold
- Cleaning products

■ Radon or methane off-gassing from the soil underneath the building

■ Pollutants from specific processes used in laboratories, hospitals, and factories

■ Pollutants tracked in on occupants' shoes

■ Occupants (bioeffluents) and their activities

Create a flashcard to remember the different types of air contaminant sources.

Studies have shown that poor indoor air quality can lead to respiratory disease, allergies and asthma, and **sick building syndrome,** and can therefore impact the performance and productivity of employees. The LEED green building certification program addresses components from a triple bottom line perspective, to improve air quality during construction and operations to avoid effects on human health and to improve the quality of life. Since there are so many variables inherent in the connection between the indoor environment and occupant comfort, the EQ category tackles the challenge from both a prescriptive and performance based approach.

Strategies for Designing for Good IAQ

When designing a project, project teams are encouraged to address the following as a means to create a great indoor environment[6]:

1. *Prohibit smoking* inside the building and around building entrances, windows, and air intakes (Figure 12.2).

2. *Properly size the ventilation system* (natural or mechanical) to deliver enough fresh air by calculating the number of occupants in each space and considering the activity performed by the occupants.

3. *Protect the air coming into the building* by locating air intakes away from exhaust sources and design a ventilation system that will remove contaminants with air filtration.

TIP **Study:** Possible exhaust sources can be idling vehicles or exterior smoking areas.

TIP Create a flashcard to remember MERV. Using filters with a high **Minimum Efficiency Reporting Value** rating will capture particulates. The higher the MERV the better.

TIP **Career:** Interested in building systems? Mechanical engineers typically are responsible for sizing ventilation systems and locating air intakes. Commissioning agents typically have a mechanical engineering background.

Figure 12.2 Owners need to prohibit smoking in the building and within 25 feet of building entrances, operable windows, and air intakes during construction and occupancy.

Figure 12.3 This entryway system getting installed at the Waterfront Tech Center in Camden, New Jersey, will help to reduce dust, dirt, and other contaminants typically carried into a facility by foot. *Photo courtesy of Stephen Martorana, LEED AP BD+C*

 Create a flashcard to remember the six design strategies to improve IAQ.

 TIP **Career:** Interior designers and architects typically compile specifications for the general contractor to follow to ensure low-emitting products, such as paints and adhesives that are used onsite. There are many roles of the construction team that are necessary, including management and administrative individuals.

 Create a flashcard to remember the three strategies to improve IAQ during construction.

 Increasing ventilation may improve the overall IAQ, but it may increase the energy demand of HVAC systems at the same time. It is important for project teams to find the balance between energy, water, and material conservation and a great indoor experience.

4. Test for radon.

5. Design for entryway systems, such as grilles, grates, or mats to reduce contaminants (Figure 12.3)

6. *Specify low-emitting materials* with low or no VOCs (Figure 12.4).

Strategies for Improving IAQ during Construction

During construction, project teams are encouraged to implement the following strategies to protect the indoor air quality[7]:

1. Keep the building clean (Figure 12.5).

2. *Protect absorptive materials* from moisture exposure (Figure 12.6) and protect ductwork from dust and contaminants (Figure 12.7).

3. *Conduct a flush-out,* before occupancy, to eliminate any off-gassed contaminants from construction. Opening the windows is not enough to remove construction pollutants! Ductwork should be flushed out with a large amount of outside air.

Strategies for Improving IAQ during Operations and Maintenance

During building operations, indoor air pollutants should also be monitored to continue to reduce impacts on occupants. Incorporating green cleaning products with low or no VOCs helps to reduce pollutants and contaminants from entering the indoor airflow. Also, MERV filters should be changed regularly and carbon dioxide levels should be monitored to help ensure good air quality. Maintenance strategies should also employ low or no VOC products, such as paints and

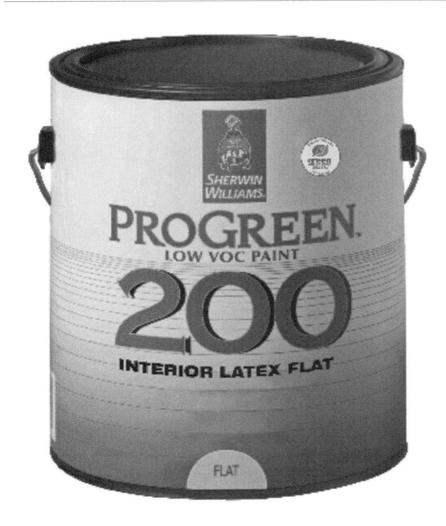

Figure 12.4 Specifying materials with low to no VOCs helps to maintain good indoor air quality. *Photo courtesy of Sherwin-Williams*

Figure 12.5 Using a sweeping compound helps to control dust.

Figure 12.6 Elevate products for storage to protect against damage.

adhesives. Integrated pest management strategies avoid the use of pesticides to eliminate human exposure; nonchemical monitor and bait strategies should be implemented instead.

Project teams and facility managers are encouraged to design for and provide adequate ventilation for occupants without compromising energy use efficiencies, not to be a burden on the environment by contributing to the need for fossil fuels. Mechanical systems should work to thermally balance outdoor air with every air change; therefore, the key is to find the right balance. Too many air changes are

Figure 12.7 Construction teams must protect ductwork prior to installation and once installed.

wasteful and would impact economic and environmental bottom lines. However, too little ventilation can result in reduced quality of the indoor air, which would impact the health and satisfaction of occupants, thus also affecting the triple bottom line components. Therefore, project teams designing green buildings use the industry standard, **ASHRAE 62.1, Ventilation for Acceptable Indoor Air Quality**, to adequately and appropriately size mechanical systems that will deliver the proper amounts of outside air while balancing energy demands.

Project teams are encouraged to implement the following nine strategies to maintain the indoor air quality throughout the life of the building continuing to protect the occupants according to the *Green Building and LEED Core Concepts Guide*[8]:

1. *Ensure adequate ventilation.* Think ASHRAE 62!

2. *Monitor airflow.* Incorporate airflow measurement devices to measure and control the minimum airflow rate.

3. *Monitor carbon dioxide.* Incorporate **demand-controlled ventilation** where airflow is increased if maximum set points are exceeded.

4. *Calibrate sensors.*

5. *Prohibit smoking.* Reinforce the no-smoking policy with signage (Figure 12.8).

6. *Employ a green cleaning program.* No harmful chemicals! Equipment and products should follow environmental standards and requirements such as Green Seal (Figures 12.9 and 12.10), California Code of Regulations and certification from the Carpet and Rug Institute (CRI).

7. *Conduct a Custodial Effectiveness Assessment.*

8. *Maintain entryway systems.*

9. *Use integrated pest management.* To eliminate contaminants indoors, no pesticides should enter the facility.

Study: Any time you see ASHRAE 62, think IAQ! Say it out loud: IAQ 62, 62 IAQ!

Create a flashcard to remember the standards for green cleaning standards.

Create a flashcard to remember the nine strategies to improve IAQ during operations. Remember, Appendix D summarizes all of the strategies to remember.

Career: Maintenance teams may not necessarily be based onsite at a property. Some aspects are subcontracting out, such as cleaning. Independent cleaning companies are just as responsible to research and use compliant green cleaning products and equipment and possibly conducting custodial effectiveness assessments.

Figure 12.8 Owners need to continue to prohibit smoking in the building and within 25 feet of building entrances, operable windows, and air intakes after construction.

Figure 12.9 Requiring the use of green cleaning products will ensure that no harmful chemicals are used to contaminate the air. *Image courtesy of Absolute Green*

Figure 12.10 Be sure to look for qualifying standards, such as Green Seal. *Image courtesy of Green Seal, Inc.*

THERMAL COMFORT

Although temperature settings should vary with the seasons, buildings should allow for occupants to control their thermal conditions to optimize satisfaction and comfort. Think about that fellow classmate or coworker that is always cold when everyone else is comfortable. Everyone's needs vary during the day, and having the ability to control is critical to comfort and satisfaction. Remember, occupants who are satisfied and comfortable tend to be more productive! For the purposes of LEED, occupants must be able to control one of the three components of thermal comfort.

Strategies

The *Green Building and LEED Core Concepts Guide* describes three strategies to offer thermal comfort to occupants[9]:

1. *Install operable windows* for fresh air access (Figure 12.11).

2. *Give occupants temperature and ventilation control.* If operable windows are not feasible, give occupants control over mechanically supplied and delivered warm or cool air by employing strategies such as raised access floors (Figure 12.12).

3. *Conduct occupant surveys.* Discover the overall satisfaction of the thermal comfort levels of the majority of the occupants to determine areas for improvement.

Create a flashcard to remember the three strategies for thermal comfort.

Figure 12.11 Wausau's LEED Silver facility in Wausau, Wisconsin, employs operable windows to give their employees access to fresh air. *Photo courtesy of Wausau Windows and Wall Systems*

Figure 12.12 Raised access floors provide the flexibility to grant occupants individual control of the amount of air supplied through diffusers for their thermal comfort. *Photo courtesy of Tate Access Floors, Inc.*

TIP **Study:** A study found students' scores improved by 7 to 18 percent in daylit classrooms as compared to students studying in artificially lit classrooms.[10]

When one is designing, **nonregularly occupied spaces** should be placed at the core to allow offices, classrooms, and other **regularly occupied areas** to be placed along the window line.

LIGHTING

The LEED green building certification program addresses lighting in terms of naturally available daylight and artificially supplied light. When debating whether to incorporate daylighting strategies, project teams are advised to conduct a life-cycle cost analysis to determine the up-front costs and operational savings.

For example, when using daylighting strategies, sensors could be installed to trigger alternative light sources when needed, which would impact up-front costs, although the costs can be offset by the energy saved during operations since less artificial light would be required. Daylighting can also result in improved occupant satisfaction and health due to access and connection to the exterior environment, also affecting the economic bottom line over time (Figure 12.13).

Besides daylighting, providing occupants with the ability to control their lighting needs can also benefit the triple bottom line. Occupant-controlled lighting contributes to employee satisfaction, as well as productivity, as light

 Remember, building orientation and passive design strategies impact the opportunities to utilize daylighting to supply ambient lighting for occupants.

 TIP **Career:** Qualified in building information modeling (BIM)? Software tools, such as BIM, allow project teams to model and design daylight strategies.

Figure 12.13 A classroom at Northland Pines High School in Eagle River, Wisconsin, provides students and teachers accessibility to views of the outdoor environment, as well as daylighting to improve their satisfaction and productivity. *Photo courtesy of Hoffman Planning, Design, & Construction, Inc.*

levels can be altered for specific tasks, needs, and preferences. Therefore, providing overall ambient light, as well as individual task lighting (Figure 12.14), is the best strategy to address lighting needs. Facilities can also see a reduction in energy usage for lighting needs by educating employees on the benefits of turning off fixtures after use.

Figure 12.14 Providing occupants with task lighting allows for more individual control of work environments to improve their satisfaction and productivity. *Photo courtesy of BASF Corporation.*

Figure 12.15 Providing interior environments with access to natural daylight not only improves the occupants' satisfaction and productivity levels but also helps to reduce the need for artificial lighting to reduce operating costs. *Photo courtesy of Steelcase Inc.*

Study: Project teams should design the overall illumination light level to be about 40 to 60 footcandles on an office work surface.

Create a flashcard to remember the three strategies to improve lighting in reference to EQ.

V3V4: LEED 2009 addressed acoustics in the LEED for Schools rating system, where as V4 offers credit compliance in most of the rating systems.

Strategies

The *Green Building and LEED Core Concepts Guide* suggests the following strategies to address lighting for a green building project[11]:

1. *Use daylighting.* Remember passive design strategies and benefits (Figure 12.15).

2. *Give occupants lighting control* for economic benefits from energy savings while improving occupant satisfaction.

3. *Conduct occupant surveys.* Discover the overall satisfaction of the lighting levels of the majority of the occupants to determine areas for improvement.

ACOUSTICS

For those who have worked in an open plan office environment, there is an appreciation for attention to proper acoustic design components. The ability to communicate effectively, in person or via telecommunications, is impacted by the quality of acoustics. Just as with thermal comfort and lighting controls, delivering high-performing interior acoustic environments adds to the satisfaction and well-being of building occupants and employees (Figure 12.16).

Strategies

The *Green Building and LEED Core Concepts Guide* provides the following strategies to address acoustics and therefore increase occupant comfort[12]:

1. *Consider acoustical impacts.* Consider interior finishes, building geometry, and duct insulation that will impact the ability for employees and staff to communicate and work effectively.

2. *Conduct occupant surveys.* Discover the overall satisfaction of the interior acoustic quality of the majority of the occupants to determine areas for improvement.

Create a flashcard to remember the two strategies to improve acoustics in reference to IEQ.

Figure 12.16 Designing for proper acoustic performance also helps to improve the satisfaction and comfort levels of occupants by improving the ability to effectively communicate. *Photo courtesy of Steelcase Inc.*

QUIZ TIME!

These questions are formatted just as they would be on the exam. Notice the question indicates how many answers to select. The proper number of correct answers is required on the exam, as partial credit is not awarded.

In an effort to present information to you in multiple ways and help you learn, you may find questions asking about information that is new to you, that you did not read about throughout the book.

Q12.1   Which of the following is consistent with the range of MERV filter ratings? (Choose one)

A. 1–30

B. 0–50

C. 1–110

D. 1–16

E. 1–100

Q12.2   Which of the following are consistent with the requirements of Low-Emitting Materials? (Choose three)

A. All adhesives and sealants must not exceed the VOC limits set by ASHRAE 62.1: Ventilation for Acceptable Indoor Air Quality.

B. Nonaerosol adhesives and sealants must be in compliance with VOC limits set by SCAQMD, Rule 1168.

C. Paints and coatings must contain no phenol-formaldehyde.

D. Adhesives and sealants must carry a Green Spec seal of approval.

E. Paints must meet VOC limits established by the Green Seal Standard (GS-36).

F. While projects are encouraged, but not required, to use low-VOC adhesives and sealants on exterior building elements, all adhesives and sealants inside of the building envelope weather seal must meet the requirements of the referenced standards.

Q12.3   Which of the following are standards for indoor air quality? (Choose two)

A. ASHRAE 90.1

B. CRI Green Label Plus

C. Green Seal

D. ENERGY STAR

E. California's Title 24

Q12.4   Which of the following should be considered to promote good lighting design? (Choose two)

A. Surface colors within the space

B. Furnishings

C. The type of ceiling finish

D. VOC level

Q12.5 Which of the following statements is not a strategy to maintain indoor air quality? (Choose one)

A. Open all windows to flush contaminated air out of a building for at least two weeks prior to occupancy.

B. Coordinate a green cleaning program.

C. Install high-efficiency filters.

D. Specify adhesives and sealants with low or no VOCs.

Q12.6 When addressing thermal comfort, which of the following are not addressed? (Choose two)

A. Humidity

B. Daylighting controls

C. Air movement

D. Artificial light

E. Average temperature

Q12.7 An environmental tobacco smoke control policy *best* addresses which of the following? (Choose one)

A. Providing ventilation requirements to effectively remove tobacco smoke

B. Providing dedicated smoking rooms 25 feet away from building entrances

C. Preventing tobacco smoke from contaminating indoor environments

D. Preventing tobacco smoke from entering the air occupied by nonsmokers

Q12.8 Which of the following help to bounce and diffuse daylight? (Choose two)

A. Task lighting

B. Light shelves

C. Clerestory windows

D. Where an occupant's desk is located

Q12.9 Which of the following would typically cause discomfort? (Choose three)

A. Glare

B. Operable window

C. Direct daylight

D. Stagnant air

E. Task lighting

Q12.10 Which of the following best describes the LEED strategy applicable to ASHRAE Standard 62.1? (Choose one)

A. Exterior lighting levels

B. Thermal comfort by means of controllability of systems

    C. Environmental tobacco smoke control

    D. Ventilation and indoor air quality

    E. Building flush-out parameters and guidelines

Q12.11 A tenant fit-out project seeking certification under the LEED for Commercial Interior rating system plans to use a raised access floor to include underfloor air distribution, allowing the use of floor-mounted operable diffusers at each workstation and therefore eliminating overhead ducts, thus maximizing the interior floor-to-ceiling height. The moderate supply air temperature required at the diffusers would reduce the amount of energy associated with cooling a consistently greater quantity of outside air needed to improve air quality. Which LEED strategy is addressed? (Choose one)

    A. Construction IAQ management

    B. Regional priority

    C. Thermal comfort

    D. Acoustical performance

Q12.12 Which of the following design-team deliverables and team members are most likely to play a significant role in achieving a Construction IAQ Management Plan? (Choose two)

    A. Project specifications

    B. Civil engineer

    C. Construction documents

    D. Lighting designer

    E. General contractor

    F. Electrical engineer

Q12.13 Which of the following most closely represents an appropriate level of overall illumination on an office work surface, including daylighting, ambient artificial lighting, and task lighting? (Choose one)

    A. 1–2 footcandles

    B. 5–10 footcandles

    C. 15–25 footcandles

    D. 40–60 footcandles

    E. 75–120 footcandles

    F. 150–200 footcandles

Q12.14 To which standard should engineers design the ventilation systems for a LEED project? (Choose one)

    A. California Air Resources Board

    B. ASHRAE 62.1

    C. ASHRAE 90.1

    D. SCAQMD

    E. California's Title 24

Q12.15 Which of the following strategies have proven to increase productivity and occupant satisfaction in green buildings? (Choose two)

    A. Providing access to daylight

    B. Selecting a site adjacent to a shopping center

    C. Improving indoor air quality

    D. Implementing a recycling program

    E. Offering incentives for carpooling

Q12.16 When conducting occupant surveys, which of the following is applicable? (Choose two)

    A. Provide adjustable task lighting.

    B. Provide ergonomic furniture.

    C. Include a plan for corrective action.

    D. Conduct confidential surveys.

Q12.17 Which of the following are examples of regularly occupied spaces? (Choose two)

    A. Bank teller station and a natatorium

    B. Break room and a copy room

    C. Dorm room and an operating room

    D. Lobby and a locker room

Q12.18 Which of the following are examples of multioccupant spaces? (Choose two)

    A. Bank teller station or a hotel room

    B. Natatorium and a conference room

    C. Hotel lobby and hotel front desk

    D. Open workstation and nursing station

Q12.19 Which of the following are examples of unoccupied spaces? (Choose three)

    A. Mechanical rooms

    B. Stairway

    C. Exhibition hall

    D. Data center floor area

Q12.20 Which of the following LEED strategies would it be important to determine regularly occupied spaces? (Choose two)

    A. Thermal comfort strategies

    B. Interior lighting strategies

    C. Integrative process

    D. Commissioning

NOTES

1. USGBC, *LEED Core Concepts Guide: An Introduction to LEED and Green Building,* 3rd ed. (2014), 77.

2. Ibid. p. 6.

3. Ibid.

4. Ibid.

5. Ibid. pp. 76–77.

6. Ibid. p. 77.

7. Ibid.

8. Ibid. p. 79.

9. Ibid. p. 81.

10. Ibid.

11. Ibid.

12. Ibid.

CHAPTER 13

INNOVATION AND REGIONAL PRIORITY

THE PREVIOUS SIX CHAPTERS DETAILED THE MAIN categories of the Leadership in Energy and Environmental Design (LEED®) green building certification program, while this chapter focuses on the two bonus categories of the rating systems: Innovation and Regional Priority (RP). These categories are treated as bonus categories, as neither contains any prerequisites. The Innovation category encourages projects to explore new and innovative strategies and technologies, while the RP category offers additional point-earning opportunities focused on geographic environmental achievements.

Remember to switch back to the white flashcards for Innovation and RP topics.

INNOVATION

The Innovation category encourages the exploration and implementation of new green building technologies, as well as exceeding the thresholds defined in the existing LEED credits. The LEED green building certification program offers up to six points for projects within the Innovation category by addressing four different strategies:

1. Exemplary performance

2. Innovative strategy

3. Pilot credit

4. Including a LEED Accredited Professional on the project team

Create a flashcard to remember the four strategies to earn Innovation points.

Two of the six available Innovation points can be used toward the achievement of Exemplary Performance. Exemplary Performance credits are achieved once projects surpass the minimum performance-based thresholds defined in the existing LEED credits, typically the next incremental percentage threshold. For example, projects can earn exemplary performance credits (within the Innovation category) for achieving the following:

■ Reuse 95 percent of the building.

■ Reduce parking capacity by 60 percent.

■ Provide at least 15 percent of total energy from renewable sources on the project site.

If the team uses either of the three opportunities for exemplary performance achievements, they still have up to three more point opportunities for implementing innovative strategies. Innovative strategies are not addressed by existing LEED credits. The teams should research credit interpretation rulings (CIRs) to see if their proposed strategy has been incorporated or presented in the past, or

Figure 13.1 Providing opportunities to educate the end users and community about the benefits and strategies of green building helps to further transform the market and therefore contributes to earning LEED certification. *Photo courtesy of Scott Strawbridge, Housing Authority of the City of Fort Lauderdale*

issue a new CIR to inquire about the award potential. Some examples previously submitted and awarded include:

- Implementing an educational program for the community, occupants and visitors (Figure 13.1)
- Achieving LEED prerequisites from other rating systems, such as Site Management Policy and Green Cleaning Policy
- Defining and implementing a waste management program that diverts a significant amount of waste generated from outside sources from landfills (Figure 13.2)

A third strategy to earning points in the Innovation category includes the pursuit of pilot credits, which are credits proposed and tried for the next version of LEED. Projects can earn up to three points for achieving the requirements of a pilot credit. Pilot credits are available for each rating system and can be found on the U.S. Green Building Council's (USGBC's®) website.

Finally, the LEED green building certification program also offers another point opportunity for including a LEED Accredited Professional (AP) on the project team. Including a LEED AP® on the project team can add efficiencies, as they are aware of the requirements of the LEED certification process. They are familiar with integrated design processes and understand how to evaluate the trade-offs and synergies of green building strategies and technologies. For the purposes of the exam, it is critical to remember that only one point can be awarded to projects for this credit; it does not matter how many LEED APs are on the project team, just as long as there is one. Unfortunately, LEED Green Associates™ do not qualify for the extra point under this credit.

Figure 13.2 Wyndham Worldwide uses compost bins for biodegradable materials to help reduce the amount of waste generated at the LEED Silver certified corporate campus in Parsippany, New Jersey.

REGIONAL PRIORITY

The Regional Priority category offers the opportunity to earn bonus points for achieving compliance of previously mentioned existing LEED credits. When the RP category was originally developed for the 2009 version of the LEED green building certification program, USGBC's® eight Regional Councils had consulted with the local chapters to determine which existing LEED credits were more challenging to achieve within certain zip codes. Based on the results of their findings, USGBC compiled a database of all the zip codes in the United States and chose six existing LEED credits to coordinate with each corresponding geographic region. This obviously presented a challenge for international projects and for changing zip codes due to population changes. In order to address this problem, the RP credit zones for LEED v4 were created using a "GIS-based program that allowed for environmental issues to be empirically mapped. This process created RP credit zones that are based on these issues rather than physical location."[1] Under the version 4 of the LEED green building certification program, a project could earn up to four Regional Priority credits (RPCs) out of the six opportunities presented based on the coordinating physical coordinates (X,Y) of the project.

Do you remember the point structure for the different certification levels of LEED? How many points does a project need to achieve to earn Platinum status?

Study: For the purposes of the exam, it is critical to remember that RPCs are not new credits.

QUIZ TIME!

These questions are formatted just as they would be on the exam. Notice the question indicates how many answers to select. The proper number of correct answers is required on the exam, as partial credit is not awarded.

In an effort to present information to you in multiple ways and help you learn, you may find questions asking about information that is new to you, that you did not read about throughout the book.

Q13.1 Exemplary performance generally requires which of the following? (Choose one)

- A. Develop an innovative strategy not presented in any existing LEED credit.
- B. Achieve either 20 percent or the next incremental percentage threshold established by the existing LEED credit that is being exceeded, whichever is greater.
- C. Meet or exceed the next percentage threshold as listed within the existing credit.
- D. Surpass the defined threshold of an innovative strategy being proposed by the team.
- E. Regardless of the LEED credit being pursued, achieve at least double the minimum effort described within the existing LEED credit, regardless of which credit is being exceeded.

Q13.2 Pursuing an Innovation credit is appropriate when *at least one* of which of the following are true? (Choose two)

- A. The project is unable to meet the requirements established by an existing LEED credit.
- B. The compliance paths offered within an existing LEED credit are not possible to pursue.
- C. The project has exceeded or is projected to exceed the minimum performance established by an existing LEED credit.
- D. The project has achieved measurable performance in a LEED credit within another rating system.

Q13.3 Is it possible for the same building to earn multiple LEED certifications?

- A. Yes
- B. No

Q13.4 Which of the following statements are true regarding RPCs? (Choose two)

- A. Earning an RPC adds a bonus point to the project's total points.
- B. RPCs are new credits included in the LEED rating systems.

C. RPCs are only earned if an Innovation credit is pursued and awarded.

D. A project may earn up to four RPC bonus points.

E. RPCs are only available to projects located in North America.

Q13.5 How many points can be earned in the Regional Priority category?

A. Six

B. Three

C. Two

D. Four

E. Ten

Q13.6 There are five LEED APs on the Botanical Center project, including three from the architectural firm, one from the mechanical engineering firm, and another one from the electrical engineering firm. How many points can be achieved within the Innovation category for achieving this effort?

A. One

B. Two

C. Three

D. Four

ONLINE RESOURCES

Curious to see what the latest pilot credits are? Visit www.usgbc.org/pilotcredits.

Interested to learn the regional priority credits available in your zip code? Visit www.usgbc.org/rpc.

NOTES

1. LEED user website, www.leeduser.com/credit/NC-v4/RPc1.

PART III

STUDY
TIPS AND
APPENDICES

CHAPTER 14

STUDY TIPS

AS MENTIONED EARLIER IN THE INTRODUCTION OF this book, this chapter is dedicated to providing an approach for the rest of your study efforts during Week Seven. It includes tips for taking online practice exams and resources on where to find additional information while you continue to study, as well as providing an insight to the Prometric testing center environment and the exam format structure.

PREPARING FOR THE LEED® GREEN ASSOCIATE™ EXAM: WEEK SEVEN

By the time you read this section, it should be Week Seven of your study efforts. You should have your white set of flashcards covering the basics of Leadership in Energy and Environmental Design (LEED®) (including Integrative Process, Innovation, and Regional Priority [RP] bonus categories) and your color-coded cards separated into the six main categories of the LEED rating systems. This week will be a great opportunity to rewrite your cheat sheet at least three times. Note that your cheat sheet may evolve as you take a few online practice exams.

During Week Seven, you may want to reference additional resources while studying. For example, if you want to learn more about an overview of the development of the impact categories and point allocation process, refer to *LEED v4 Impact Category and Point Allocation Development Process* by the U.S. Green Building Council (USGBC®). It is quite a complex issue of how the different strategies are weighted within the LEED green building certification program. Another resource you may want to look at is the section overviews of the *LEED Reference Guide for Building Design and Construction*. This might give you a good summary of Part II of this book. Finally, the LEED V4 User Guide offers an introduction to LEED v4 and a comparison of changes from LEED V3. All of these references are available to download from the *LEED Green Associate Candidate Handbook* on the USGBC website for free. Again, it is highly recommended that you download the most current *Candidate Handbook* from the USGBC website to be sure you have the most up to date information while preparing for your exam. The following was referenced throughout the preceding chapters of this book, but is available for sale and is a reference listed in the *Candidate Handbook*:

■ Green Building and LEED Core Concepts Guide, 3rd ed. (USGBC, 2014)

Some other resources include:

■ www.usgbc.org. You will need to visit this site when you are ready to register for the exam. In the meantime, you may also want to check out some of the rating system scorecards or download the current *Candidate Handbook*. The USGBC website is also your primary source to learn about any updates to the LEED rating systems.

TIP **Study:** If you have the time and are eager to dive in deeper, feel free to download and read through three of the references from the *Green Associate Candidate Handbook*:
- Reference Guide Introductory and Overview Sections www.usgbc.org/guide/bdc#cc_overview
- LEED v4 Impact Category and Point Allocation Process Overview www.usgbc.org/resources/leed-v4-impact-category-and-point-allocation-process-overview
- LEED v4 User Guide www.usgbc.org/resources/leed-v4-user-guide

TIP **Study:** Be sure to check out the different groups at www.Linkedin.com, such as The LEED Green Associate for another resource for study tips: https://www.linkedin.com/company/5238674?trk=tyah&trkInfo=tarId%3A1409705641556%2Ctas%3Aleed%2Cidx%3A4-2-13

■ www.leedonline.com. Even if you do not have any projects assigned to you, you will still be able to see what it looks like (your USGBC login info is the same on this site) and watch a v3 demo video.

Practice Exam Approach

TIP **Study:** Be sure to take online practice exams to simulate your exam day environment.

Also during Week Seven, you should take some online practice exams. Although there are many sample exam questions provided in this book, it is helpful to practice for the real-life testing environment scenario. Search online, as you will find that there are a few options from which to choose. When you are taking a practice exam, pretend as if it is the real thing. For example, time yourself, have scratch paper and a pencil available, make a cheat sheet in about two to three minutes, do not use this book or your flashcards, and avoid any disruptions. Most of the online practice exams allow you to flag questions you are doubtful of, so take advantage of this for practice.

Most of the questions include multiple choices with multiple answers required. When approaching these types of questions, it is best advised to hide or cover up the provided answer options and formulate your own answers to help avoid getting sidetracked by the answer selection choices. Once you uncover or reveal the answer choices, make sure to read through all of the options before selecting your final answer(s). Be sure to read each question carefully and select the proper number of answers. After taking the practice exam, go through the answer key and evaluate your score. On the first practice exam, read through each question and answer one by one to understand how you decided on the correct answer and where you went wrong on the incorrect ones. Try to notice a pattern on your strengths and weaknesses to determine where your study efforts need to be devoted to improve your score. After taking the first practice exam, you may just want to focus on the questions you answered incorrectly.

THE TESTING CENTER ENVIRONMENT

The introduction of this book described the opportunity to make a cheat sheet after you completed the tutorial at the testing center, and Chapter 1 detailed how to schedule your exam date with a Prometric testing center. Hopefully, your exam date is still not scheduled at this point, as one more week of prep time is suggested to review your flashcards, refine your cheat sheet, and have the opportunity to take a few online practice exams. As stated earlier, it is best to assess your knowledge before scheduling your exam date.

During Week Eight, the week of your test date, there are a few things to remember before you sit for the exam:

■ Remember to visit the USGBC website and download the latest version of the *LEED Green Associate Candidate Handbook*.

■ Confirm your exam date at least one day prior.

■ Find the Prometric testing center and map your path to make sure you know where you are going on your exam day. Be sure to note any construction along your path that may cause delays. Be sure to note traffic patterns depending on the time of your exam.

■ Keep rewriting your cheat sheet and studying your flashcards. Take your flashcards everywhere with you!

To be prepared on the day of your exam, please note the following:

- Bring your picture ID with matching name, just as it is on your Green Building Certification Institute (GBCI™) profile.

- Dress comfortably and bring a sweater or a jacket, as the testing center may be cold.

- Be sure to get plenty of rest and eat something, as you will not want to take any breaks during the exam to grab a bite or a drink (the clock cannot be paused).

- Be sure to check in at least 30 minutes prior to your testing time. If you miss your scheduled exam time, you will be considered absent and will have to forfeit your exam fees and the opportunity to take the exam.

- Be sure to use the restroom after checking in and prior to being escorted to your workstation. Remember, no breaks!

- You will be observed during your testing session and will be audio and video recorded as well.

- You will not be allowed to bring any personal items to your workstation such as calculators, paper, pencils, purses, wallets, food, or books.

EXAM STRUCTURE

The exam is structured to test you on three components, as described in the *Candidate Handbook* provided by USGBC. You will be tested on recognition items, application items, and analysis items. The recognition items test your ability to remember factual data once presented in a similar environment to the exam references. For example, you may need to provide the definition for a term or recall a fact. The application items present a situation for you to solve using the principles and elements described in the exam format. These questions may require you to perform a calculation or provide the process or sequence of actions (i.e., CIRs, registration, certification). The analysis items are presented to evaluate your ability to evaluate a problem to create a solution. These question types are more challenging, as you must be able to decipher the different components of the problem and also assess the relationships of the components.

 TIP **Study:** The formulas and an on-screen calculator will be provided should you be required to perform any calculations.

Although the exam questions are delivered randomly, the questions are separated into two categories of focus areas (task domains and knowledge domains) and then are coordinated with an applicable rating system category (as applicable). Within the task domain, there might be questions pertaining to working on a LEED project such as navigating LEED-Online. Knowledge domains are broken into nine categories:

 TIP **Study:** Remember, the exam is composed of multiple-choice questions, just like the practice questions in this book. No written answers are required!

1. *LEED Process.* Focuses on the structure of the rating systems, the development process, impact categories, and the certification process.

2. *Integrative Strategies.* Questions could include topics such as the integrative process, team members, reference standards within LEED.

3. *Location and Transportation.* Site Selection and transportation strategies are tested.

4. *Sustainable Sites.* Includes site assessment plus design and development strategies, such as light pollution and rainwater management.

5. *Water Efficiency.* Focuses on water design measures for both indoor and outdoor use, as well as water performance management strategies.

6. *Energy and Atmosphere.* Topics include energy efficiency, environmental concerns, and renewable energy practices.

7. *Materials and Resources.* Questions could include reuse, life-cycle impacts, and purchasing policies.

8. *Indoor Environmental Quality.* Indoor air quality, lighting, sounds, and occupant comfort strategies are tested.

9. *Project Surroundings and Public Outreach.* This category tests regional design aspects, the relationship between building codes and LEED, and triple bottom line concepts.

When at the Testing Center

To give you an idea of what to expect, once you are at your workstation:

- You should dedicate 2 hours and 20 minutes to take the exam:
  - 10-minute tutorial
  - 2-hour exam
  - 10-minute exit survey

- The tutorial is computer based so make sure your workstation's monitor, keyboard, and mouse are all functioning properly. After completing the tutorial, remember to then create your cheat sheet in the time left over.

- The 2-hour exam is composed of 100 multiple-choice questions. Just like with the practice exam questions, in order for the question to be counted as CORRECT, you must select **all** of the correct answers within each question, as there is no partial credit for choosing two out of the three correct answers.

- Although some of the practice exam questions in this book are formatted with a true or false statement or "All of the above" as an answer selection, you are less likely to find this on the real exam, as the questions tend to be straightforward and clear, to avoid any confusion.

- You will not see any credit numbers listed on their own, as all credit names will include the full name.

- Appendix I includes a list of commonly used acronyms. Although most of them are spelled out on the exam, it is still helpful to know what they are!

- During the exam, you will have the opportunity to mark or flag questions to come back to later. It is advised that you take advantage of this, as you may be short on time and want to revisit only the questions you were doubtful about. Please note that any unanswered questions are marked INCORRECT, so it is best to at least try.

- The 10-minute exit survey is followed by your exam results—yes, instant and immediate results!

 Study: Remember to rely on your instincts. Typically, the first answer that comes to mind is often the right one!

Exam Scoring

The exams are scored on a scale from 125 to 200, where 170+ is considered passing. Please do not worry about how the questions are weighted, just do your best! Should you need to retake the exam, your application is valid for one year and therefore you will have three chances within the year to earn a score of 170 or more. Please consult the *Candidate Handbook* for more information.

After the Exam

Once you have passed the LEED Green Associate exam, remember to change your signature to reflect earning the credential! Remember, it is not appropriate to use "LEED GA," but instead use "LEED Green Associate." Although your certificate will not arrive immediately, remember—you must fulfill 15 hours of continuing education over the next two years. Please refer to the Credential Maintenance Program (CMP) handbook found on the USGBC website for more information. There is also a code of conduct you must abide by, as stipulated in the Disciplinary Policy posted on the GBCI website at www.gbci.org/Files/Disc_ExamAppeals_Policy.pdf. It states that individuals with LEED credentials must:

 TIP

Study: Although the Candidate Handbook includes some information about exam appeals, the Disciplinary Policy found on the GBCI website also includes the Exam Appeals Policy if needed.

- Be truthful, forthcoming, and cooperative in their dealings with GBCI.

- Be in continuous compliance with GBCI rules (as amended from time to time by GBCI).

- Respect GBCI intellectual property rights.

- Abide by laws related to the profession and to general public health and safety.

- Carry out their professional work in a competent and objective manner.

ONLINE RESOURCES

Visit this page from Business Insider for more study tips: www.businessinsider.com/study-hacks-for-final-exams-2013-12.

Visit this page for some additional study tips from USGBC: http://www.usgbc.org/articles/essential-leed-green-associate-cheat-sheet?mkt_tok=3RkMM JWWfF9wsRonuavJZKXonjHpfsX54u8qXa%2Bg38431UFwdcjKPmjr1YIASMF 0aPyQAgobGp5I5FENTLLYX7Nwt6AFUg%3D%3D

Appendix A

RATING SYSTEMS OVERVIEW

LEED® Green Building Certification Program Overview

REFERENCE GUIDE	RATING SYSTEM	APPLICABLE PROJECT TYPES
BD+C		**LEED for New Construction and Major Renovations™**
		• New buildings
		• Major renovations: HVAC, envelope and interior habitation
		• Commercial occupancies: offices, institutional, residential with nine or more stories
		• Complete more than 60% of leasable SF
		• Does not include K–12 schools, retail, data centers, warehouses and distribution centers, hospitality, or healthcare facilities
		LEED for Core & Shell™
		• Developer controls exterior shell and core mechanical, electrical, and plumbing units but not tenant fit-out
		• Control less than 40% of leasable SF
		LEED for Schools™
		• K–12 typically
		• Can also be used for nonacademic buildings: admin offices, maintenance facilities, dorms
		LEED for Healthcare™
		LEED for Retail: New Construction™
		LEED for Data Centers™
		LEED for Warehouses and Distribution Centers™
		LEED for Hospitality™
		LEED for Homes and Multifamily
		• Homes and Multifamily Lowrise for one to three stories
		• Multifamily Midrise for four to eight stories
O+M		**LEED for Existing Buildings: Operations & Maintenance™**
		• Applies to buildings new to LEED or previously certified under New Construction and Major Renovations, Core & Shell, or Schools
		• Commercial occupancies: offices, institutional, residential with nine or more stories

REFERENCE GUIDE	RATING SYSTEM	APPLICABLE PROJECT TYPES

O+M (*continued*)		• Applicable for:
		  • Building operations
		  • Process and system upgrades
		  • Minor space-use changes, facility alterations, and additions
		• Individual tenant spaces do not apply

	LEED for Existing Buildings: Schools™	
	LEED for Existing Buildings: Retail™	
	LEED for Existing Buildings: Hospitality™	
	LEED for Existing Buildings: Data Centers™	
	LEED for Existing Buildings: Warehouses and Distribution Centers™	
ID+C	LEED for Commercial Interiors™	

		• For tenant spaces:
		  • Office, retail, and institutional
		  • Tenant spaces that don't occupy entire building
		• Works hand-in-hand with LEED for Core & Shell

	LEED for Retail: Commercial Interiors™	
	LEED for Commercial Interiors: Hospitality™	
ND	LEED for Neighborhood Development™	
		• Neighborhoods (whole, fraction, or multiple)
		• Smaller infill projects
		• Larger mixed-use developments
		• Plan and Built Project

Appendix B

MINIMUM PROGRAM REQUIREMENTS (MPRs)

Minimum Program Requirements		
1	**MUST BE IN A PERMANENT LOCATION ON EXISTING LAND**[1]	
	ALL	All LEED projects must be designed for, constructed on, and operated on a permanent location on already existing land.
		No building or space that is designed to move at any point in its lifetime may pursue LEED certification.
2	**MUST USE A REASONABLE SITE BOUNDARY**[2]	
	ALL	The LEED project boundary must include all contiguous land that is associated with the project and supports its typical operations. This includes land altered as a result of construction and features used primarily by the project's occupants, such as hardscape (parking and sidewalks), septic or rainwater treatment equipment, and landscaping. The LEED boundary may not unreasonably exclude portions of the building, space, or site to give the project an advantage in complying with credit requirements. The LEED project must accurately communicate the scope of the certifying project in all promotional and descriptive materials and distinguish it from any non-certifying space.
3	**MUST COMPLY WITH PROJECT SIZE REQUIREMENTS**[3]	
	BD+C AND O+M	The LEED project must include a minimum of 1,000 square feet of gross floor area.
	ID+C	The LEED project must include a minimum of 250 square feet of gross floor area.
	ND	The LEED project should contain at least two habitable buildings and be no larger than 1,500 acres.
	HOMES	The LEED project must be defined as a "dwelling unit" by all applicable codes. This requirement includes, but is not limited to, the International Residential Code stipulation that a dwelling unit must include "permanent provisions for living, sleeping, eating, cooking, and sanitation."

NOTES

1. USGBC website, www.usgbc.org/node/2742910?return=/credits/new-construction/v4/minimum-program-requirements.

2. USGBC website, www.usgbc.org/node/2742911?return=/credits/new-construction/v4/minimum-program-requirements.

3. USGBC website, www.usgbc.org/node/2742912?return=/credits/new-construction/v4/minimum-program-requirements.

Appendix C

LEED® CERTIFICATION PROCESS

The Basic Steps in the LEED Certification Process

PROJECT REGISTRATION	
	Access to LEED Online
	❖ LEED Scorecard ❖ LEED Credit Templates
DESIGN APPLICATION PHASE (OPTIONAL)	
	Submit Credits and Prerequisites via LEED Online
	❖ Comes back "Anticipated" or "Denied" (25 days) ❖ No points awarded
	Clarification Request (25 days)
	Final Design Review (15 days)
	❖ Project team can: —ACCEPT: goes to Construction Application phase —APPEAL: goes to Design Appeal phase
DESIGN APPEAL PHASE	
	Changes made and submitted once again
	❖ Comes back "Anticipated" or "Denied" (25 days)
	No clarification requests
	Final Design Review (15 days)
CONSTRUCTION APPLICATION PHASE	
	Submit via LEED Online (both design and construction)
	❖ Comes back "Anticipated" or "Denied" (25 days) ❖ No points awarded yet
	Clarification Request (25 days)
	Final Construction Review (15 days)
	❖ Project team can: —ACCEPT: goes to Certification/Denial phase —APPEAL: goes to Construction Appeal phase

CONSTRUCTION APPEAL PHASE	
	Changes made and submitted once again
	❖ Comes back "Anticipated" or "Denied"
	No clarification requests
	Final Construction Review (15 days)
CERTIFIED/DENIAL PHASE	
	After Final Construction Review is ACCEPTED:
	❖ Certification Level Awards: Certified, Silver, Gold, or Platinum ❖ Denied: project closed (appeals should be done in prior phases)

Appendix D
MAIN CATEGORY SUMMARIES

Location & Transportation

Location

  Increase density

  Redevelopment and infill development

  Locate near existing infrastructure

  Protect habitat

  Increase diversity of uses

  Encourage multiple modes of transportation

Transportation (Design and Planning)

  Choose a site adjacent to mass transportation

  Limit parking capacity

  Encourage bicycling

Transportation (Operations)

  Encourage carpooling

  Encourage or provide alternative fuel vehicles

  Incentivize building user/employees

  Support alternative transportation

Neighborhood Pattern and Design

  Design walkable streets

  Include pedestrian amenities

  Use compact development strategies

  Promote connectivity

  Provide diverse land uses

  Create diverse community

  Support access to sustainable food

  Ensure easy access to grocery stores

Sustainable Sites

Site Design & Management

  Preserve open space and sensitive areas

  Minimize hardscape

  Use native landscaping

  Prevent light pollution

  Protect and restore habitat

Site Maintenance and Operations

Development a sustainable management plan

Implement conservation programs

Maintain site lighting to prevent light pollution

Rainwater Management (Design)

Minimize impervious areas

Control rainwater

Incorporate rainwater management into site design

Rainwater Management (Operations)

Redirect rainwater

Harvest rainwater

Heat Island Effect

Use reflective roof materials

Reduce the area of paved surfaces exposed to sunlight

Plan an urban forest or a green roof

Water Efficiency

Indoor Water Use Reduction

Install efficient plumbing fixtures

Use nonpotable water

Submeters

Outdoor Water Use Reduction

Implement native and adaptive plants

Xeriscaping

Install high-efficiency irrigation systems

Use nonpotable water

Submeters

Energy & Atmosphere

Energy Demand

Establish design and energy goals

Size the building appropriately

Use free energy

Insulate

Energy Efficiency

Address the envelope

Install high-performance mechanical systems and appliances

Use high-efficiency infrastructures

Capture efficiencies of scale

Use energy simulation

Monitor and verify performance

Renewable Energy

Generate onsite renewable energy

Purchase green power or RECs

Ongoing Energy Performance

Adhere to OPR

Training for staff

Preventative maintenance

Incentives for tenants and occupants

Materials & Resources

Conservation of Materials

Reuse existing buildings and salvaged materials

Plan for smaller, more compact communities

Design smaller, more flexible homes and buildings

Use efficient framing techniques

Environmentally, Socially, and Locally Preferable Materials

Identify local sources of environmentally preferable products

Specify green materials

Specify green custodial products

Waste Management and Reduction (Design)

Design buildings that produce less waste

Develop a construction waste management policy

Establish a tracking system

Waste Management and Reduction (Operations)

Develop a solid waste management policy

Conduct a waste stream audit

Maintain a recycling program

Monitor, track, and report

Compost

Recycle durable goods

Indoor Environmental Quality

Indoor Air Quality (Design)

Prohibit smoking

Properly size the ventilation system

Protect the air coming into the building

Test for radon

Design for entryway systems

Specify low-emitting materials

Indoor Air Quality (Construction)

Keep the building clean

Protect absorptive materials

Conduct a flush-out

Indoor Air Quality (Operations)

Ensure adequate ventilation

Monitor airflow

Monitor carbon dioxide

Calibrate sensors

Prohibit smoking

Employ a green cleaning program

Conduct a custodial effectiveness assessment

Maintain entryway systems

Use integrated pest management

Thermal Comfort

Install operable windows

Give occupants temperature and ventilation control

Conduct occupant surveys

Lighting

Use daylighting

Give occupants lighting control

Conduct occupant surveys

Appendix E

TRADE-OFFS AND SYNERGIES

Trade-offs and Synergies Summary

RAINWATER MANAGEMENT
Synergies:
Reuse for flushing toilets or urinals
Reuse to water landscaping
Increase pervious pavement to recharge groundwater
Reduces pollutants from entering water bodies
CAPTURING RAINWATER
Synergies:
Reuse for flushing toilets or urinals
Reuse to water landscaping
Reduces rainwater runoff
CHOOSING A BROWNFIELD SITE OR PREVIOUSLY DEVELOPED SITE
Synergies:
Development density (infrastructure exists)
Community connectivity
Public transportation access
Preserves open space, habitat, and greenfield sites
LIMIT PARKING
Synergies:
Helps to maximize open space
Reduces heat island effect
Rainwater management opportunities with paving materials
Encourages the use of mass transit
VEGETATED ROOF
Synergies:
Reduces rainwater runoff from roof
Reduces heat island effect
Provides thermal barrier to save energy
Qualifies as open space and preserved habitat

Trade-offs:

Can be costly and challenging to coordinate

Reduces the amount of rainwater to be captured for nonpotable water uses

WATER EFFICIENT LANDSCAPING

Synergies:

Xeriscaping can provide buffers can help to optimize energy performance

Xeriscaping can add efficiencies to passive designs

Vegetation can restore habitat

Reduces demand for potable water

INCREASED VENTILATION

Synergies:

Improves air quality

Operable windows contribute to earning Thermal Comfort credit

Natural ventilation reduces operating costs

Trade-offs:

Requires mechanical systems to work harder to heat and cool

Increases HVAC capacity

Increases capital and operating costs

BUILDING AND MATERIAL REUSE

Synergies:

Reduces the need for virgin raw materials

Reduces burden on budget as new typically costs more

Reduces landfill contribution

DAYLIGHTING

Synergies:

Reduces need for artificial lighting

Provides connection to exterior environment for occupants

Trade-offs:

Windows provide poor thermal break

Increases glare problems for occupants

Requires increased heating loads in winter and higher cooling loads in summer

PROVIDING OPERABLE WINDOWS

Synergies:

Increases natural ventilation

Operable windows contribute to earning Thermal Comfort credit

Trade-offs:

Can cause acoustic issues

Appendix F

SAMPLE LEED FOR NEW CONSTRUCTION™ SCORECARD

LEED for New Construction and Major Renovations (v4)

	POSSIBLE: 1
Credit Integrative process	1

LOCATION & TRANSPORTATION	POSSIBLE: 16
Credit LEED for Neighborhood Development location	16
Credit Sensitive land protection	1
Credit High priority site	2
Credit Surrounding density and diverse uses	5
Credit Acccess to quality transit	5
Credit Bicycle facilities	1
Credit Reduced parking footprint	1
Credit Green vehicles	1

SUSTAINABLE SITES	POSSIBLE: 10
Prereq Construction activity pollution prevention	REQUIRED
Credit Site assessment	1
Credit Site development - protect or restore habitat	2
Credit Open space	1
Credit Rainwater management	3
Credit Heat island reduction	2
Credit Light pollution reduction	1

WATER EFFICIENCY	POSSIBLE: 11
Prereq Outdoor water use reduction	REQUIRED
Prereq Indoor water use reduction	REQUIRED
Prereq Building-level water metering	REQUIRED
Credit Outdoor water use reduction	2
Credit Indoor water use reduction	6
Credit Cooling lower water use	2
Credit Water metering	1

ENERGY & ATMOSPHERE	POSSIBLE: 33
Prereq Fundamental commissioning and verification	REQUIRED
Prereq Minimum energy performance	REQUIRED
Prereq Building-level energy metering	REQUIRED
Prereq Fundamental refrigerant management	REQUIRED
Credit Enhanced commissioning	6
Credit Optimize energy performance	18
Credit Advanced energy metering	1
Credit Demand response	2
Credit Renewable energy production	3
Credit Enhanced refrigerant management	1
Credit Green power and carbon offsets	2

MATERIAL & RESOURCES	POSSIBLE: 13
Prereq Storage and collection of recyclables	REQUIRED
Prereq Construction and demolition waste management planning	REQUIRED
Credit Building life-cycle impact reduction	5
Credit Building product disclosure and optimization - environmental product declarations	2
Credit Building product disclosure and optimization - sourcing of raw materials	2
Credit Building product disclosure and optimization - material ingredients	2
Credit Construction and demolition waste management	2

INDOOR ENVIRONMENTAL QUALITY	POSSIBLE: 16
Prereq Minimum IAQ performance	REQUIRED
Prereq Environmental tobacco smoke control	REQUIRED
Credit Enhanced IAQ strategies	2
Credit Low-emilling materials	3
Credit Construction IAQ management plan	1
Credit IAQ assessment	2
Credit Thermal comfort	1
Credit Interior lighting	2
Credit Daylight	3
Credit Quality views	1
Credit Acoustic performance	1

INNOVATION	POSSIBLE: 6
Credit Innovation	5
Credit LEED Accredited Professional	1

REGIONAL PRIORITY	POSSIBLE: 4
Credit Regional priority	4

TOTAL	110

40-49 Points	50-59 Points	60-79 Points	80+ Points
CERTIFIED	SILVER	GOLD	PLATINUM

Appendix G

SAMPLE CREDIT[1]

SS CREDIT OPEN SPACE

1 Point

Intent

To create exterior open space that encourages interaction with the environment, social interaction, passive recreation, and physical activities.

Requirements

Provide outdoor space greater than or equal to 30 percent of the total site area (including building footprint). A minimum of 25 percent of that outdoor space must be vegetated (turf grass does not count as vegetation) or have overhead vegetated canopy.

The outdoor space must be physically accessible and be one or more of the following:

- A pedestrian-oriented paving or turf area with physical site elements that accommodate outdoor social activities
- A recreation-oriented paving or turf area with physical site elements that encourage physical activity
- A garden space with a diversity of vegetation types and species that provide opportunities for year-round visual interest
- A garden space dedicated to community gardens or urban food production
- Preserved or created habitat that meets the criteria of SS Credit Site Development—Protect or Restore Habitat and also includes elements of human interaction

For projects that achieve a density of 1.5 floor-area ratio (FAR), and are physically accessible, extensive, or intensive, vegetated roofs can be used toward the minimum 25 percent vegetation requirement, and qualifying roof-based physically accessible paving areas can be used toward credit compliance.

Wetlands or naturally designed ponds may count as open space if the side slope gradients average 1:4 (vertical:horizontal) or less and are vegetated.

For projects that are part of a multitenant complex only, open space can be either adjacent to the building or at another location in the site master plan. The open space may be at another master plan development site as long as it is protected from development. If the open space is not adjacent to the building, provide documentation showing that the requirements have been met and the land is in a natural state or has been returned to a natural state and conserved for the life of the building.

NOTES

1. USGBC website, www.usgbc.org/node/2613129?return=/credits/new-construction/v4/sustainable-sites.

Appendix H

REFERENCED STANDARDS

Referenced Standards for the LEED® Green Associate Exam

LT		
	KEYWORDS	**STANDARD**
	Site Selection	USDA, U.S. Code of Federal Regulations Title 7, Volume 6, Parts 400 to 699, Section 657.5
		U.S. Fish and Wildlife Service, List of Threatened and Endangered Species
		NatureServe Heritage Program, GH, G1, and G2 species and ecological communities
		FEMA Flood Zone Designations
		U.S. Environmental Protection Agency, National Priority List
		U.S. Housing and Urban Development, Federal Empowerment Zone, Federal Enterprise Community; and Federal Renewal Community
		U.S. Department of Treasury, Community Development Financial Institutions Fund
		U.S. Department of Housing and Urban Development, Qualified Census Tracts and Difficult Development Areas
	Reduced Parking Footprint	Institute of Transportation Engineers, *Transportation Planning Handbook*, 3rd ed., Tables 18-2 through 18-4
	Green Vehicles	American Council for Energy Efficient Economy (ACEEE)
		Society of Automotive Engineers, SAE Surface Vehicle Recommended Practice J1772, SAE Electric Vehicle; Conductive Charge Coupler
		International Electrical Commission 62196
SS		
	KEYWORDS	**STANDARD**
	Construction Activity Pollution Prevention	EPA, Construction General Permit
	Site Assessment	ASTM E1527-05 Phase I Environmental Site Assessment
		ASTM E1903-97 Phase II Environmental Site Analysis
		Natural Resources Conservation Service, Soils
		TR-55 Initial Water Storage Capacity
	Site Development	US EPA ecoregions
		Land Trust Alliance accreditation
		Sustainable Sites Initiative (SITES™)
		Natural Resources Conservation Service, web soil survey

	Rainwater Management	U.S. EPA Technical Guidance on Implementing the Rainwater Runoff Requirements for Federal Projects under Section 438 of the Energy Independence and Security Act
	Heat Island Effect	ASTM E903-96 and E892
		Cool Roof Rating Council Standard (CRRC-1)
	Light Pollution Reduction	Illuminating Engineering Society and International Dark Sky Association (IES/IDA) Model Lighting Ordinance User Guide and IES TM-15-11, Addendum A

WE		
	KEYWORDS	**STANDARD**
	Water Use Reduction	Energy Policy Act (EPAct) 1992 became law in 2005
		Energy Policy Act (EPAct) 2005
		International Association of Plumbing and Mechanical Officials Publication (IAPMO)
		International Association of Plumbing and Mechanical Officials Publication IAPMO/ANSI UPC 1-2006, Uniform Plumbing Code 2006, Section 402.0, Water-Conserving Fixtures and Fittings
		ICC, International Plumbing Code (IPC), 2006
		ENERGY STAR
		Consortium for Energy Efficiency
		WaterSense
		IgCC/ASHRAE 189.1 cooling tower and evaporative condenser requirements

EA		
	KEYWORDS	**STANDARD**
	Commissioning	ASHRAE Guideline 0–2005, The Commissioning Process
		ASHRAE Guideline 1.1–2007, HVAC&R Technical Requirements for the Commissioning Process
		NIBS Guideline 3–2012, Exterior Enclosure Technical Requirements for the Commissioning Process
	Energy Performance	ASHRAE/IESNA 90.1-2010
		ASHRAE 50% Advanced Energy Design Guides
		Advanced Buildings Core Performance Guide
		COMNET Commercial Buildings Energy Modeling Guidelines
	Metering	Electricity. American National Standards Institute, ANSI C12.20, Class 0.2
		Natural gas. American National Standards Institute, ANSI B109
		Thermal energy (Btu meter or heat meter). EN Standard, EN-1434

	Refrigerant Mgmt, CFCs, HCFCs, HFCs	U.S. EPA Clean Air Act, Title VI, Section 608, Refrigerant Recycling Rule
	Renewable Energy	Center for Resource Solutions Green-e Program
		Commercial Building Energy Consumption Survey (CBECS)
	Green Power and Carbon Offsets	Green-e Energy and Green-e Climate
		U.S. Department of Energy's Commercial Buildings Energy Consumption Survey (CBECS)
		Building Owners and Managers Association (BOMA)
		ENERGY STAR Portfolio Manager: Methodology for Greenhouse Gas Inventory and Tracking Calculations
		Inventory of U.S. Greenhouse Gas Emissions and Sinks: 1990–2010. Annex 2 Methodology and Data for Estimating CO2 Emissions from Fossil Fuel Combustion
		2006 IPCC Guidelines for National Greenhouse Gas Inventories
		eGRID2012 Version 1.0—U.S. Environmental Protection Agency
		WRI-WBCSD Greenhouse Gas Protocol
MR		
	KEYWORDS	**STANDARD**
	Construction and Demolition Waste Management	Certification of Sustainable Recyclers
		European Commission Waste Framework Directive 2008/98/EC
		European Commission Waste Incineration Directive 2000/76/EC
		EN 303-1—1999/A1—2003, Heating boilers with forced draught burners, terminology, general requirements, testing and marking
		EN 303-2—1998/A1—2003, Heating boilers with forced draught burners, special requirements for boilers with atomizing oil burners
		EN 303-3—1998/AC—2006, Gas-fired central heating boilers, assembly comprising a boiler body and a forced draught burner
		EN 303-4—1999, Heating boilers with forced draught burners, special requirements for boilers with forced draught oil burners with outputs up to 70 kW and a maximum operating pressure of three bar, terminology, special requirements, testing and marking
		EN 303-5—2012, Heating boilers for solid fuels, manually and automatically stoked, nominal heat output of up to 500 kW
		EN 303-6—2000, Heating boilers with forced draught burners, specific requirements for the domestic hot water operation of combination boilers with atomizing oil burners of nominal heat input not exceeding 70 kW

		EN 303-7—2006, Gas-fired central heating boilers equipped with a forced draught burner of nominal heat output not exceeding 1000 kW
	Life-Cycle Impact	ISO 14044
		National Register of Historic Places
		Secretary of Interior's Standards for the Treatment of Historic Properties
	Product Disclosure: EPDs	International Standard ISO14021-1999: Environmental Labels and Declarations—Self Declared Claims (Type II Environmental Labeling)
		International Standard ISO 14025–2006, Environmental Labels and Declarations (Type III Environmental Declarations—Principles and Procedures)
		International Standard ISO 14040–2006, Environmental Management, life-cycle assessment principles, and frameworks
	Product Disclosure: Sourcing of Raw Materials	Global Reporting Initiative (GRI) Sustainability Report
		Organization for Economic Co-operation and Development (OECD) Guidelines for Multinational Enterprises
		U.N. Global Compact, Communication of Progress
		ISO 26000—2010 Guidance on Social Responsibility
		Forest Stewardship Council
		Sustainable Agriculture Network
		The Rainforest Alliance
		ASTM Test Method D6866
		International Standards ISO 14021–1999, Environmental Labels and Declarations—Self Declared Environmental Claims (Type II Environmental Labeling)
	Product Disclosure: Material Ingredients	Chemical Abstracts Service
		Health Product Declaration
		Cradle-to-Cradle Certified CM Product Standard
		Registration, Evaluation, Authorization and Restriction of Chemicals (REACH)
		GreenScreen
EQ		
	KEYWORDS	**STANDARD**
	IAQ Performance	ASHRAE 62.1-2010
		ASHRAE Standard 170–2008
		CEN Standard EN 15251–2007

	CEN Standard EN 13779–2007
	CIBSE Applications Manual AM10, March 2005
	ASHRAE Standard 52.2–2007
	Chartered Institution of Building Services Engineers (CIBSE) Applications Manual AM10, March 2005
	Chartered Institution of Building Services Engineers (CIBSE) Applications Manual 13, 2000
	National Ambient Air Quality Standards (NAAQS):
IAQ Assessment	ASTM D5197–09e1 Standard Test Method for Determination of Formaldehyde and Other Carbonyl Compounds in Air (Active Sampler Methodology)
	ASTM D5149–02(2008) Standard Test Method for Ozone in the Atmosphere: Continuous Measurement by Ethylene Chemiluminescence:
	ISO 16000-3, Indoor air–Part 3: Determination of formaldehyde and other carbonyl compounds in indoor air and test chamber air—Active sampling method
	ISO 16000-6, Indoor air–Part 6: Determination of volatile organic compounds in indoor and test chamber airby active sampling on Tenax TA sorbent, thermal desorption and gas chromatography using MS or MS-FID
	ISO 4224 Ambient air—Determination of carbon monoxide—Nondispersive infrared spectrometric method
	ISO 7708 Air quality—Particle size fraction definitions for health-related sampling
	ISO 13964 Air quality—Determination of ozone in ambient air—Ultraviolet photometric method
	U.S. EPA Compendium of Methods for the Determination of Air Pollutants in Indoor Air, IP-1: Volatile Organic Compounds, IP-3: Carbon Monoxide and Carbon Dioxide, IP-6: Formaldehyde and other aldehydes/ ketones, IP-10 Volatile Organic Compounds
	U.S. EPA Compendium of Methods for the Determination of Inorganic Compounds in Ambient Air, TO-1: Volatile Organic Compounds, TO-11: Formaldehyde, TO-15: Volatile Organic Compounds, TO-17: Volatile Organic Compounds
	California Department of Public Health, Standard Method for the Testing and Evaluation of Volatile Organic Chemical Emissions from Indoor Sources using Environmental Chambers, v1.1–2010
Environmental Tobacco Smoke Control	Standard Test Method for Determining Air Leakage Rate by Fan Pressurization, ASTM E779-03
	Standard Test Methods for Determining Airtightness of Buildings Using an Orifice Blower Door, ASTM E1827-11

		Nondestructive testing, leak testing—Criteria for method and technique selection, CEN Standard EN 1779—1999
		Nondestructive testing, leak testing, tracer gas method, CEN Standard EN 13185—2001
		Nondestructive testing, leak testing, calibration of reference leaks for gases, CEN Standard EN 13192—2001
		RESNET Standards
		ENERGY STAR Multifamily Testing Protocol
	Acoustics	AHRI Standard 885–2008, Procedure for Estimating Occupied Space Sound Levels in the Application of Air Terminals and Air Outlets
		American National Standards Institute (ANSI)/ASHRAE Standard S12.60–2010, Acoustical Performance Criteria, Design Requirements, and Guidelines for Schools
		2011 HVAC Applications, ASHRAE Handbook, Chapter 48, Noise and Vibration Control
		NRC-CNRC Construction Technology Update No. 51, Acoustic Design of Rooms for Speech, 2002
		ASHRAE 2011, HVAC Applications Handbook, Chapter 48, Noise and Vibration Control
		AHRI Standard 885–2008
		ANSI S1.4, Performance Measurement Protocols for Commercial Buildings
		2010 Noise and Vibration Guidelines for Health Care Facilities
		FGI Guidelines for Design and Construction of Health Care Facilities, 2010 edition
		ANSI T1.523–2001, Telecom Glossary
		E966, Standard Guide for Field Measurements of Airborne Sound Insulation of Building Facades and Facade Elements
	Construction IAQ Management, Pollutant Control, MERV	Sheet Metal and Air-Conditioning National Contractors Association (SMACNA) IAQ Guidelines for Occupied Buildings under Construction, 2nd edition, 2007, ANSI/SMACNA 008–2008 (Chapter 3)
		ASHRAE 52.2–2007
		CEN Standard EN 779–2002
		British Standard 5228—2009 (Healthcare)
		Infection Control Risk Assessment (ICRA) Standard, published by the American Society of Healthcare Engineering (ASHE) and the U.S. Centers for Disease Control and Prevention (CDC) (Healthcare)
		NIOSH, Asphalt Fume Exposures During the Application of Hot Asphalt to Roofs, Publication No. 2003-112 (Healthcare)

VOCs, IAQ, Low-emitting materials	CDPH Standard Method v1.1–2010
	ISO 17025
	ISO Guide 65
	AgBB—2010
	ISO 16000 parts 3, 6, 7, 11
	Hong Kong Air Pollution Control Regulation
	CARB 93120 ATCM
Low-Emitting Materials, Adhesives and Sealants, IAQ	Coast Air Quality Management District (SCAQMD) Rule 1168
	Green Seal Standard 36 (GS-36) Commercial Adhesives
Low-Emitting Materials, Paints and Coatings	South Coast Air Quality Management District (SCAQMD) Rule 1113
IAQ	European Decopaint Directive
	Canadian VOC Concentration Limits for Architectural Coatings
Low-Emitting Materials, Furniture, IAQ	ANSI/BIFMA M7.1 Standard Test Method for Determining VOC Emissions from Office Furniture Systems, Components and Seating
	ANSI/BIFMA e3–2011 Furniture Sustainability Standard
Thermal Comfort	ASHRAE Standard 55–2010, Thermal Environmental Conditions for Human Occupancy
	"ASHRAE *HVAC Applications Handbook,* 2011 ed., Chapter 5, Places of Assembly, Typical Natatorium Design Conditions"
	ISO 7730–2005 Ergonomics of the thermal environment, Analytical determination and interpretation of thermal comfort using calculation of the PMV and PPD indices and local thermal comfort criteria
	EuropeanStandard EN 15251: 2007, Indoor environmental input parameters for design and assessment of energy performance of buildings addressing indoor air quality, thermal environment, lighting and acoustics
Interior Lighting	*The Lighting Handbook,* 10th ed., Illuminating Engineering Society of North America
Daylighting	IIES Lighting Measurements (LM) 83-12, Approved Method: IES Spatial Daylight Autonomy (sDA) and Annual Sunlight Exposure (ASE)
	The Lighting Handbook, 10th ed., Illuminating Engineering Society
Views	Windows and Offices: A Study of Office Worker Performance and the Indoor Environment

Appendix I

ABBREVIATIONS AND ACRONYMS

AFV	alternative fuel vehicle
AIA	American Institute of Architects
ALP	ENERGY STAR Advanced Lighting Package
ANSI	American National Standards Institute
AP	LEED® Accredited Professional
ASE	annual sun exposure
ASHRAE	American Society of Heating, Refrigerating, and Air-Conditioning Engineers
ASTM	American Society for Testing and Materials
BAS	building automation system
BD+C	Building Design + Construction (LEED AP credential and also a reference guide)
BEES	Building for Environmental and Economic Sustainability software by NIST
BIFMA	Business and Institutional Furniture Manufacturer's Association
BIPV	building integrated photovoltaics
BIM	building information modeling
BMP	best management practice
BOD	basis of design
BOMA	Building Owners and Managers Association
BUG	backlight-uplight glare
CAE	combined annual efficiency
CBECS	Commercial Building Energy Consumption Survey (by DOE)
CDL	construction, demolition, and land clearing
CFA	conditioned floor area
CFC	chlorofluorocarbon
CFL	compact fluorescent light
CFM	cubic feet per minute
CFR	U.S. Code of Federal Regulations
CI	Commercial Interiors (LEED rating system)
CIR	Credit Interpretation Ruling
CMP	Credentialing Maintenance Program
CO	carbon monoxide
CO_2	carbon dioxide
COC	chain of custody
COP	coefficient of performance
CRI	Carpet and Rug Institute
CS	Core & Shell (LEED rating system)
CSI	Construction Specifications Institute

CWMP	construction waste management plan
Cx	commissioning
CxA	commissioning agent or authority
DHW	domestic hot water
DOE	U.S. Department of Energy
EA	Energy & Atmosphere category
ECB	energy cost budget
ECM	energy conservation measures
EER	energy efficiency rating
EERE	U.S. Office of Energy Efficiency and Renewable Energy
EF	energy factor
EPA	U.S. Environmental Protection Agency
EPAct	U.S. Energy Policy Act of 1992 or 2005
EPD	environmental product declaration
EPEAT	electronic product environmental assessment tools
EPP	environmentally preferable purchasing
ESA	environmental site assessment
ESC	erosion and sedimentation control
ET	evapotranspiration
ETS	environmental tobacco smoke
EQ	Indoor Environmental Quality category
FEMA	U.S. Federal Emergency Management Agency
FF&E	fixtures, furnishings, and equipment
FSC	Forest Stewardship Council
FTE	full-time equivalent
GBCI	Green Buildings Certification Institute
GF	glazing factor
GHG	greenhouse gas
GI	green infrastructure
GIS	Geographic Information System
GPF	gallons per flush
GPM	gallons per minute
GWP	global warming potential
HCFC	hydrochlorofluorocarbon
HEPA	high-efficiency particle absorbing
HERS	Home Energy Rating Standards
HET	high-efficiency toilet
HFC	hydrofluorocarbon
HPD	health product declaration
HVAC	heating, ventilation, and air conditioning
HVAC&R	heating, ventilating, air conditioning, and refrigeration

IAP	ENERGY STAR with Indoor Air Package
IAQ	indoor air quality
ICF	insulated concrete form
ID	Innovation category
ID+C	Interior Design + Construction (LEED AP credential and also a reference guide)
IDR	Innovative Design Request (only for LEED for Homes)
IEQ	Indoor Environmental Quality category
IESNA	Illuminating Engineering Society of North America
IGCC	International Green Code Council
IPD	integrated project delivery
IPM	integrated pest management
IPMVP	International Performance Measurement and Verification Protocol
ISO	International Organization for Standardization
KW	kilowatt
KWH	kilowatts per hour
LCA	life-cycle assessment
LCC	life-cycle cost
LCGWP	life-cycle global warming potential
LCODP	life-cycle ozone depletion potential
LED	light-emitting diode
LEED	Leadership in Energy and Environmental Design
LEFE	low-emitting fuel-efficient vehicle
LID	low-impact development
LPD	lighting power density
LT	Location & Transportation category
MDF	medium-density fiberboard
MERV	minimum efficiency reporting value
MPR	Minimum Program Requirement
MR	Materials & Resources category
MSDS	material safety data sheet
M&V	measure and verification
NBI	New Building Institute
NC	New Construction (LEED for New Construction & Major Renovations rating system)
ND	Neighborhood Development (LEED for Neighborhood Development rating system)
NIST	National Institute of Standards and Technology
ODP	ozone-depleting potential
O&M	operations and maintenance
O+M	Operations + Maintenance (LEED AP credential and also a reference guide)
OPR	owner's project requirements
OSB	oriented strand board
PMV	predicted mean vote

PPD	predicted percentage dissatisfied
PV	photovoltaic
PVC	polyvinyl chloride
REC	renewable energy certification
RESNET	Residential Energy Services Network
RFP	request for proposal
RP	Regional Priority category
SCAQMD	South Coast Air Quality Management District
SCS	Scientific Certification Systems
SDA	spatial daylight autonomy
SEER	seasonal energy efficiency rating
SHGC	solar heat gain coefficient
SIP	structural insulated panel
SMACNA	Sheet Metal and Air-Conditioning Contractor's Association
SS	Sustainable Sites category
SR	solar reflectance
SRI	solar reflectivity index
TAG	Technical Advisory Group
TASC	Technical Advisory Subcommittee
TP	total phosphorus
TRACI	Tool for the Reduction and Assessment of Chemical and Other Environmental Impacts
TSS	total suspended solids
Tvis	visible transmittance
UL	Underwriter's Laboratory
USGBC	U.S. Green Building Council
VOC	volatile organic compound
WE	Water Efficiency category
WF	water factor
WFA	window-to-floor ratio
WWR	window-to-wall ratio
ZEV	zero emission vehicle

Appendix J

ANSWERS TO QUIZ QUESTIONS

CHAPTER 1: UNDERSTANDING THE CREDENTIALING PROCESS

Q1.1   **A.** The credentialing system is composed of five types of LEED® APs at the second tier: BD+C, ID+C, Homes, ND, and O+M.

Q1.2   **A.** Yes, it is possible to sit for two exams in one day: the LEED Green Associate and any of the LEED AP + exams.

Q1.3   **B.** No, LEED project experience is no longer required in order to sit for any of the LEED AP + exams, according to the LEED candidate handbooks.

Q1.4   **D.** You will have one year after you register and paid for the exam to schedule and sit for the LEED Green Associate™ exam.

Q1.5   **C.** Leadership in Energy and Environmental Design.

CHAPTER 2: INTRODUCTION TO THE CONCEPTS OF SUSTAINABLE DESIGN

Q2.1   **E.** All of the four options listed are environmental benefits of green building design, construction, and operational efforts.

Q2.2   **B.** According to the EPA website, Americans typically spend about 90 percent of their time indoors.

Q2.3   **A.** Thirty-eight percent of energy in the United States is used for space heating, followed by lighting with 20 percent of energy usage.

Q2.4   **E.** All of the four options listed describe high-performance green building strategies.

Q2.5   **A and C**. When studying about LEED, you will see multiple references to the built environment and must understand what the term is referring to.

Q2.6   **A.** Incorporating green building strategies and technologies is best started from the very beginning of the design process. Schematic Design is the earliest phase of the design process, and therefore the correct answer.

Q2.7   **A.** It is important to remember that LCAs not only look at the present impacts and benefits during each phase of the process but future and potential impacts as well.

Q2.8   **B and C**. LCAs include the purchase price, installation, operation, maintenance, and upgrade costs for each technology and strategy proposed.

CHAPTER 3: INTEGRATIVE PROCESS

Q3.1   **A and B**. Charrettes are an important part of the iterative process to ensure an integrative approach for green building projects. An agenda and stipulated goals are needed in order to produce specific deliverables. The facilitator has an extremely important role as his or her approach can dictate a charrette's success.

Q3.2   **C.** Stakeholder meetings typically include those with a vested interest in the project, such as neighbors and members of the community.

Q3.3   **B and C.** Goals can be both quantitative and qualitative.

Q3.4   **D.** Goals should be clear and measurable.

Q3.5   **B and D.** Remember, the ideal strategy is to award to the best low bid, not necessarily the lowest bid, when working on an IPD project.

Q3.6   **A and C.** The integrative process encourages more collaboration up front to avoid changes later.

Q3.7   **C and D.** Biomimicry is the science of using nature to solve human problems by imitating life. Permaculture encompasses the concepts of ecological design and construction practices to embrace nature and not work against it. Think about how hot air rises, how water moves, or the natural pattern of tree growth. By understanding how nature would respond, project teams can apply the same concepts to evaluate strategies and technologies to implement into sustainable projects.

Q3.8   **B and C.** The LEED Green Associate exam can be a bit overwhelming if you are not familiar with green building terms and acronyms. Refer to Appendix I and make flashcards for any acronyms you are not familiar with.

CHAPTER 4: THIRD-PARTY VERIFICATION

Q4.1   **E.** It is not possible to register a project with a certification level indicated.

Q4.2   **D.** Refer to the USGBC® website to download the Trademark Policy at www.usgbc.org/Docs/Archive/General/Docs3885.pdf.

Q4.3   **A.** GBCI™ is responsible for the appeals process as well as managing the certification bodies. It is best to remember USGBC as an education provider for the LEED rating systems they create, and GBCI as being responsible for the professional accreditation and project certification processes.

Q4.4   **A and C.** CIRs are submitted electronically to the project's assigned GBCI™ certification body for review through LEED-Online. CIRs are limited to 600 words and should not be formatted as a letter. Since the CIR is submitted electronically through LEED-Online, the project and credit or prerequisite information is tracked; therefore, the CIR does not need to include this type of information. It is critical to remember that CIRs are submitted specific to one credit or prerequisite.

Q4.5   **B and C.** Certification bodies are managed by GBCI and are assigned to a project team after registration, to assist with the process for a project seeking LEED certification, including the review of and response to CIRs. GBCI is responsible for the appeals process.

CHAPTER 5: THE LEED GREEN BUILDING CERTIFICATION PROGRAM

Q5.1   **A.** A project's LEED certification can expire, but only within one rating system: LEED for Existing Buildings: Operations & Maintenance. Certification is valid for five years, at which time (or before) recertification can be pursued.

Q5.2   **C.** LEED for Commercial Interiors is best suited for tenant spaces within office, retail, and institutional project types, specifically tenant spaces that do not occupy an entire building. LEED for Commercial Interiors goes hand-in-hand with the LEED for Core & Shell rating system.

Q5.3   **D.** The LEED for Core & Shell rating system is best suited for new construction projects where the developer/owner will occupy less than 40 percent of the leasable square footage.

Q5.4   **B and D.** LEED for Neighborhood Development has different categories than the other rating systems including: Smart Location & Linkages, Neighborhood Pattern and Design, and Green Infrastructure and Buildings.

Q5.5   **A.** LEED for Homes is the only rating system where a project can earn or lose points according to the number of bedrooms and the size of the house. Project teams use the Home Size Adjustment tool detailed in the LEED for Homes Reference Guide to determine if their project will have points credited or deducted based on the proposed size of the home.

Q5.6   **B.** Prerequisites are absolutely required just as minimum project requirements (MPRs) are for any project seeking LEED certification.

Q5.7   **B.** LEED for Existing Buildings: Operations & Maintenance is the best rating system for this project, as it involves only HVAC replacement and no other renovations. For the purposes of the exam, it is important to remember the project types applicable for each of the rating systems.

Q5.8   **B, C, and D.** USGBC consulted with NIST and the U.S. EPA's TRACI tool to determine the credit weightings for LEED 2009, not V4.

Q5.9   **C.** Ultimately, it is up to the project team to decide which rating system is best suited to their project. A LEED for Universities rating system does not exist.

Q5.10   **E.** The *LEED Reference Guide for Building Design and Construction* (BD+C) is the resource for projects seeking LEED for New Construction and Major Renovations, LEED for Core & Shell, LEED for Schools, LEED for Healthcare, LEED for Hospitality, LEED for Data Centers, LEED for Warehouses and Distribution Centers, or LEED for Retail certification.

Q5.11   **B and D.** This question relates to the goals of LEED. Be sure to make a flashcard to remember the seven impact categories used to weigh credits.

Q5.12   **A and B.** Although the strategies listed will increase the first costs for a project, it is important to remember the life-cycle costs, including purchase price, installation, operation, maintenance, and upgrade costs.

Q5.13   **A.** Make sure to remember the point range scales of the LEED certification levels for the purposes of the exam.

Q5.14   **D.** Use Appendix A to refer to some key concepts to remember about the rating systems for the purposes of the exam.

Q5.15   **B and C.** Make a flash card to remember the three association factors used to weight the credits of the LEED v4 rating systems: relative efficacy, duration, and control.

CHAPTER 6: ESSENTIAL LEED CONCEPTS

Q6.1   **C.** LEED BD+C and LEED O+M projects must include a minimum of 1,000 square feet of gross floor area, while LEED ID+C projects must include a minimum of 250 square feet of gross floor area. LEED for Neighborhood Development projects are required to contain at least two habitable buildings and cannot be larger than 1,500 acres.

Q6.2   **D.** LEED for Core & Shell is the only rating system that can be precertified in order to help marketing efforts to lease the building.

Q6.3   **C and E.** Make a note on your cheat sheet or create a flashcard to help you to remember rating system specific details.

Q6.4   **A and E.** LEED BD+C and LEED O+M projects must include a minimum of 1,000 square feet of gross floor area, while LEED ID+C projects must include a minimum of 250 square feet of gross floor area.

Q6.5   **B.** All projects seeking LEED certification must agree to comply with the three minimum program requirements.

Q6.6   **B and E.** Appeals are electronically submitted to GBCI through LEED-Online for a fee, within 25 business days after the final results from a design or construction certification review are posted to LEED-Online.

Q6.7   **B and D.** Make a note on your cheat sheet or create a flashcard to help you to remember rating system specific details. MPRs exist for each of the rating systems. Each project team member will log into LEED Online using their USGBC account login information and then will be able to access each of the projects they have been invited to and/or registered.

Q6.8   **B.** Although design reviews can be beneficial, points are not awarded until final review after construction.

Q6.9   **D and E.** Registering with GBCI indicates a project is seeking LEED certification. GBCI assigns a certification body to help a project team through the process and to answer any CIRs. Project registration can be completed at any time, although it is strongly encouraged to do so as early as possible. GBCI does not grant the award of any points regardless when registration occurs. Registration will, however, grant the project team access to a LEED-Online site specific for the project, but does not include any free submissions of CIRs.

Q6.10   **A and C.** Although registering a project requires some information, including contact information, project location, and indication of compliance with MPRs, a team must submit all credit templates for all prerequisites and attempted credits during the certification application. Required supplemental documentation, such as plans and calculations, must be uploaded as well.

Q6.11   **C.** The earliest construction prerequisites and credits can be submitted, along with design prerequisites and credits, for certification review is after substantial completion.

Q6.12   **C.** It is important to remember that points are awarded only once the project team submits for construction review, not at the design phase certification review. Design-side review is optional and therefore not required.

Q6.13   **B.** Project teams have 25 business days to issue an appeal to GBCI after receiving the final review comments.

Q6.14   **B, C, and F.** CIRs can be submitted through LEED-Online's formal inquiry page, to the GBCI certification body assigned to the project, any time after registration. CIRs specifically address one MPR, prerequisite, or credit. Although the project administrator submits the CIR, the credit interpretation ruling is viewable by all team members invited to the LEED-Online site for the project. CIRs are project specific, and therefore will not be published to the online database as they once were.

Q6.15   **A, D, and E.** Although it is strongly encouraged to begin the integrative design process and to incorporate green building technologies and strategies as early as possible in the design process, it is not intended to be an elaborate process. Value engineering should not be needed if the triple bottom line principles are applied.

CHAPTER 7: LOCATION AND TRANSPORTATION

Q7.1   **B.** A project's location can have multiple impacts on the ecosystem and water resources required during the life of a building.

Q7.2   **B.** Make a flashcard to remember these statistics.

Q7.3   **D and E.** Be sure to read through the question carefully to be sure the correct answers are selected.

Q7.4   **A.** LEED for Neighborhood Development projects are encouraged to provide a higher street density, with narrow streets interconnecting to prevent sprawl.

Q7.5   **A, B, and C.** According to the *Green Building and LEED Core Concepts Guide*, transportation is most impacted by location, vehicle technology, fuel, and human behavior.

Q7.6 **A, C, D, and E.** If a LEED project's site does not offer mass transit accessibility, and is therefore dependent on car commuting, it is best to encourage the occupants to carpool, offer alternative fuel–efficient vehicles, or incorporate conveniences within the building or onsite.

Q7.7 **A, B, and C.** Selecting a site near public transportation, limiting parking, and encouraging carpooling are all strategies to consider when working on a project seeking LEED certification. It is always best to redevelop a previously developed site, avoiding greenfield sites.

Q7.8 **A, C, and D.** In addition, project teams should consider the standard they setting and avoid encouraging others to contribute to urban sprawl.

Q7.9 **B and C.** Brownfield site development conserves undeveloped land, while infill development actually decreases the amount of land covered. Finally, although sites without access public transportation will have to be more creative with their transportation strategies, they are still able to pursue certification.

Q7.10 **E.** Sometimes you have to choice the best answer as the choices could seem confusing. Owners typically see a cost savings by selecting an infill site or redeveloping an existing site as the infrastructure is already in place. Occupants are encouraged to bike or walk, thereby increasing their physical activity. Locating the building close to services and amenities can increase happiness and productivity. Owners that redevelop land or invest in disadvantaged areas within an existing community help to conserve undeveloped land.

Q7.11 **B, D, and E.** All new and existing parking spaces must be included, whether they are in a new or existing garage or surface lot. Any parking that is available to the building users (including visitors) must be included. On-street parking, whether parallel or pull-in, should be excluded from calculations. Fleet and inventory vehicles' reserved spaces also should be excluded from calculations unless the vehicles are used for commuting.

Q7.12 **C, D, and F.** Shortest path analysis takes into account safety, convenience, and obstructions to movement as compared to the single straight-line radius used in LEED 2009. Make a flashcard to quiz yourself and help you to remember these components.

CHAPTER 8: SUSTAINABLE SITES

Q8.1 **C.** The key to reducing heat island effects is to avoid implementing materials that will absorb and retain heat. Deciduous trees lose their leaves and therefore are not the best decision. Xeriscaping to reduce evaporation, and increasing impervious surfaces to recharge groundwater, are great strategies for sustainable site design, but do not help to reduce heat island effects. They, in turn, reap the benefits of reduced heat island effects. Implementing paving and roofing products with a higher SRI, is therefore the best answer to reduce heat island effects.

Q8.2 **F.** It is best to involve all the players related to designing and installing a green roof in a collaborative setting. Understanding the requirements of a green roof will indicate the team members required and especially what type of vegetation will be utilized. Remember, a green roof impacts the thermal elements of a building, structural integrity, rainwater management, and the coordination of construction trades.

Q8.3 **D.** Emissivity is the ability of a material surface to emit energy in the form of radiation. It may be helpful to remember that emittance is the opposite of reflectivity. Infrared reflectivity applies to low-emissivity materials. Therefore, these materials reflect the majority of long-wave radiation and emit very little, such as metals or special metallic coatings. High-emissivity surfaces, such as painted building materials, absorb a majority of long-wave radiation as opposed to reflecting it, and emit infrared or long-wave radiation more willingly.

Q8.4 **A, B, and C.** The LEED rating systems recommend to combine strategies to reduce heat island effects, such as providing shade, install paving materials with a high SRI, and implement an open-grid pavement system.

Q8.5   **A, C, and D.** Impervious asphalt does not allow rainwater to percolate through and therefore allows rainwater to leave the site, carrying pollutants and debris, heading to storm sewers and nearby bodies of water. Increasing open space and the pervious land would reduce runoff.

Q8.6   **B, C, and E.** Sometimes the process of elimination works best for these types of questions.

Q8.7   **C and E.** Project teams can evaluate location and site-specific information prior to the beginning of designing a structure and the site, to determine the efficiencies of strategies and technologies for a green building project. These issues include the availability of mass transit and public transportation, and brownfield redevelopment. Strategies to reduce heat island effects, provisions for preferred parking, and technologies to reduce water use can all be addressed during the design process.

Q8.8   **D and E.** Selecting products with the highest SRI values is best suited for compliance with LEED.

Q8.9   **A, B, and D.** Be sure to read through the questions slowly to pick up on the key terms to help you select the correct answers.

Q8.10   **A, C, and D.** LID refers to low-impact development. Sometimes you will be tested on how well you know the many acronyms used in the LEED green building certification program. Be sure to use your flashcards and Appendix I to help you remember them.

CHAPTER 9: WATER EFFICIENCY

Q9.1   **A and E.** Aerators and flush valves are the two most economically feasible options if fixtures cannot be replaced.

Q9.2   **B and F.** Remember flow fixture and flush fixture types for the exam.

Q9.3   **A, B, and E.** Turf grass poses a maintenance, economic, and environmental concern by the amount of watering it requires. Reducing pervious surfaces does not address saving water for landscaping, and from an environmental aspect, project teams are encouraged to *increase* pervious surfaces to recharge groundwater.

Q9.4   **A, B, C, and D.** The site design strategies do not address increasing the density factor. Density can be increased by development design strategies, such as increasing floor-to-area ratio (FAR).

Q9.5   **C, D, and E.** Installing open-grid pavers in lieu of asphalt minimizes the contributions to the urban heat island effect, as pavers do not absorb the heat from the sun as opposed to asphalt. By reducing heat gain, energy use is optimized, as the building has less of a demand for cooling loads. The pavers also allow rainwater to penetrate through to reduce runoff.

Q9.6   **A, B, and C.** Process water is the water needed for building systems and business operations.

Q9.7   **B, C, and E.** Blackwater is wastewater from a toilet. Remembering the different types of nonpotable water can help answer other questions about specific design strategies as related to water efficiency.

Q9.8   **B and D.** Sometimes the process of elimination helps to determine the correct answers. Although captured rainwater is used for custodial purposes, cleaning dishes and clothes is best with potable water sources.

Q9.9   **B and E.** Sometimes the process of elimination helps to determine the correct answers.

Q9.10   **C.** Remember to read each question slowly and carefully to ensure the correct answers are selected.

CHAPTER 10: ENERGY AND ATMOSPHERE

Q10.1   **A, B, and D.** Process energy is not included in minimum LEED requirements for the EA Minimum Energy Performance prerequisite. Process energy uses include computers, office equipment, kitchen refrigeration and cooking, washing and drying machines, and elevators and escalators. Miscellaneous items, such as waterfall pumps and lighting that is exempt from lighting power allowance calculations such as lighting integrated into equipment, are also categorized as process energy uses.

Q10.2 **B, D, and E.** Refrigerants do not apply to boilers, fan motors, or variable-frequency drives, which eliminates answer options A and C.

Q10.3 **C.** Remember each of the referenced standards and what each applies to. Remember to think "energy" every time you read "ASHRAE 90.1"!

Q10.4 **B, D, and E.** Regulated energy uses include lighting, HVAC, and service water for domestic or space heating.

Q10.5 **C.** Demand response programs can help when renewable energy sources are not available, such as calm days with no wind. Utility companies could announce a curtailment event to encourage a lower energy demand.

Q10.6 **B and D.** Remember, commissioning agents should be independent third parties to perform their responsibilities for the owner. A CxA is responsible for minimizing design flaws and assessing the installation, calibration, and performance for the main building systems.

Q10.7 **A.** Using thermal storage and energy simulation helps to use energy more efficiently. Purchasing offsite renewable energy is a strategy to offset what cannot be produced onsite.

Q10.8 **B, E, and F.** Passive solar design features and offsite strategies do not contribute to earning the On-Site Renewable Energy credit. Ground-source heat pumps do not qualify either, as they require power to function the pump.

Q10.9 **C.** Green power should be remembered with offsite renewable energy, as green power is purchased and not installed.

Q10.10 **B.** Think of when you go to purchase gas for your car, as you are charged by the gallon and not by the liter.

Q10.11 **C and E.** Although a commissioning agent will be responsible for verifying the installation, calibration, and performance of the cogen system, the strategy described in the question does not indicate any information involving a commissioning agent. The question does not indicate any renewable energy to be generated onsite, nor does it refer to any offsetting green power procurement.

Q10.12 **B.** Remember to make a flashcard to help remember this statistic.

Q10.13 **A.** Remember, it is advised to incorporate integrative design strategies as early as possible in the design process.

Q10.14 **A, C, and D.** Remember to make a flashcard to help remember this fact.

Q10.15 **B and C.** Sometimes the process of elimination will help you answer these types of questions if you are unsure of the correct answers. CFCs and HCFCs destroy the ozone layer; commissioning needs to start as early as possible in the design phase (programming or schematic design); and when purchasing RECs, project teams should look for a Green-e certified provider.

CHAPTER 11: MATERIALS AND RESOURCES

Q11.1 **C, D, and E.** Remember, preconsumer recycled content refers to scrap and trim material generated from the manufacturing process, but does not enter into the consumer cycle of goods. Preconsumer recycled materials are used to manufacture a different product than what it was originally intended for.

Q11.2 **A and D.** Regional materials, salvaged materials, and rapidly renewable materials are calculated as a percentage of the total material cost for a project for the purposes of LEED.

Q11.3 **B.** Rapidly renewable products can be grown or raised in 10 years or less.

Q11.4 **A and D.** For the purposes of LEED, FSC wood products are calculated as a percentage of the total cost of materials purchased for a specific project. Chain-of-custody documentation should be tracked and the certification number entered into the credit submittal form for proof of compliance.

Q11.5 **A, C, and E.** The EPA's ENERGY STAR Portfolio Manager is used to compare energy use consumptions for similar-type buildings.

Q11.6 **B.** Landfills produce methane, a powerful greenhouse gas. Although methane can be captured and burned to generate energy, if it is emitted, it is harmful to the environment.

Q11.7 **B and C.** Cradle-to-cradle products can be recycled, while cradle-to-grave materials are landfilled. Products with either or both preconsumer and postconsumer recycled content can contribute to earning a LEED credit.

Q11.8 **B and C.** Rainwater management plans are typically the responsibility of the civil engineer, while the energy modeling calculations are typically provided by the mechanical engineer.

Q11.9 **B, D, and E.** Project teams are required to upload the solar reflectance index (SRI) of the roof under the SS category. The CEO's automobile choice is not evaluated or assessed for LEED compliance.

Q11.10 **A, B, and E.** Furniture is not considered permanently installed but can be included in MR credit calculations if included consistently across all cost-based credits.

Q11.11 **C.** Furniture and electronics are not considered ongoing consumables.

Q11.12 **D.** Waste is calculated in tonnage for the purposes of LEED documentation.

Q11.13 **D.** Recycling. Construction debris has become a commodity and is no longer considered a waste.

Q11.14 **A.** By minimizing the use of materials, source reduction has the least environmental impact as compared to the other waste management strategies.

Q11.15 **B and D.** Be sure to read through these types of questions slowly and carefully to ensure that the correct answers are selected.

Q11.16 **A and B.** Infill projects and dense neighborhood designs reduce the need for miles of new roads and infrastructure. Remember, you want to space framing members farther apart and use insulation between for a more resource- and energy-efficient building. FSC wood is sustainably harvested but not a strategy to conserve.

Q11.17 **E.** A product extracted, processed, and manufactured within 100 miles of a project site and that meets at least one of the sustainable criteria can be included at 200 percent of its value.

Q11.18 **C, D, and F.** Create a flashcard to remember this calculation's components.

Q11.19 **A and D.** Furniture is not required to be included in the calculations but if it is, the furniture must be applied consistently across all cost-based MR credits. Special equipment, such as elevators, escalators, process equipment, and fire suppression systems, must be excluded from calculations.

Q11.20 **C and D.** MEP items are also optional but project teams may choose to exclude some products in calculations (as long as the total project cost is consistent across credits).

CHAPTER 12: INDOOR ENVIRONMENTAL QUALITY

Q12.1 **D.** LEED requires a minimum of MERV 8 to be installed for compliance.

Q12.2 **B, E, and F.** Remember the specifics of the referenced standards and what they apply to.

Q12.3 **B and C.** ASHRAE 90.1 = Energy! ENERGY STAR applies to energy-efficient appliances, products, and buildings.

Q12.4   **A and B.** There are at least five other factors of good lighting design, such as the activities to be conducted in the space, building orientation, the layout of the room, the type of glass, and configuration of the windows.

Q12.5   **A.** Opening the windows is not sufficient means to eliminate contaminants, as the mechanical system (ductwork) and indoor environment needs to be flushed out with fresh air as well.

Q12.6   **B and D.** Remember to read questions and answer options carefully to eliminate the incorrect answers and to depict the correct answer.

Q12.7   **D.** Remember to read questions and answer options carefully to eliminate the incorrect answers and to depict the correct answer.

Q12.8   **B and C.** Reflective paint and materials also need to be considered when introducing natural light within a space.

Q12.9   **A, C, and D.** Although good intentions may be behind green building strategies, design teams need to be aware of good design techniques to avoid discomfort. For example, although the thermostat may read a desired temperature, the ventilation and aim of the air needs to be considered as well. It is also important to choose the best answers as it might appear there are many correct ones.

Q12.10   **D.** 62 IAQ, IAQ 62!

Q12.11   **C.** Remember the BAIT tip to point out the trade-offs and synergies of increased ventilation strategies: better IAQ but reduced energy efficiency for mechanical systems to condition outside air.

Q12.12   **A and E.** Project specifications will give the contractor direction on how to comply with the IAQ credit requirements such as MERV filters, flush-out, and low-emitting materials.

Q12.13   **D.** Create a flashcard to remember this technical information.

Q12.14   **B.** Remember ASHRAE 62 = IAQ as it relates to ventilation system design.

Q12.15   **A and C.** Proximity to a shopping mall may increase satisfaction due to convenience, but not necessarily increase production as related to work. Carpooling and recycling are benefits to the environment and operations, not necessarily related to productivity or satisfaction.

Q12.16   **C and D.** A and B are encouraged to provide on a daily basis, not just for conducting surveys.

Q12.17   **A and C.** A regularly occupied space is typically used more than an hour per person per day and is not intended to be passed through.

Q12.18   **B and C.** A multioccupant space typically includes a place of "overlapping or collaborative tasks. . . . Occupied spaces that are not regularly occupied or not used for distinct or collaborative tasks are neither individual occupant nor shared multioccupant spaces."[1]

Q12.19   **A, B, and D.** Unoccupied spaces are inactive areas.

Q12.20   **A and B.** Be sure to read through the questions slowly and carefully to stay focused and not get distracted by the terminology.

CHAPTER 13: INNOVATION AND REGIONAL PRIORITY

Q13.1   **C.** Earning exemplary performance is credit specific, so be aware of statements such as "regardless of which credit is being exceeded."

Q13.2   **C and D.** For more information and examples of Innovation credits, download the archived Innovation in Design Credit catalog from the USGBC website at www.usgbc.org/Docs/Archive/General/Docs3569.pdf.

Q13.3 **A.** A new green building project can earn certification under the LEED for New Construction rating system and then earn certification under the LEED for Existing Buildings: O&M rating system during operations or a LEED Core & Shell building can be built and then earn multiple LEED for Commercial Interiors rating system certifications.

Q13.4 **A and D.** Remember, the Regional Priority category does not include any new credits. RPCs are earned by achieving existing LEED credits from other categories. Although earning a maximum of four RPCs is allowed, there are six opportunities available to choose from.

Q13.5 **D.** Although earning a maximum of four RPCs is allowed, there are six opportunities available to choose from based on the physical coordinates (X,Y) of the project.

Q13.6 **A.** Regardless of how many LEED AP®s are on a project, only one point can be earned.

NOTES

1. USGBC website, www.usgbc.org/guide/bdc#cc_overview.

Index

The abbreviation fig. following a page number indicates an illustration or a photograph, while a letter t after a page number denotes a table.

Sample Flashcards

1 **Q.** What does USGBC stand for?	**2** **Q.** What does LEED stand for?
3 **Q.** What code has been developed to overlay existing, traditional building codes?	**4** **Q.** What savings have green buildings achieved?
5 **Q.** What are the environmental benefits of green buildings?	**6** **Q.** What are the economic benefits of green buildings?
7 **Q.** What are the health and community benefits of green buildings?	**8** **Q.** What is a positive feedback loop?

2

A. Leadership in Energy and Environmental Design

1

A. U. S. Green Building Council

4

A. 26 percent energy use reduction
27 percent higher levels of satisfaction
33 percent lower CO2 emissions
13 percent reduction in maintenance costs

3

A. International Green Construction Code (IGCC)

6

A. Reduce operating costs.
Enhance asset value and profits.
Improve employee productivity and satisfaction.
Optimize life-cycle economic performance.

5

A. Enhance and protect ecosystems and biodiversity.
Improve air and water quality.
Reduce solid waste.
Conserve natural resources.

8

A. A perpetual and ongoing cycle of cause and effect. Examples include urban sprawl, population growth, and climate change.

7

A. Improve air, thermal, and acoustic environments.
Enhance occupant comfort and health.
Minimize strain on local infrastructure.
Contribute to overall quality of life.

9

Q. What is USGBC's mission statement?

10

Q. Describe USGBC.

11

Q. What is GBCI's mission statement?

12

Q. Describe GBCI.

13

Q. What is a TAG?

14

Q. What are the two primary roles of USGBC?

15

Q. What are the two primary roles of GBCI?

16

Q. What are the five additional strategies of the LEED for Existing Buildings: O&M rating system as compared to the other rating systems?

10

A. A 501(c)(3) nonprofit composed of leaders from every sector of the building industry working to promote buildings and communities that are environmentally responsible, profitable, and healthy places to live and work.

9

A. To transform the way buildings and communities are designed, built, and operated, enabling an environmentally and socially responsible, healthy, and prosperous environment that improves the quality of life.

12

A. Provides third-party project certification and professional credentials recognizing excellence in green building performance and practice.

11

A. To support a high level of competence in building methods for environmental efficiency through the development and administration of a formal program of certification and recertification.

14

A. Develop LEED rating systems.
Provide education and research programs.

13

A. Technical advisory group within USGBC to help the LEED rating systems to evolve.

16

A. Evaluating their exterior site maintenance programs
Purchasing policies for environmentally preferred services and products
Cleaning programs and policies
Waste stream
Ongoing indoor environmental quality

15

A. Administering the project certification process with the help of certification bodies
Administering the professional accreditation process

17

Q. What is a negative feedback loop?

18

Q. What are the categories of the LEED for Neighborhood Development rating system?

19

Q. What are the two differences between prerequisites and credits?

20

Q. What are the seven impact categories credit weightings are based on?

21

Q. What are the certification levels and coordinating point ranges for LEED?

22

Q. What is the Prius effect?

23

Q. What is an RFI?

24

Q. What is a CIR?

18

A. Smart Location & Linkage
Neighborhood Pattern & Design
Green Infrastructure & Buildings
Innovation
Regional Priority

17

A. A self-regulating system. Examples include a thermostat's change due to a sensor input.

20

A. Climate Change, Human Health, Water Resources, Biodiversity, Material Resources, Greener Economy, and Community

19

A. Prerequisites are mandatory, as they address minimum performance achievements, and credits are optional.
Prerequisites are not worth any points, while credits are.

22

A. A user's reaction when given real-time information

21

A. Certified: 40–49 points
Silver: 50–59 points
Gold: 60–79 points
Platinum: 80 and higher

24

A. Credit Interpretation Ruling

23

A. Request for information

25

Q. Most of the _____ rating systems require at least _____ percent of the project's gross floor area to be complete by the time of certification (except _____ rating system)?

26

Q. What are the three types of boundaries associated with LEED projects?

27

Q. According to the MPRs, what is the minimum project size requirement for the BD+C and O+M rating systems?

28

Q. According to the MPRs, what is the minimum project size requirement for the ID+C rating systems?

29

Q. What are the guidelines for referencing LEED in product literature?

30

Q. What must be achieved in order for a project to be eligible for certification?

31

Q. The distance boundary from an existing feature or natural body that a development is required to abide by is referred to as what?

32

Q. What is a zero lot line?

26

A. Building footprint, LEED boundary line, and property line

25

A. BD+C; 60; LEED for Core & Shell

28

A. 250 square feet

27

A. 1,000 square feet

30

A. Complying with all minimum program requirements, achieving all prerequisites, and earning a minimum of 40 points.

29

A. Manufacturers may reference LEED in their product literature providing that the language neither states nor implies endorsement by USGBC or the LEED program. The language must clearly acknowledge that LEED credit requirements do not cover the performance of individual products or brands. Products meeting LEED performance criteria can only contribute toward earning points needed for LEED certification; they cannot earn points individually for LEED certification.

32

A. A development in which the building footprint is the same as the lot boundary. This is common in urban areas.

31

A. Setback. Common setbacks include minimum distance from the street and sidewalk, or minimum distance from a wetland or water body.

33

Q. In a construction project, what is the site area?

34

Q. What is the tool in which project teams utilize to communicate with GBCI?

35

Q. What is an LPE?

36

Q. What are the six characteristics of credit interpretation rulings?

37

Q. What are the three factors certification fees are based on?

38

Q. What are the three factors to address within the SS category?

39

Q. What is floor-to-area ratio (FAR)?

40

Q. What are the six strategies of Site Selection?

34

A. LEED Online

33

A. The total area within the project boundary of the applicant building including all areas of the property, both constructed and nonconstructed.

36

A. Issued after a project is registered
Issued for a fee
Applicable only to the project submitting the inquiry
Submitted for clarification referencing *one* credit or prerequisite
Ruling not final
Submitted via LEED-Online

35

A. Licensed-professional exemption. Path decided on a submittal template to reduce documentation requirements.

38

A. Site Design & Management
Rainwater Management
Heat Island Effect

37

A. Rating system, membership, and square footage

40

A. Increase density.
Choose redevelopment and infill development.
Locate near existing infrastructure.
Protect habitat.
Increase diversity of uses.
Encourage multiple modes of transportation.

39

A. The proportion of the total floor area of a building to the total land area the building can occupy.

41

Q. What is community connectivity?

42

Q. What is development density?

43

Q. What is a brownfield?

44

Q. What are the four strategies to earn Innovation points?

45

Q. What are the four strategies to promote sustainable purchasing during design and operations?

46

Q. What are the six strategies to reduce waste during operations?

47

Q. What are the eight characteristics of environmentally preferred material and products?

48

Q. What is greenwashing?

42

A. The total square footage of all buildings within a particular area, measured in square feet per acre or units per acre

41

A. Proximity of project site to local businesses and community services such as parks, grocery stores, banks, cleaners, pharmacies, and restaurants.

44

A. Exemplary performance
Innovative strategy
Pilot credit
Including a LEED AP

43

A. Real property, the expansion, redevelopment, or reuse of which may be complicated by the presence or potential presence of a hazardous substance, pollutant, or contaminant. Cleaning up and reinvesting in these properties protects the environment, reduces blight, and takes development pressures off green spaces and working lands.

46

A. Develop a solid waste management policy.
Conduct a waste stream audit.
Maintain a recycling program.
Monitor, track, and report.
Compost.
Provide recycling for durable goods.

45

A. Identify local sources of environmentally preferable products.
Develop a sustainable materials policy.
Specify green materials and equipment.
Specify green custodial products.

48

A. Implying a material or product is more sustainable than it actually is

47

A. Support local economy
Sustainably grown and harvested
Have intended end-of-life scenarios that avoid landfills
Contain recycled content from industrial or consumer resources
Made of bio-based materials
Free of toxins
Long lasting, durable, and reusable
Made in factories that support human health and workers' rights

49

Q. What are the four impacts of transportation?

50

Q. What is shortest path analysis?

51

Q. What are the three strategies to reduce the transportation impacts associated with the built environment during design and construction?

52

Q. What is street grid density?

53

Q. What are the three strategies to address for site maintenance?

54

Q. What are native and adaptive plantings?

55

Q. What is potable water?

56

Q. What is imperviousness?

50

A. When determining the maximum walking and bicycle distances, take into account safety, convenience, and obstructions to movement to ensure use of amenities (as compared to the straight line radius).

49

A. Location
Vehicle technology
Fuel
Human behavior

52

A. The number of centerline miles (length of a road down the center) per square mile

51

A. Choose site adjacent to mass transit.
Limit parking capacity.
Encourage bicycling.

54

A. Native vegetation occurs naturally, while adaptive plantings are not natural; they can adapt to their new surroundings. Both can survive with little to no human interaction or resources.

53

A. Develop a sustainable management plan.
Implement conservation programs.
Maintain site lighting to prevent light pollution.

56

A. Surfaces that do not allow water to pass through them

55

A. Drinking water supplied by municipalities or wells

57

Q. What is perviousness?

58

Q. What is rainwater runoff?

59

Q. What is a footcandle?

60

Q. What is the heat island effect?

61

Q. What is emissivity as described in the *Green Building and LEED Core Concepts Guide*?

62

Q. What is the solar reflective index (SRI) and the associated scale?

63

Q. What is evapotranspiration?

64

Q. What is a building footprint?

58

A. Rainwater that leaves a project site flowing along parking lots and roadways, traveling to sewer systems and water bodies.

57

A. Surfaces that allow water to percolate or penetrate through them

60

A. Heat absorption by low-SRI, hardscape materials that contribute to an overall increase in temperature by radiating heat.

59

A. A measurement of light measured in lumens per square foot

62

A. A material's ability to reflect or reject solar heat gain measured on a scale from 0 (dark, most absorptive) to 100 (light, most reflective).

61

A. The ability of a material to emit energy through radiation.

64

A. The amount of land the building structure occupies, not including landscape and hardscape surfaces such as parking lots, driveways, and walkways.

63

A. The return of water to the atmosphere through evaporation from plants' leaves.

65

Q. What are the five strategies to address for site design?

66

Q. What are the three design strategies to manage rainwater?

67

Q. What are the two types of water uses described in the WE category?

68

Q. What is the reference standard for the WE category?

69

Q. What is baseline versus design case?

70

Q. What are examples of flow fixtures?

71

Q. How are flow fixtures measured?

72

Q. What are examples of flush fixtures?

66

A. Minimize impervious areas.
Control rainwater.
Incorporate rainwater management into site design.

65

A. Preserve open space and sensitive areas.
Minimize hardscape.
Use native landscaping.
Reduce light pollution.
Protect and restore habitat.

68

A. EPAct 1992

67

A. Indoor water
Outdoor water

70

A. Sink faucets, showerheads, and aerators

69

A. The amount of water a conventional project would use as compared to the design case

72

A. Toilets and urinals

71

A. Gallons per minute (gpm)

73

Q. How are flow fixtures measured?

74

Q. What is graywater?

75

Q. What are the strategies to reduce indoor water consumption?

76

Q. What are the five strategies to reduce outdoor water consumption?

77

Q. How can nonpotable water use reduce water consumption?

78

Q. What are the uses for process water?

79

Q. What are the nine strategies to improve IAQ during operations?

80

Q. What are the benefits of utilizing a CxA?

74

A. Wastewater from showers, bathtubs, lavatories, and washing machines. This water has not come into contact with toilet waste according to the International Plumbing Code (IPC).

73

A. Gallons per flush (gpf)

76

A. Implement native and adapted plants.
Use xeriscaping.
Install/specify high-efficiency irrigation systems.
Use nonpotable water.
Install submeters.

75

A. Use efficient fixtures.
Use nonpotable water.
Install submeters.

78

A. Industrial uses, such as chillers, cooling towers, and boilers
Business operations, such as washing machines, ice machines, and dishwashers

77

A. Indoor: toilet and urinal flushing
Outdoor: irrigation
Process: building systems

80

A. Minimize or eliminate design flaws.
Avoid construction defects.
Avoid equipment malfunctions.
Ensure preventative maintenance is implemented during operations.

79

A. Ensure adequate ventilation.
Monitor airflow.
Monitor carbon dioxide.
Calibrate sensors.
Prohibit smoking.
Employ a green cleaning program.
Conduct a custodial effectiveness assessment.
Maintain entryway systems.
Use integrated pest management.

81

Q. What is the baseline standard for energy performance?

82

Q. What are the uses for regulated energy?

83

Q. What are the uses for process energy?

84

Q. What two components should be evaluated when determining which refrigerants to use?

85

Q. What is ODP?

86

Q. What is GWP?

87

Q. What is the requirement for existing building projects that have CFC refrigerants?

88

Q. What are the four components of the Energy & Atmosphere category?

82

A. Lighting: interior and exterior applications (parking garages, facades, site lighting)
HVAC: space heating, cooling, fans, pumps, toilet exhaust, ventilation for parking garages
Domestic and space heating for service water

81

A. ASHRAE 90.1 2010, Appendix G

84

A. Refrigerants should be evaluated based on ODP and GWP impacts.

83

A. Computers, office equipment, kitchen refrigeration and cooking, washing and drying machines, and elevators and escalators. Miscellaneous items, such as a waterfall pump, and lighting that is exempt from lighting power allowance calculations such as lighting integrated into equipment, are also categorized as process energy uses.

86

A. Global warming potential

85

A. Ozone-depleting potential

88

A. Energy demand
Energy efficiency
Renewable energy
Ongoing energy performance

87

A. The CFCs must be phased out.

89

Q. What are the four strategies to reduce energy demand?

90

Q. How are electricity, natural gas, and liquid fuel each measured?

91

Q. What are the six strategies to use energy more efficiently?

92

Q. What are the six types of eligible renewable energy sources for LEED projects?

93

Q. What are the two ways to incorporate renewable energy into a green building project?

94

Q. What is an REC?

95

Q. What are the four strategies to ensure optimal performance for a LEED project?

96

Q. What are the three components to address within the Materials & Resources category?

90

A. Electricity is measured in kilowatts per hour, natural gas in therms, and liquid fuel in gallons.

89

A. Establish design and energy goals.
Size the building appropriately.
Use free energy.
Insulate.

92

A. Solar, wind, wave, biomass, geothermal power, and low-impact hydropower

91

A. Address the envelope.
Install high-performance mechanical systems. and appliances.
Use high-efficient infrastructure.
Capture efficiencies of scale.
Use energy simulation.
Monitor and verify performance.

94

A. Renewable energy credit

93

A. Generate on-site renewable energy and/or purchase green power or RECs.

96

A. The conservation of materials
Environmentally, socially, and locally preferable materials
Waste management and reduction

95

A. Adhere to the OPR.
Provide staff training.
Conduct preventative maintenance.
Create incentives for occupants and tenants.

97

Q. What is a rapidly renewable material?

98

Q. Define recycled content.

99

Q. What referenced standard declares a material having postconsumer/preconsumer recycled content?

100

Q. Recycled material that was generated from a manufacturing process is referred to as _____.

101

Q. Recycled material that was generated by household, commercial, industrial, or institutional end users, which can no longer be used for its intended purpose, is referred to as _____.

102

Q. What are considered regional materials according to LEED?

103

Q. What type of documentation is required to prove compliance for FSC wood?

104

Q. Which type of products must be excluded from MR category compliance calculations?

98

A. The percentage of materials in a product that are recycled from the manufacturing waste stream (preconsumer waste) or the consumer waste stream (postconsumer waste) and used to make new materials. Recycled content is typically expressed as a percentage of the total material volume or weight.

97

A. Fiber or animal materials that must be grown or raised in 10 years or less.

100

A. Preconsumer. Examples include planer shavings, sawdust, bagasse, walnut shells, culls, trimmed materials, over issue publications, and obsolete inventories. Not included are rework, regrind, or scrap materials capable of being reclaimed within the same process that generated them.

99

A. ISO 14021-1999—Environmental Label and Declarations

102

A. The amount of a building's materials that are extracted, processed, and manufactured close to a project site, expressed as a percentage of the total material cost. LEED considers regional materials as those that originate within 100 miles of the project site.

101

A. Postconsumer. Examples include construction and demolition debris, materials collected through recycling programs, and landscaping waste (ISO 14021).

104

A. Special equipment, such as elevators, escalators, and fire suppression systems

103

A. FSC wood requires chain-of-custody documentation.

105

Q. What are the five strategies to conserve materials throughout a project's life-cycle?

106

Q. What are the minimum types of items to be recycled during operations to meet the requirements of the MR prerequisite?

107

Q. What are the 3Rs of waste management?

108

Q. What are the three strategies to reduce waste during construction?

109

Q. What are the four components discussed in the EQ category?

110

Q. What are the sources of air contaminants?

111

Q. What are the different referenced standards for products that emit VOCs?

112

Q. What are the eight strategies to address sustainable pattern and design?

106

A. Paper, corrugated cardboard, glass, plastics, and metals

105

A. Reuse existing buildings and salvaged materials.
Plan for smaller, more compact communities.
Design smaller, more flexible homes and buildings.
Use efficient framing techniques.
Promote source reduction in operations.

108

A. Design buildings that produce less waste.
Develop a construction waste management policy.
Establish a tracking system.

107

A. Reduce, reuse, and recycle

110

A. Carbon dioxide, tobacco smoke, mold, radon, bioeffluents, and VOCs emitted from carpet, paints, adhesives, glues, sealants, coatings, cleaning products, furniture, and composite wood products.

109

A. Indoor air quality (IAQ)
Lighting
Acoustics
Occupant experience

112

A. Design walkable streets.
Include pedestrian amenities.
Use compact development strategies.
Promote connectivity.
Provide diverse land uses.
Create a diverse community.
Support access to sustainable food.
Ensure that all residents have easy access to grocery stores.

111

A. Paints and Coatings—Green Seal 11
Adhesives—Green Seal 36
Sealants—SCAQMD 1168
Carpet—Carpet & Rug Institute (CRI)
Other Flooring—FloorScore
Furniture—Greenguard™ and SCS Indoor Advantage

113

Q. What are the two strategies to manage rainwater during operations?

114

Q. What is MERV? What is the range?

115

Q. What are the six strategies to improve IAQ?

116

Q. What are the three strategies to improve lighting?

117

Q. What are the three strategies to address thermal comfort?

118

Q. What are the three strategies to improve IAQ during construction?

119

Q. What are the two acoustical strategies to improve occupant comfort?

120

Q. Of the six available Regional Priority credits, how many can count toward a project's LEED certification?

114

A. Minimum Efficiency Reporting Value (MERV) filters range from 1 (low) to 16 (highest).

113

A. Redirect rainwater.
Harvest rainwater.

116

A. Use daylighting.
Give occupants lighting control.
Conduct occupant surveys.

115

A. Prohibit smoking.
Properly size the ventilation system.
Protect air coming into the building.
Test for radon.
Specify low-emitting materials.
Design for entryway systems.

118

A. Keep the building clean.
Protect absorptive materials.
Conduct a flush-out.

117

A. Install operable windows.
Give occupants temperature and ventilation control.
Conduct occupant surveys.

120

A. Four

119

A. Consider acoustic impacts.
Conduct occupant surveys.

121

Q. A project's available Regional Priority points are determined by what project-specific element?

122

Q. How does a project team find out the Regional Priority point opportunities for a LEED project?

123

Q. How many Innovation points can a LEED Green Associate earn for a project seeking LEED certification?

124

Q. A project team diverts 97 percent of the nonhazardous construction waste away from a landfill. They earn all the points that are within the credit and an additional point that will be included in which category?

125

Q. What are the two components of a zoning requirement?

126

Q. What are some examples of uses that are defined in zoning ordinances?

127

Q. Within the SS category, LEED encourages a project team not to exceed the minimum number of _____, but encourages the team to exceed the minimum amount of _____, both as required by zoning.

128

Q. What best describes a regulation that restricts the height of a building?

122

A. Refer to the USGBC website and enter a project's geographic coordinates or refer to LEED-Online for registered projects.

121

A. Geographic coordinates

124

A. Innovation

123

A. Zero, only LEED APs are eligible.

126

A. Single-family residential, multifamily residential, commercial, and industrial

125

A. The map of the zones and a text description of the requirements

128

A. Zoning ordinance

127

A. Parking spaces; open space